TEX SMITH'S

Roaring Roadsters

By Don Radbruch

Illustrations by Loren Kreck

Printed and bound in the United States of America

First printed in 1994 by co-publishers: CarTech, Inc. 11481 Kost Dam Rd., North Branch, MN 55056; and Tex Smith Publishing, P.O. Box 726, Driggs, ID 83422.

CarTech, Inc., and Tex Smith Publishing Company books are also available at discounts in bulk quantity for industrial or sales-promotional use. For details, contact the marketing director at:
CarTech, Inc., 11481 Kost Dam Rd., North Branch, MN 55056; telephone (612) 583-3471, FAX (612) 583-2023.

Overseas distribution by:
BROOKLANDS BOOKS, LTD., P.O. Box 146, Cobham, Surrey, KT11 1LG, England; telephone 0932 865051, FAX 0932 868803.
BROOKLANDS BOOKS LTD. 1/81 Darley St., P.O. Box 199, Mona Vale, NSW 2103, Australia; telephone 2 997 8428, FAX 2 452 4679.

ISBN 1-884089-06-2

Printed and bound in the United States of America.

AUTHOR	DON RADBRUCH
PUBLISHER	LEROI TEX SMITH
EDITOR	BRIAN BRENNAN
TECH. EDITOR	RON CERIDONO
ART DIRECTOR	GREG COMPTON
ART ASSISTANT	LISA HANKS

Roaring Roadsters

TABLE OF CONTENTS

6   **A WORD UP FRONT—LEROI TEX SMITH**

7   **INTRODUCTION**
- ROADSTER HISTORY • A HOT ROD MYSTERY
- SOME TERMINOLOGY • LOREN KRECK

10   **ABOUT THE AUTHOR—DON RADBRUCH**

11   **ARIZONA**

16   **CALIFORNIA, SOUTHERN**
- WALT JAMES • THE DAY BOB CROSS BECAME BOB DENNY • A SOUTHERN CALIFORNIA MYSTERY
- THE CRA'S FIVE HUNDREDS • THE BIG WHEEL • A CHAIN-DRIVE ROADSTER • THE AGOURA ROAD RACE

34   **CALIFORNIA, CENTRAL**
- A REAR-ENGINED ROADSTER

42   **CALIFORNIA, NORTHERN**
- RICK • STOCKTON SPITFIRE • AAA ROADSTER RACES • CCRA & PALM BEACH • THE HUDSON THAT WASN'T • THE VERY DIFFERENT ROADSTER
- OAKLAND STADIUM • NUMBER 119 ON ROUTE 66
- THE OUTLAWS AT ALEMAND

66   **COLORADO**
- REVERSE CAM CRAGAR • AN INDY CAR MYSTERY

74   **FLORIDA**
- NASCAR AND THE ROADSTERS
- ROADSTERS ON THE BOARDS

78   **ILLINOIS**
- A HISTORY LESSON

82   **INDIANA**
- DICK FRAZIER, #32 & THE SMITHSONIAN • HOT RODDERS & AAA • BURTON AND THE VACANT POLE
- ROADSTER DRIVERS AT INDY
- THE LITTLE 500 • THE OTHER LITTLE 500
- RETURN OF THE ROADSTER

104 **IOWA**
- THE FRIENDLY INFIELD FENCE

108 **KANSAS**

110 **MICHIGAN**
- WHISKEY RIDGE

116 **MINNESOTA**

122 **MISSOURI**
- THE WILSON-HOWER-CUNNINGHAM SHOW

128 **NEBRASKA**
- THE RACES AT ORD: A SEMI-MYSTERY • FRANZ SCHULZE—INNOVATOR • A STAR-STUDDED FIELD

134 **NEW MEXICO**
- THE LOST SUPER SPEEDWAY

138 **NEW YORK**
- A FINGER LAKES MYSTERY
- FROM PENNEY-ROYAL TO NASCAR

142 **NORTH DAKOTA**

144 **OHIO**
- BUD CLAYPOOL'S ROCKET • A KENTUCKY MYSTERY
- THE LANDECK RACERS

152 **OKLAHOMA**

154 **OREGON**
- CROSS DRESSING • AN IDAHO MYSTERY

162 **PENNSYLVANIA**
- A RARE ROADSTER

170 **SOUTH DAKOTA**
- THE BIJOU BOBTAIL

175 **TEXAS**
- A LOUISIANA MYSTERY • A MEXICAN ROAD RACE

180 **VIRGINIA & MARYLAND**
- ROADSTER RACING IN THE 1940S
- A NEW ENGLAND MYSTERY

186 **WASHINGTON**
- HOT RODS TO FORMULA I • BIG LEAGUE RACING
- A FIASCO AT PORT ANGELES
- THE STORY OF #55

196 **WISCONSIN**
- ROADSTER RACERS AND THE LAW

198 **MORE MYSTERIES**

A WORD UP FRONT

This is a book too long overdue. For the automotive historian, for the race car enthusiast, for the hard core hot rodder.

I've wanted to do this book for more than 30 years, first as a writer and later as a publisher. There was never enough time. I grew up with track roadsters, just one of the many facets of cars and my generation. Racing was everywhere, so were hot rods, and California was the obvious melting pot for all. But track roadsters really came to my attention in the mid-1940s. My father was a bodyman sometimes called on to modify roadster bodies for oval competition, but information on the cars and the races was hard to come by. Mostly, it was word of mouth, often direct from the racers. This was before *Hot Rod Magazine,* before widespread publicity on any form of hot rod racing. No wonder that the history of track roadsters has languished in the shadows. No more.

Track roadsters were not jalopies. Neither were they Indy 500 style Big Cars. They were simply track racing hot rod roadsters. Open to the air, so spectators could see the driver wrestling with horsepower and traction and position. Most of the cars, especially in the western states, were well built, on a par with midgets and sprinters. But there were some places where they were less than well engineered. No matter, wherever and whatever they were, track roadsters were a major part of race car history.

While I was working on Tom Medley's first *Hot Rod History* book, I mentioned to an acquaintance my interest in track roadsters. He, in turn, knew someone who had been gathering material for just such a book. Last year, we got together on the project. Welcome to one of my very first love affairs, and welcome to track roadster historian Don Radbruch.

Thank you, Don, for being here when we all needed you the most!

—LeRoi Tex Smith
Publisher

Roaring Roadsters

I n a way this book started in 1938. I was a race crazy kid who couldn't find an article in the newspaper about a roadster race I'd seen the previous day. I typed out the following rather messy piece for my scrapbook.

The "article" starts out with an error. The winning driver was "Ameral," not "Amerald." I can promise that this book won't START with an error.

Almost no official records of roadster racing exists. With but three exceptions, dozens of associations or clubs that sanctioned the races are gone. Recordkeeping was sparse to begin with, as for the most part, the people involved with the roadsters were interested in racing—period.

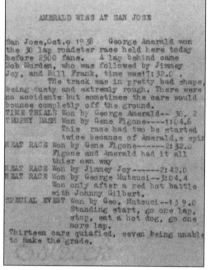

AMERALD WINS AT SAN JOSE

San Jose, Oct.o 19 5 George Amerald won
the 30 lap roadster race held here today
before 2500 fans. A lap behind came
Bob Warden, who was followed by Jimmy
Joy, and Bill Frank, time was 7:32.0.
        The track was in pretty bad shape,
being dusty and extremely rough. There were
no accidents but sometimes the cars would
bounce completly off the ground.
TIME TRIALS Won by George Amerald-- 30. 2
TROPHY DASH Won by Gene Figone----1:04.6
        This race had two be started
        twice because of Amerald,s spin.
HEAT RACE Won by Gene Figone--------2:32.0
        Figone and Amerald had it all
        thier own way
HEAT RACE Won by Jimmey Joy------2:42.0
HEAT RACE Won by George Mutouci--3:04.4
        Won only after a red hot battle
        with Johnny Gilbert.
SPECIAL EVENT Won by Geo. Mutouci--13 9.0
        Standing start, go one lap,
        stop, eat a hot dog, go one
        more lap.
Thirteen cars quiafied, seven being unable
to make the grade.

Some records might have been kept of race results, payoffs, point standings and champions, but these cold scarcely be expected to survive some 40 years. A few official records of the Mutual Racing Association in the Midwest and the Nebraska Hot Rod Racing Association have turned up, but that is about it. Published information of roadster racing is available in copies or microfilms of the racing publications like *National Speed Sport News* and *Illustrated Speedway News*. These publications depended on material sent in by correspondents for the various tracks or racing groups. Usually nobody bothered, so it is doubtful if even 10 percent of the roadster racing results ever made it into the pages of these newspapers. *Hot Rod Magazine* came along in 1948 and did give considerable space to the track roadsters. Except for Southern California, *Hot Rod* was dependent on material received by mail. A few people sent in copy and some articles were printed, but this did not begin to cover the racing that was going on at that time. Local newspapers, especially in small towns, did give some space to roadsters but researching this is nearly impossible.

I have researched *National Speed Sport News, Illustrated Speedway News* and *Hot Rod Magazine,* but most of the material for this book has come from individuals who were involved with roadster racing. A few of these people had scrapbooks to refer to and a few had kept records of their racing careers. Most people had only their memories of events that happened 40 to 60 years ago, so errors are bound to exist. I've resigned myself to errors. I've tried to avoid big errors. When there are conflicting "facts" I've used what seems the most logical.

It is fortunate that many people kept their photographs. These are the backbone of the book. I can't thank people enough for lending me the more than 1,000 photos that appear here. When it is known, the photographer has been credited, as has the person who supplied the photos. Driver identification should be reasonably accurate. Except in a few cases, the identity of the car owners has been lost to history—the poor guys paid all the bills and now they are forgotten!

In two years of research, I've had a lot of help from many very nice people. Racing historians have helped, famous racers have helped, not-so-famous racers have helped and so have just plain fans. Even though I live in the wilds of northern Idaho, I've managed to contact a number of people personally. There has been a great number of phone calls and something like a thousand letters. Even non-racing people have been marvelous—like editors of some 100 newspapers in various parts of the country. When all else failed I wrote a "Letter to the Editor" to newspapers in cities where I knew, or thought, roadsters ran. I'm sure that these editors never heard of roadsters, but these letters, asking for information on the races, were printed. Response was excellent and many voids in hot rod history were filled in this manner.

Historian and *National Speed Sport News* writer and columnist, Bill Hill, got me started on this thing. We talked about the roadsters we both drove way back when and lamented the fact that racing historians had almost completely ignored these cars and their drivers. We agreed that roadster history was fast on the way to being forgotten forever and that a book should be written on the hot rods. Frankly, I hoped that Bill would do it and I'd help out, but he was busy with other matters and urged me to do it. I'd been a racing history nut for many years and had done a number of historical articles, but I remember pleading that I wasn't qualified to do a book on roadsters. Bill replied, "You are as well qualified as anybody." Indicative of the sad state of affairs is that I guess I was, even though I knew almost nothing about roadsters.

Despite all the effort that has gone into this book, I know there are omissions. Perhaps a longer research period would dig out some more information, but I was advised against it. Publisher Tex Smith was smart enough to tell me, "Hey you can't get it all or the book will never get finished!"

He was right. The book is finished, and I hope that I got most of it. I also hope that I got most of it right. I hereby apologize for what I got wrong. Let's get on with Roaring Roadsters!

Hundreds of people helped make this book happen. Special thanks to the following:

Wayne Alspaugh	Bruce Craig	Harley Gunkle	Dick Liebfritz	Bill Rexford	Bill Smith
Red Amick	Bob Cross	Johnny Haigler	Marty Little	Ernie Reyes	Tex Smith
Andy Anderson	Dannny Daniels	Wyatt Harris	Pete Lovely	Dick Richardson	Marion Spencer
Randy Anderson	Alan Darr	Ray Hiatt	Bob Machin	Kevin Richardson	Ken Stansberry
Mike Ashley	Phyllis Devine	Bill Hill	Ralph Mapes	Eric Rickman	Gordy Sutherland
Archie Bado	Bob Eby	Ralph Hobbs	Dick Martin	Hal Robson	Len Sutton
Bonnie Bailey	Chris Economaki	Alice Holtkamp	Flenn McGlonie	Jack Rook	George Tichenor
Bob Barkhimer	Dixie Emmons	Bob Hoover	Bob McMurty	Rosie Roussel	Larry "Toby" Tobias
Bob Bartlett	Lou Ensworth	Dick Houser	Tom Medely	Bob Rushing	Ray Valasck
Wade Bedell	Rod Eschenburg	Forrest Hurd	Lloyd Moore	Troy Ruttmann	Ken VanWoert
Mike Bell	Ray Erickson	Sam Jacobs	Tommy Morrow	B.C. Ryan	Herc Vigienzone
Bob Blake	Erwin Eszlinger	Walt James	Tom Motter	Doris Schindler	Dick Vineyard
Paul Blake	Dale Fairfax	Larry Jendras Jr.	Bob Noe	Carl Schmidt	Dick Wallen
Ken Boydstun	Dick Frazier	Jim Johansson	Dan Norgaarden	Henry Schroeder	John Way
Ray Boyes	Bill Fitzgerald	Brandon Johnston	Don O'Rielly	Gordy Schuck	Charles Weeks
Frank Brennfoerder	Joe Gemsa	Paul Kamm	James Park	Scotty Scovill	Wayne Weiler
Arnold Bremler	Don Gilchrest	Adrain Ketchem	Lynn Paxton	Tim Sexton	Paul Weisner
Allan Brown	Andy Granatelli	Lee Kirk	Frank and Eldora	Greg Sharp	Mary West
Leroy Byers	Nate Gassfield	Johnny Klann	Peieto	Jeff Sharpe	Gordon White
Bob Chaddock	Al Gray	Jay Koch	Jim Penney	Doug Shaw	Lee Wick
Sonny Coleman	Myra Gray	Loren Kreck	Bill Peters	Bob Sheldon	Joe Winkler
Ken Coles	Elton Green	Steve Larson	Al Powell	Bob SIlvia	Crocky Wright
Don Connolly	Jon Gullihier	Bill LeVrier	Jim Rathmann	Al Slinker	Zeke Ziegler

Last, but not least, a very special thanks to my wife, Naida, for correcting my spelling, seemingly endless proofreading and for putting in most of the commas that appear in *Roaring Roadsters.*

ROADSTER HISTORY

This book could be called "Roaring Roadsters II." It starts in 1924, but actually "track roadsters" existed some two decades before this.

In general, racing on the European Gran Prix circuits started around 1905, and a few years later the Vanderbuilt Cup Races were held on New York's Long Island. The Indianapolis Speedway opened in 1909, and the first 500-mile race was held in 1911. The cars in these races were, for the most part, modified stock cars. The body types were early versions of a roadster, they were stripped of unnecessary parts and the engines were souped up. Isn't that a track roadster? We could call these early race cars "hot rods," but that term wouldn't even exist for another 40 years.

Racing hasn't changed over the years in that cars will evolve to go faster and faster. In 1905, there was plenty of evolving to do, and things changed in a hurry. By about 1915, the cars running in the major road races and at Indy were strictly race cars. The "track roadsters" had disappeared—for the first time.

A HOT ROD MYSTERY

There are a number of mysteries in this book and one of them is the term "hot rod" itself. Where did it come from?

The word definitely did not exist before World War II. The "hot rodders" called their cars many things, but "hot rod" was not one of them. The word appears to have cropped up around 1946. Applying logic to the origin of "hot rod" helps a little but does not solve the puzzle. "Hot" sounds easy enough to figure out, but how did "rod" come to mean car?

I've asked a number of people about the origin of the term "hot rod," and Publisher Tex Smith came up with the best answer. He thinks the term was dreamed up by newspaper writers to describe any modified car—especially if the car was involved in a highway accident. Usually the car involved wasn't a true "hot rod," but that didn't stop some newspaper from editorializing against street roadsters. This could have been an outgrowth of the anti-auto racing policy that some newspapers had at that time. This was especially true of the Hearst newspaper chain. This "yellow journalism" carried over to the highway. Tex Smith thinks that the *San Francisco Examiner* first used "hot rod" and used it in a very derogatory manner.

The name somehow caught on, hot rodders used it, and soon promoters started using it to describe the track roadsters. With some trepidation about the name, *Hot Rod Magazine* came out in 1948. It took only a few years for hot rod to make it to the pages of *Webster's Dictionary*, but it took many years to make the name respectable.

In this book, I've used the term hot rod only in the time period after the word was coined.

SOME TERMINOLOGY

There are many references to sprint cars in this book. This term did not exist prior to about 1950. Sprint cars were called "big cars." Why "big cars"? Because they were bigger than midgets—simple but logical thinking!

For the most part in order to avoid confusion, I've used the term "sprint car," even though I may be referring to a time period before 1950. In some instances, when the reference is to racing in the 1930s or early 1940s, I just couldn't bring myself to write "sprint car," so they are (properly) "big cars."

To carry history a bit further back—the midgets didn't come on the racing scene until the early 1930s. What were "big cars" called before then? Just plain "race cars" or sometimes "one mans" to separate them from the two-man Indianapolis cars.

LOREN KRECK

As a teenager in Southern California during the 1930s, I vividly remember the excitement from the roar of Ascot's big cars and Gilmore's midgets. That was enough to launch a life-long interest in sketching crossed-up roadsters, spinning race cars, and splintered guard rails. Early on, it was an effective substitute for reality, while scrimping to save enough money for a forty-dollar Cragar head (safely ensconced under the bed) and eventually, a twenty-five dollar 1928 Ford roadster.

In the future were to be street drags, dry lakes meets, and what is best described as "lights out adventures in avoidance," shared with Hollywood and Beverly Hills police. These late night exercises were to prove their training usefulness during World War II while flying a Marine Corsair from a carrier in the pre-dawn darkness off Okinawa.

Now retired from a career in dentistry and living in Montana, I still remember the skinny-tire circa by drawing and scratch building models of old race cars. Along with author Don Radbruch, I belong to the Golden Wheels antique racing association.
—*Loren Kreck*

ABOUT THE AUTHOR

● ●

I got hooked on auto racing in the 1930's, when my parents took me to races in the San Francisco Bay area. I watched great drivers, like Rex Mays and Fred Agabashian, drive big cars and midgets at Oakland, San Jose, and the San Francisco Motordrome. Right then, I decided that someday I would drive such cars. Sometimes, after witnessing one of the violent crashes so common in those deadly times, I would have doubts. But not for long. World War II interrupted, and I spent time as an infantryman in Germany, earning the Combat Infantry Badge and a Bronze Star.

I began racing in earnest in 1948, when my brother, Les, and I converted my street roadster into a track roadster. We were both complete neophytes at building a racer... all we knew we had seen from the grandstands! A trip through a fence and an end-over-end flip during our third race quickly taught us that welding on the steering gear was a very bad idea!!

Better track roadsters were built over the next two years, with me at the wheel for some success. We ran on the Northern California circuit, as well as in Oregon and Washington. Even though I did better than many racers, my winnings did not begin to cover the costs. Payoffs varied from a high of $98.60 to a low of $1.34.

Late in the 1950 season, I switched to sprint cars. That winter, Les helped me build a Mercury V8-powered sprinter that carried us to the 1951 American Racing Association (now the Northern Auto Racing Club) championship. In 1951 and '52, I usually ran up front, and the sprint car payoffs averaged around $100 per race. My career high payoff of $670 came for a third place finish at a 500-lap race in Oakland. I raced some stocks and hardtops in the early 1950s, but eventually I confined my activities to the Bay Cities Racing Association indoor midgets and to sports cars. I quit

driving in 1967. I had been upside down seven times in those pre-rollcage days, but I had escaped with relatively minor injuries.

I've been interested in automobile racing history for many years. I wrote historical articles for *Speed Age Magazine* in the 1950s, and more recently I've been doing material for Phyllis Devine's *The Alternate,* as well as for *Auto Racing Memories*.

Publisher Tex Smith warned me that a book of this scope would be difficult. I found soon enough that there was lousy recordkeeping by those early racing organizations (if there were any records at all). To boot, most of those organizations no longer exist. Thank goodness there are a few people out there who care about racing history, and who have been willing to help. Even so, I found that compiling this book has been an awesome task. On more than once occasion I have sworn I would never again attempt such a task. Now, I find that new information on roadsters keeps coming in, and to my horror, a Roaring Roadsters II file has appeared!

The photos show my continuing interest, my current appearance is shown in the cockpit of Les Stern's Offy sprinter (Donaven Stark photo) at Meridian, Idaho. The older picture is my 1950 track roadster at Seattle. Along with a partner in California, I am restoring the car. Well, restoring is cheating a lot, as most of the parts on number 23 went into a sprint car and are long gone. But, the '23 T body remains, and all this is happening so I can run with the Golden Wheels in Washington state.

I worked as a soil engineer for San Francisco Bay area firms for 25 years before retiring to northern Idaho, near Sagle, with my wife Naida and our cats Maxwell and Harrison.

—Don Radbruch

ARIZONA

● ●

It is probable that there was some form of roadster racing in Arizona in the 1930s. It appears that there were roadster races at Holbrook as early as 1936, but research in that eastern Arizona city came up with no specific information.

After World War II, there was roadster racing at Prescott on a quarter-mile dirt track at the Yavapai County Fairgrounds. This was in the early summer of 1946 and in one race the winner was Bobby Ball. The future Indy driver drove his A-V8 from Phoenix and raced complete with windshield and headlights. Photos indicated that there was a capacity crowd at Prescott that day so Bobby Ball started off a very illustrious racing career with a payoff that probably exceeded a hundred dollars.

Roadster racing continued at Prescott in 1946 and 1947 and there was also racing at Flagstaff and Holbrook. There was not as much roadster racing in the big cities of Phoenix and Tucson as might be expected. The roadsters apparently ran only occasionally, and then it was in dual shows with the midgets. The reason for this is unclear, but perhaps the hot rods just did not have enough cars to run races in areas where the promoters, and fans, would expect large fields. In Phoenix, the roadsters ran with the Arizona Midget Drivers and Owners Club at the fifth-mile Phoenix Midget Speedway and Bobby Ball and Jimmy Bryan were winners here. The Arizona midgets also ran at Safford, Yuma and Globe so the roadsters may have also raced in these cities.

On September 14, 1947, a roadster race billed as the Arizona State Championship was held at Prescott on the fairgrounds half-mile track. Future Indy winner Jimmy Bryan had the fast time of 36.0 seconds and also won the 50-lap main event in the McIlvain Chrysler Six. The *Prescott Evening Courier* reported that, "Showers of dust made progress of the races difficult and at times impossible to follow." Bryan's time of 29 minutes and 5 seconds indicates that he ran laps a second faster than his qualifying speed or that somebody kindly knocked a few laps off the

Action on the one-mile track at the Arizona State Fairgrounds in Phoenix in 1954. An unidentified driver in #98 battles with Hank Henry. (Al Gray collection)

Rosie Roussel slides under Johnny Paulson in #42 at South Mountain Speedway, circa—1952. Roussel won a lot of races in this Riley Four Port-powered car. He has recently restored the roadster and will soon be competing in vintage races. (Rosie Roussel collection)

More Phoenix action. Johnny Paulson fights to hold off Don O'Reilly in the Merc-powered #36. (Rod Eschenburg collection)

1946 at Prescott and Bobby Ball is leading Lional Alderton in #7 and another very street-like hot rod.
(Bob Blake collection)

Complete with windshield and headlights Bobby Ball is in action at Prescott. Ball appears to be wearing a World War II tank driver's helmet.
(Leroy Winslow photo—Greg Welsh collection)

Augie Chemas leads an unidentified competitor at Prescott in 1946 or 1947. Chema's car had a four-cylinder Chevy engine with an Olds three-port head. The car still exists and is owned by Bob Blake of Phoenix. *(Bob Blake collection)*

One of the Prescott roadsters in 1947. Left to right—Jerry Arman, driver, Harold (Gordo) Vichem and Joe Ilvain. *(Alan Neff collection)*

After winning a race at Prescott in 1946 Bobby Ball prepares to drive his A-V8 home to Phoenix. That's the battery alongside the Merc engine. Note the liberal use of plumber's tape and telephone wire.
(Bob Blake collection)

advertised 50-lap distance. Also in the field that day was Dempsey Wilson and Bobby Ball who would be Bob Bell in the newspaper accounts.

In 1948 it appears that an attempt was made to bring wintertime roadster racing to the Tucson area, and there may have been a roadster organization formed at that time. A three-quarter-mile dirt oval was constructed at Kinsley Ranch just south of Tucson. Two of Arizona's Indy drivers, Bill Cheeseburg and Roger McCluskey, got their start in the Kinsley Ranch Roadsters. The only specific information on roadster races at this track comes from a tragic report in *National Speed Sport News* in early 1948, "2 Die In Hot Rod Race Accident." A spectator was killed by a loose wheel, and later that same day, driver Eugene Gasser was killed in a four-car pileup on what sounds like a very dusty track. It is not known if there was further racing of any kind at Kinsley Ranch after this tragedy.

Some California cars must have raced in Arizona in the 1940s, but it was not until April of 1950 that a major invasion took place. At that time the California Roadster Association sanctioned a 100-mile roadster race on the one-mile dirt oval at the

Jimmy Bryan gets what may be his first trophy at Prescott in 1947. The 1958 Indy winner drove a Chrysler Six-powered car that day.
(Bob Blake collection)

Danny Waite died in this crash at Flagstaff. Note that the driver's body has apparently pushed the steering column and the cowl forward. Although technically a jalopy, this car competed with the full-bodied roadsters.
(Joe Winkler collection)

Arizona State Fairgrounds in Phoenix. The race attracted an excellent field of cars and drivers from all over the West Coast. Roy Prosser had a fast lap of 40.17 seconds to outpace 35 qualifiers. (This time was only about two seconds off of the time of the AAA Championship cars of that era.) The 100-mile race turned out to be an endurance contest as the rough track took its toll of the hot rods. Bobby Ball wasn't the fastest but he drove his '27 T-Merc to victory by a comfortable margin as only 11 cars finished the long grind. Ball was still having troubles with the press as *Hot Rod Magazine* had Bob "Hall" winning the race. (This may have been deliberate as Ball was running AAA midgets and perhaps should not have been driving the hot rods.)

Manzanita Speedway had been built in Phoenix in 1949 and it was lighted for night racing—ideal for the torrid Arizona summers. A few roadster races were held there in 1949 with mostly Arizona cars and it appears that fields were short. In 1950, the California Roadster Association took over that sanction at Manzanita (and later at South Mountain Speedway) and from that time on the CRA made regular trips to Arizona. Arizona drivers like Wayne Weiler, Roger McCloskey and Donnie Davis were usually outnumbered by the Californians but they usually won their share of races. CRA regulars such as Bob Cross and Rosie Roussel took home lots of Arizona cash during the early 1950s. In 1951, the CRA started allowing sprint cars to compete with the roadsters. From 1951 until the roadsters were phased out in 1956 most CRA races were combined roadster-sprint car events.

In eastern Arizona, roadster racing continued at Holbrook with local and New Mexico cars until about 1951 when the stock cars took over at that track.

The 100-mile races at the Arizona State Fairgrounds were not held for several years but in 1954 the CRA was back for a race on May 9. The race was billed as the second Western States Roadster Championships and was not open to the sprint cars. It is safe bet that some sprint cars with temporary roadster bodies took part in the

The dusty start of the 1947 Arizona State Championships at Prescott. Jimmy Bryan has already grabbed the lead as Lee Sorrells (arrow) battles on the outside. (Bonnie Sorrells collection)

race. Ronnie Allyn's story in *Desert Dust Magazine* reported that 7,000 fans saw Johnny Paulson drive a steady race to win over Art Bisch, Steve Owens and midget driver Lyle Dickey.

The CRA returned to the fairgrounds in Phoenix for another 100 miler in 1955. This time it was a combined roadster-sprint car race and there were even some Offy sprinters in the race. (Don Olds was killed when his Offy flipped during this race). Wayne Weiler won this race in a roadster and, thanks to him, the hot rods went out a winner in Arizona. Perhaps Weiler remembered the tough 1950 race and figured that "strong is better." He'd been running and winning "jalopy" races with his Merc powered '32 Ford Coupe. For the 100 miler Weiler replaced the coupe body with a Model A roadster body. Weiler today admits that he didn't outrun too many cars but "was in front at the end of 100 miles." He took home $460 for his victory.

The roadsters competed with the sprinters in other Arizona races during 1955, but at the end of that year the roadsters were gone.

In addition to the Eugene Gasser crash at Kinsley Ranch in 1948, there were other roadster fatalities in Arizona. Danny Waite died at Prescott in about 1947 and, at Holbrook, Lional Alderton lost his life a couple of years later. At Globe Raceway, Speed Millet was killed in about 1949 and this was probably in a roadster.

Note: *Most of this information for this chapter came from Arizona racing historian, Bob Blake of Phoenix.*

The Los Angles-based CRA made many trips to the Phoenix area in the early 1950s. The CRA has become the California Racing (not roadster) Association and the sprint cars are replacing the roadsters. *(Joe Winkler collection)*

The lineup for the Arizona State Championships at Prescott on September 14, 1947. Jimmy Bryan is on the pole with Lee Sorrells in #18 on the outside. (Bob Blake collection)

At Holbrook, it was "Run What Ya Brung"

There was hot rod racing at Holbrook on a fairly regular basis from 1947 until about 1950. For the most part the cars that competed were local or came from neighboring New Mexico. As the program cover indicates the races were billed as "Hot Rod Jalopy Races"—these terms covered a multitude of car designs at Holbrook. The artist's drawing on the program looks like an Indy Novi—this is about the only type of car that did not race at Holbrook.

(Joe Winkler collection)

Stan Owens prepares to qualify the H.D. Morris and Ray Ashley car. This roadster had rear torsion bars that were made from Ford driveshafts. *(Bob Noe collection)*

This is obviously a Model A Ford chassis, but no further information is available. The less said about that roll bar the better. *(Joe Winkler collection)*

This Holbrook car appears closer to a sprint car than a roadster. Lional Alderton may have been the driver. *(Bob Noe collection)*

Stan Owens is congratulated after a victory at Holbrook in 1948. This jalopy appears to have a stock engine. *(Joe Winkler collection)*

It is not known who drove #113. It appears that there is no seat belt and that the fuel tank serves as a rear bumper. *(Bob Noe collection)*

This car has been shortened and is technically a "modified." Pappy Noe usually ran #14, but this is not his car. *(Bob Noe collection)*

The start of a race at Holbrook in about 1948. It looks as unsafe for the spectators as it does for the drivers. *(Bob Noe collection)*

Pappy Noe in his nice looking roadster from Gallup, New Mexico is on the outside of a Holbrook "jalopy." *(Joe Winkler collection)*

Another unidentified driver at Holbrook. That's probably a Buick Eight engine in what can be called a sprint car. *(Joe Winkler collection)*

This car came from the Phoenix area to race at Holbrook. The engine is a 320 cubic-inch Buick Eight. Lee Sorrells usually drove the car. *(Bob Noe collection)*

The body work is crude, but this is a sprint car. Pete Jaramilo usually drove the car—it can be assumed that Pete was not superstitious. *(Bob Noe collection)*

SOUTHERN CALIFORNIA

There was more roadster racing in Southern California than in any other part of the United States. The first roadster raced there in 1924 and the last in 1956. There were hundreds of roadsters, hundreds of drivers, and they raced on nearly a hundred tracks.

It all began in the summer of 1924 when three Model T Ford roadsters lined up for a race at the Culver City one-mile dirt track. Bud Winfield was one of the drivers and the rider in his T was his brother Ed—a pioneer builder of race cars and racing equipment. Ed Winfield had some of his early speed parts on that Model T, so it is a safe bet that the Winfield brothers won the first Southern California roadster race.

In the mid- to late 1920s, there were occasional exhibition roadster races at Ascot Speedway during the race car events. Clarence Downing ran his Rajo T roadster there, and his times were probably faster than those of some of the race cars. Around 1930, roadster racing really got going and for the next several years races were held at several tracks. Races were held at Huntington Beach, Colton, Riverside and Culver City. Races were also held on a regular basis at Jefferies Ranch in Burbank. This usually dusty five-eighths-mile track was built on a

ranch owned by former heavyweight champion Jim Jefferies. Thanks to historian Johnny Klann, who drove in some of these races, some information on the purses is available. Klann remembers that on a good day the feature winner might get $65—on a bad-paying day, $15. Usually the cars were guaranteed $5 for showing up—in those depression days that would buy groceries for a week. Johnny Klann raced against some very good drivers in

This is the first roadster race—Culver City one-mile dirt track in 1924. Bud Winfield with his brother Ed riding with him is on the pole.
(Johnny Klann collection)

It's a stretch to call #33 a roadster. This is a "claiming race" at Banning, California, on July 4, 1924. Any car could be claimed for $25.
(Johnny Klann collection)

Johnny Klann in his bobtail—circa 1930. Klann ran this car in race car events and put the roadster body shown in the background (upper left corner) on for roadster races.
(Johnny Klann collection)

Indy legend Jack McGrath was a regular at Southern California roadster races
(LCS collection)

those roadster races. There were drivers like Rex Mays, George and Hal Robson, Floyd Roberts, Mel Hansen, Roy Russing and Bayliss Leverett. There are some famous racing and Indy names in that batch of roadster racers.

Most of the roadsters were Model T Fords with a few four-cylinder Chevys and an occasional Essex or Dodge. Speed equipment was available for these motors. Johnny Klann recalls that it was just like today—the more money you had the faster you went. The cars were fast—a semi-stock Model T could hit 70 mph and a full race T would easily top 100 mph. Many of the roadsters, especially the Model T Fords, were flimsy things and something was always breaking. Things like spindles, steering parts and axles broke with frightening regularity and the result was often a bad crash. The mechanical failures combined with narrow, rutted and often dusty tracks took a heavy toll of roadster drivers. In about three years of racing, five roadster

Jefferies Ranch in 1933. (Left to right) Bayliss Leverett, Ray Pixley and George Robson. All later raced at Indianapolis. (Johnny Klann collection)

A field of modified roadsters lines up at Southgate in 1935. This track was sometimes called Southern Speedway. (Norris Cook collection)

Two modified roadsters at Southgate on August 9, 1935. Wally Schock is in #31. (Norris Cook collection)

WALT JAMES

If anybody is "Mr. Roadster Racing" it has to be Walt James. James was involved with hot rod racing from 1946 until 1956. He was a driver, a car owner, an official, and a president of the California Roadster Association, but most of all he was an enthusiast.

Walt James began roadster racing in the "Ash Can Derby" races at San Bernardino in 1946. He drove a cut-down T-V8 that was much more of a track roadster than some of his competition. James got into trouble during one race when he tangled with another car and did a few flips off the track. The car came to rest right-side up and against the fence that separated the track from the spectators. James was a bit dazed, but not enough to refuse the offer of a beer from a nearby spectator. When the ambulance arrived he was enjoying a beer and completely recovered.

Walt James, along with his brother Joe, moved on to the California Roadster Association when that group began racing late in 1946. Both of the James brothers did well in roadster racing. Joe James was the better driver, but Walt usually managed to keep pace with him. Walt cheerfully admits, "I talked a better race than Joe so I usually had a better ride." Walt James stuck with the roadsters and drove for several years. Joe James moved on to a AAA sprint car championship and a shot at Indy before he was killed in a championship car race at San Jose in 1952.

Walt James almost died in the terrible highway crash that took the life of Bud Winfield in 1950. It was while he was in the hospital in Fresno that he was elected 1951 president of the California Roadster Association—a job nobody else wanted. James accepted the job with his usual good humor and set about to save an organization that most people thought was finished. The CRA had only five races in 1950.

Propped up in a hospital bed with both legs in casts James set out to find some races for the roadsters by writing to every promoter he could think of. He wrote glowingly of all the roadsters he could provide for a race—he could think of 18. He told of all the "name drivers" in the roadsters—at best only Bob Cross and Colby Scroggin could be called name drivers. By return

Walt James at a track someplace in Southern California in 1946. The engine is a Model B Ford with a Cook Head. James drove this car only a few times. (Don Radbruch collection)

mail came a few tentative OKs and the CRA wasn't quite dead. From that point on things got better for the California Roadster Association. They were soon running mixed shows with the sprint cars and would go on to become the strong organization that they are today.

Walt James is still enthusiastic about racing and is active with the Western Racing Association. This is a group of vintage race cars and vintage race car drivers—both go fast and so does Walt James.

Jefferies Ranch—1932. There are other "star-studded field" photos in this book, but this one is tops. Two Indy winners (Robson and Roberts) and a National Champion (Mays). Babe Stanyer was considered the best of the bunch but died at Ascot before reaching his full potential.
(Johnny Klann collection)

Jefferies Ranch in Burbank in 1932. Floyd Roberts leads a field of roadsters. (Johnny Klann collection)

Rajo Jack gets a big trophy from his wife Estelle at Southgate in 1936. Rajo Jack (aka Jack DeSoto) was probably the best black driver who ever raced
(Loren Kreck collection)

	LIST OF ENTRIES			
Car	No.	Driver	Owner	Address
Chevy Lee Spl	1	Bill Moore	Lee Chapel	Glendale
Rajo Ford	2	Ed Bunnell	W. Cunningham	Riverside
Rajo Ford	3	Chet Shafer	Chet Shafer	Riverside
Rajo Ford	4	C. Stewart	Forrest Pratt	Riverside
Buick Spl	7	Floyd Douglas	Floyd Douglas	Colton
Rajo Ford	9	Bob Chantlon	Rex Mays	Riverside
Rajo Ford	10	Mel Hanson	Mel Hanson	Fontana
Riley Spl	12	Ed Hanley	Ed Hanley	Colton
Fronty Spl	16	J. W. Wilson	J. W. Wilson	Colton
Rajo Ford	20	Ed. Palmer	Ed. Palmer	San Bernardino
Riley Ford "A"	26	Geo. Robson	H. Robson	Huntington Park
C & H Spl	27	Rex Mays	Mal Hare	Riverside
Chevy Spl	28	Al Horn	E. R. Ross	Fullerton
Ford "A"	29	Al Horn	Al Horn	Los Angeles
Ford "A"	30	Les Lytle	Les Lytle	Santa Monica
Rajo Ford	31	Ted Horn	A. Andregg	Los Angeles
De Soto	32	Ray Young	Ray Young	Santa Monica
Fronty Spl	33			Corona
Ford "A"	34	Ike Trone	Ike Trone	Long Beach
Chevy Spl	35	Bill Williams	Bill Williams	Long Beach

The entry list for roadster races at Ed Glaser's Race Track in 1931. There are five future Indy drivers on that list. (Hal Robson is listed as an owner.) (Jeff Sharpe collection)

drivers were killed. Frankie Gargola died at Riverside, Oliver Burton at Culver City and Wayne Gause was killed in his first race. At Jefferies Ranch, Johnny Pastovich and Johnny McCrachen died in separate crashes.

Roadster racing died out in about 1933 as many of the racers, including Johnny Klann, were more interested in race cars. (They weren't called big cars yet.) After a few years absence, roadster racing returned to Southern California. This time the cars were actually modified roadsters—actually the granddaddies of today's modifieds. The cars used a cowl from a roadster body, usually a '27 Model T. This unit was narrowed, the standard wheel base shortened and there was no tail section—just an exposed fuel tank. Most of the cars used four cylinder engines—hopped up Model A or Model B Ford with some Chevy fours. There was a new batch of drivers. An entry list for a Southgate race on September 27, 1936, lists the following drivers:

Wally Schock smiles from his modified roadster. Note that there is no tail section—just an exposed fuel tank. (Norris Cook collection)

AUTO RACES
Ed Graser's Race Track
SUNDAY DECEMBER 6th, 1931
MODIFIED STOCK CAR RACES
Sponsored by Tri-City Auto Race Club
on
McMILLAN
GASOLINE
and
MEMOIL
GUARANTEED

HOLMSTROM'S CAFES
DELICIOUS FOOD · PLEASANT SURROUNDINGS
ALWAYS OPEN

A view of the Southgate track in 1936. The modified roadsters must have been short of cars that day as there are a couple of big cars lined up at the rear.
(Norris Cook collection—Ron's Sport Pic)

A program cover for roadster races at Colton in 1931. (Jeff Sharpe collection)

Bud Sennett, Ed Barnett, Wally Schock, Pat Cunningham, Tex Peterson, Spider Webb, Rajo Jack and Bob Frame. These names would be around West Coast racing for awhile.

The Southgate modified roadsters died out about 1939. Some strange-looking apparently stock roadsters raced briefly and then jalopy races were held. The jalopy races were held on a steeplechase track built in the infield at Southgate and the cars were similar to the ones that evolved into track roadsters in other parts of the country. Evolution was backwards in Southern California. Popular big car driver Bud Minyard died during one of these races.

After World War II, the first roadster racing was on a sandy oval in the desert near San Bernardino, some 50 miles east of Los Angeles. There was no organization and it was simply a matter of "run what ya brung." A few pre-war modified roadsters raced, a few big cars and a lot of near stock street rods. The races somehow acquired the rather undignified name of "The Ash Can Derby"—odds are most of the cars were not as bad as the name sounds. Troy Ruttman drove his first race here as did Joe and Walt James.

Southern California had been a hot bed of roadster activity for many years, but most of the energy had been directed towards hot rods and the straightaway runs at the dry lakes. A group of hot rodders got together in the summer of 1946 with the intention of forming an organization so that they could race their cars on oval tracks. They formed the California Roadster Association. A list of some of the charter members reads like a racing hall of fame roster—Pop and Troy Ruttman, Pat Flaherty, Jack McGrath, Dick and Jim Rathmann, Jimmy Davies, Walt and Joe James, Manual Ayulo, Jim Rigsby, Don Freeland, Dick Vineyard and Yam Oka.

Wally Schock in #31 at Southgate—circa 1935. Schock was a two-time American Racing Association Pacific Coast champion in the late 1930s. (Norris Cook collection)

Wally Schock's slick-looking modified—circa 1935. These cars differed from true roadsters in that the bodies were narrowed. (Norris Cook collection)

Saugus—1946. Troy Ruttman in #4 and Gordon Reid in #36. Ruttman's #4 is a near-stock Model A. Today he says, "It didn't take us long to figure out that this wasn't going to get the job done."
(Greg Sharp—Vintage Racing Photos)

THE DAY BOB CROSS BECAME BOB DENNY

Despite the fact that car #54 landed upside-down, Bob Cross survived this flip with minor injuries. The problem came the next day when this photo appeared in the sports section of a Los Angeles newspaper and was seen by his bosses at the Pacific Telephone Company. He was told to quit racing or quit his job—race drivers seemed to have few civil rights in 1948.

Cross' girlfriend and future wife's name was "Denny" so that became his name on Southern California race tracks.

Cross' immediate superiors at the phone company knew what was going on—it was just the Big Brass that needed to be deceived. The ploy worked just fine and Cross continued to be a top-ranked California Roadster Association driver until about 1955. Bob Cross is now retired and living in Idaho. It is also doubtful if the Pacific Telephone Company Big Brass cares what went on 40 years ago. Bob Denny-Cross is Bob Cross in this book.
(Photo: Bob Cross collection)

Harry Stockman drove this car at Saugus—this is probably 1946. (Bill Hill collection)

Walt James towed his Ford Six roadster north to Oakland in 1948. Jimmy Davies is the driver—James is at the right in the background.
(Rod Eschenburg collection—Bruce Craig photo)

The turtle deck of a roadster serves as a workbench as the crew works on the head of a Riley four-port. (Greg Sharp—Vintage Racing Photos)

The first race was held at the half-mile Carrell Speedway on Labor Day of 1946. About 50 hot rods showed up, as well as a large crowd. The cars were fast, mostly ill-handling and all but a few of the drivers were complete novices. It was one wild show. Wally Pancratz, one of the few drivers with racing experience, won the first CRA main event. There were a number of races before winter and the roadster racing boom was on in Southern California.

During the 1947 season the California Roadster Association had as many as 80 cars at a race. Races were held up to five times a week at tracks like Carrell Speedway, Huntington Beach, Bonelli Stadium in Saugus, San Bernardino, and a half-dozen other tracks that have been forgotten. The CRA also hosted a "National Roadster Championship" at the famed Rose Bowl in Pasadena on August 7, 1947. The "National" aspect of the race required giving the regular CRA drivers some very strange hometowns. Troy Ruttman's listing as being from Mooreland, Oklahoma, was probably more honest than most—at least his dad had been born there. The race was a good one and drew a large crowd—the purse was probably around $5,000. It was the only roadster race ever held at the Rose Bowl as the cars got into the infield too often and tore up too much delicate turf. By the end of the 1947 season the California Roadster Association had run close to 100 races for a total purse of about $180,000.

In 1948, for various reasons, three more roadster groups were formed in Southern California. One of the organizations was California Hot Rods Inc. This was a fairly strong, active and well run group and had some good drivers like Dick Vineyard and Stan Kross. The CHR ran several races at Gilmore Stadium in Hollywood. Gilmore was long the home

This is the massive Packard Straight Eight in the Puffy Puffer-driven #13. Puffer later flipped this car. (Al Slinker collection)

of the midgets and these were a hard act for the roadsters to follow—apparently the crowds were not too large. Another of the spin-offs from the CRA was the Southern California Racing Association— nothing is known about this group. The third new group was called American Sports Cars Inc. Somebody apparently thought that hot rods were "American Sports Cars." (Perhaps they were, but I'm certainly glad the name didn't stick—this book would then be "The Roaring American Sports Cars.") The American Sports Cars Inc. operated for a couple of seasons and ran at the Carpenteria Thunderbowl, on a very high-banked half miler at Fresno and on a track built in a ballpark in Oceanside. Top drivers were George Seeger, Bruce Emmons, Grant Lambert and Bill Steves.

The CRA, despite the competition from the other groups, enjoyed another good year in 1948. The roadsters were racing two to three times a week, although crowds and purses were down a bit from 1947. The CRA had a 500-lap race at the half-mile dirt Carrell Speedway in May. A crowd, reported as

Lou Figero at Saugus in 1946. Figero later moved on to the NASCAR stockers and was killed in one of these cars in about 1955. (Rod Eschenburg collection)

Troy Ruttman gets another trophy. He's driving the Bert Letner Elco Twin car—two spark plugs per cylinder.
(Rod Eschenburg collection—Bruce Craig photo)

In this photo it is probably Pop Ruttman in #4 and Troy Ruttman in #7. Bonelli Stadium, Saugus, in 1946. (Rod Eschenburg collection)

Troy Ruttman gets one of his many trophies. Ruttman was about 16 when this photo was taken. (Rod Eschenburg collection)

A trio of California Roadster Association drivers in 1948. Left to right—Lou Figero, Colby Scroggin and Dempsey Wilson. Scroggin was generally called "Scroggins" but this was not his name.
(Rod Eschenburg collection—Bruce Craig photo)

Location of this photo is unknown and so is the driver of #10. Ken Stansberry is in #119.
(Ken Stansberry collection)

This looks like Bill Steves—is it? The location is unknown. *(Greg Sharp—Vintage Racing Photos)*

Carrell Speedway—circa 1950. Rosie Roussel and Yam Oka pose with some young ladies. *(Rosie Roussel collection)*

12,000 saw dark-horse Dempsey Wilson come home the winner. By mid-1948, some of the early stars of the California Roadster Association were moving on to the midgets, sprints and even to Indianapolis. There were still fine drivers and good cars competing—plenty of both. Some of the drivers starting to win races were Bob Cross (aka Bob Denny), Rosie Roussel, Roy Prosser, Walt James, Ed Lockhart and Chuck Leighton.

By 1949 and 1950, the roadsters were fading. The rival groups had folded, but the CRA was having a hard time booking races and a harder time attracting fans. There was a successful 500-lap race at Carrell Speedway and Bob Cross won that race. As might be expected the hardtop stock cars were coming on the scene. These cars appeared on local television, the fans flocked to see all the action (wrecks), and the roadsters were all but forgotten—the midgets and the sprints suffered much the same fate. In 1950, the California Roadster Association ran only five races for a total purse of less than $2000.

Late in 1950, the CRA members met to elect a new president for 1951. Most members felt that nothing could be done and that roadster racing and the CRA were finished. Several car owners and drivers were nominated for president but all turned it down—nobody wanted what certainly would be a frustrating and thankless job. Finally, perhaps somewhat in desperation, Walt James was nominated and quickly elected. James was in no

Ed Lockhart drove Al Grady's GMC to a trophy dash win at Carrell Speedway. Gray's car usually raced some 150 miles to the north at Porterville. *(Al Gray collection)*

position to say no—he'd been seriously injured in an auto accident a few weeks earlier and was 200 miles away in a hospital.

Walt James saved the CRA, but to an extent the roadsters paid a price—a price that was unavoidable anyhow. James insisted that the sprint cars be allowed to run with the roadsters. Promoters liked this and the California Roadster Association recovered to become the strong group that it is today. The roadsters were not deliberately phased out and for the next six years they

This is Don Freeland at Carrell Speedway— probably 1947.
(Rod Eschenburg collection—Bruce Craig photo)

Handsome George Seegar gets a trophy at Saugus in 1950. (Greg Sharp—Vintage Racing Photos)

A SOUTHERN CALIFORNIA MYSTERY

It was around 1939 that these strange-looking roadsters raced at Southern Speedway in Southgate.

These cars are not the modified roadsters that ran at Southgate a few years earlier. They don't look like the track roadsters that were running elsewhere in 1939. They don't even look like street roadsters.

Does anybody know the story of these cars?

This is a Hudson roadster at Southgate in 1939. No identification on the driver or the group that ran the races. (Greg Sharp—Vintage Racing Photos)

A lineup at Southgate around 1939. Car #6 looks a bit like a "normal" track roadster but check the "outrigger" on #31. The driver of #56 is probably big car pilot Ed Barnett.
(Greg Sharp—Vintage Racing Photos)

Ken Stansberry leads the main even at Huntington Beach—circa 1950. (Ken Stansberry collection)

Bob Cross in one of the roadsters he drove in CRA competition. This was in his "Bob Denny" era. (Bill Hill collection— Ted Tanner photo)

Bob Cross relaxes after a main event win—probably Carrell. (Greg Sharp—Vintage Racing Photos)

THE CRA'S FIVE HUNDREDS

In 1948 and 1949, the California Roadster Association ran 500-lap races at Carrell Speedway. Thanks to Dorothy Sloan, who wrote articles for *Speed Age* and for *Hot Rod Magazine*, information is available about these races.

In 1948, the half-mile Carrell Speedway was a dirt track, and it got very rough during the 500 laps of competition. Thirty-three cars started the race and despite the heavy traffic there were no major crashes. Drivers Roy Prosser, Andy Linden, Ed Korgan, Ed Barnett, Troy Ruttman and Jim Rigsby were all early leaders in a hotly contested race. Around mid-way in the race, Dempsey Wilson took the lead in his #37 Mercury and held it to the end of the race. Veteran Ed Barnett finished second, despite a lengthy stop to change a broken axle, and Puffy Puffer was third. The rough track took its toll of cars, although 18 of them were running at the finish. Jim Rigsby's car lost a door and the fuel tank. His crew wired the door back on and rigged a five-gallon can as a fuel tank and placed it in the cockpit of the car. Holding onto the can with one hand, Rigsby finished sixth. No margin of victory was given in the Sloan story, but it may have been close to 50 laps.

"Listen kid and I'll tell you how to do it." The veteran, Ed Barnett, gives young Dempsey Wilson some advice before the start of the 1948 500-lap roadster race at Carrell Speedway. It worked—Wilson won the race and Barnett was second.
(Rod Eschenburg collection—Bruce Craig photo)

In 1949, Carrell Speedway was paved and the CRA 500 lapper was a better show. Some 70 cars attempted to qualify for the race and only one non-local driver managed to make the starting field. The early leaders were Corky Benson, Lou Figero and Bob Cross (Denny). By mid-race Cross was pretty well in command but was in the position of having to make one more pit stop than Benson who was running second. Cross made his stop around lap 400 and was making up time on Benson but his position seemed hopeless—he was a lap behind with only 30 to go. On lap 471 Benson slammed into the spun out car of Al King and was out of the race. This was the break Cross needed and he won the 500 lapper by 11 laps over Ed Kasold. Bob Ascot was third as, once again, there were 18 cars running at the end of the long grind.

Unfortunately Sloan's stories give no information about the size of the purses for the 500-lap races. Press releases report crowds of 12,000 but publicists have been know to exaggerate. Bob Cross remembers that the most he ever won in a roadster race was around $650—odds are that this was in the 1949 500-lap race.

competed on equal terms with the sprint cars. With the future clearly sprint cars, all the new cars that were built were sprinters. It was announced that for the 1957 season that only sprint cars would be permitted to race and that the name of the organization would be changed to the California Racing Association. To an extent a roadster had the last laugh as Wayne Weiler in a hot rod won the biggest race of the 1956 season—a 100 miler at Phoenix.

Location is unknown—circa 1948. Wayne Tipton is in #25. Tipton's brother, Archie, also drove hot rods in Southern California.
(Rod Eschenburg collection)

Troy Ruttman did good once in awhile. Here he is spinning out at a CRA race someplace in Southern California. (Rod Eschenburg collection)

THE BIG WHEEL

Street roadsters have appeared in quite a few movies, but only once were track roadsters shown in a Hollywood production. This was *The Big Wheel* starring Mickey Rooney and Thomas Mitchell. The movie came out in 1949 and used California Roadster Association cars for the hot rod racing scenes. Dick Vineyard was one of the racers who did some driving in the film, and he recalls that he became quite friendly with actor Dick Lane who played the "bad guy" in the movie.

The movie starts with Mickey Rooney driving a stock Model A Ford roadster which he magically transforms into the T-Merc V8 #23. Actual night race scenes at Carrell Speedway were used in the movie and Mickey Rooney crashes while battling for the lead.

Unfortunately for us hot rodders, Rooney got a ride in a midget instead of fixing his car and doing some more roadster racing—darn!

Rosie Roussel is in the Sunset Auto Parts car #74 that was used in The Big Wheel. This is the #23 that Mickey Rooney "drove" in the movie. George Seegar is in #1.
(Rosie Roussel collection—Courtesy Hot Rod Magazine)

Great action on the dirt at Balboa Stadium in San Diego. Rosie Roussel is in the Bogosian Wayne Chevy and Johnny Paulson in the Henry and James #42. (Rosie Roussel collection)

A CHAIN-DRIVE ROADSTER

The Dick Vineyard-driven #53 was one of the most unusual roadsters to race anywhere. So far as is known, this was the only hot rod to utilize chain drive.

The car was designed and built in 1948 by Ed Walker whose racing heritage went back to the 1930s and Legion Ascot Speedway. Walker wanted to keep unsprung weight to a minimum and figured that the chain drive was the way to do this. He had his design well in mind and knew that it would work but was unsure what size chain to use. Walker consulted a mechanical

Ed Walker's #53 was one of the relatively few track roadsters to be featured on the cover of Hot Rod Magazine
(Used with permission of Hot Rod Magazine—Ray Hiatt collection)

engineer, told him he was planning to use a GMC engine, and asked for his recommendations. The engineer calculated that a massive six-inch chain was needed to handle the torque of the GMC. Ed Walker decide to trust his own common sense, instead of the numbers, and figured a double roller chain about two-inches wide would do the job. He was right—the car ran nearly 100 races with no trouble.

With Walker's design, the equivalent of a rear end was mounted right under the driver's seat. This was made from part of a Model A Ford rear end and

This undressed view of the Ed Walker car shows the '28 Chevy frame rails and the homemade manifold on the GMC engine. Note the modified Model A Ford rear end center section that transfers power from the engine to be drive chain.
(Dick Vineyard collection)

Walker even included a drum and hydraulic unit that would serve as the car's rear wheel brakes. He'd planned to change chain sprockets to get different gear ratios, but the car ran so well he used the same sprocket at all race tracks.

The front suspension was conventional Ford, but on the rear Ed Walker was once again the innovator. He used "torsilastic" suspension—Walker probably coined the term. (Torsilastic suspension was used on some Indy cars around 1948, so it is possible that Walker was working with the designers of these cars—or perhaps they copied from Ed Walkers.) He found some World War II aircraft engine mounts that had a shaft bonded to the center of a rubber "doughnut." By clamping this unit to the frame and making an arm that attached to the shaft, Walker had a lightweight and fully adjustable suspension.

The GMC engine that Walker used in #53 was nothing special. He did some porting work on the head, installed a Winfield cam, made a three-carburetor intake manifold and built some exhaust headers. For most of the car's racing existence, the engine was a small 232 cubic inches. It wasn't as fast as some of the Merc V8s, but excellent handling was the key to the car's success.

Dick Vineyard was the driver of #53, and he remembers that it was pure pleasure to drive. He recalls, "The Mercs would pull us on the straights but we'd go

Dick Vineyard tosses the Ed Walker GMC into a turn at Gilmore Stadium. The car's appearance is ungainly, but it was fast and a constant winner. *(Dick Vineyard collection)*

flying by them in the corners." Vineyard drove the car to many victories, including a few at famous Gilmore Stadium. He drove the car to the 1948 California Hot Rods Inc. championship.

Dick Vineyard's ride before stepping into #53 was his own '27 T-Merc that he justly dubbed, "The Little Beauty." So far as #53 goes, Vineyard states, "It was flat ugly!"

This view shows the chain drive and the brake drum on the transfer case. The "torsilastic" suspension was the twisting of the rubber in the units mounted to the frame. Note the simplicity of the rear end.
(Dick Vineyard collection)

The safety record of post-war roadster racing in Southern California was not good. This was especially true in the late 1940s. The cars were fast with no safety features like properly designed roll bars, the purses were good and the drivers eager to impress—a deadly combination. At one time a one carburetor rule was in effect at the half-mile Carrell Speedway in an attempt to slow the cars down. There might have been some sort of roll bar rule implemented, but nothing substantial appears in photos. The known fatalities in Southern California roadster racing are Slim Mathis on May 8, 1948, Fred Luce on August 11, 1948, and Rue Whiting on

Bert Letner is pictured in his #19. Troy Ruttman normally drove this car.
(Greg Sharp—Vintage Racing Photos)

This is probably El Monte—circa 1947.
(Greg Sharp—Vintage Racing Photos)

Jim Rathmann was a charter member of the CRA and raced roadsters for several years before moving on to bigger things—like winning Indy.
(Jim Chini collection)

Le Roy Nooks drove in the California Roadster Association as well as in the Mutual Racing Association in the Midwest.
(Marty Little collection)

This is the cover of the 1946 California Roadster Association yearbook.
(Ray Hiatt collection)

Stansberry loses a wheel at Carrell Speedway. This must have been before hubs were required.
(Ken Stansberry collection)

Chuck Burness

Jay Frank

Mitch Rodriguez

Troy Ruttman

Wayne Tipton

Dick Womack

From the 1946 CRA yearbook: Troy Ruttman needs no introduction and Jay Frank and Wayne Tipton did OK in racing. The others are typical of hot rod racers who have been all but forgotten. *(Ray Hiatt collection)*

J.C. Agajanian presents Ken Stansberry with a trophy at Carrell. (Ken Stansberry collection)

A nonchalant Howard Gardner seems to be saying, "Aw, shucks, it was easy!"
(Greg Sharp—Vintage Racing Photos)

The track looks like Bonelli Stadium in Saugus. The driver looks like Bob Cross.
(Greg Sharp—Vintage Racing Photos)

This is a 1950 publicity shot at Carrell Speedway. Can't beat Rosie Roussel's comment, "What an engine!" The "engine" is Carol Cummings. (Rosie Roussel collection)

February 3, 1952. All of these were in CRA races at Carrell Speedway. The CRA suffered two other fatal crashes in areas outside of Southern California and almost certainly there were additional fatalities that have been forgotten by history.

California Roadster Association Champions:
1946—Connie Weidell
1947—Jack McGrath
1948—Troy Ruttman
1949—Bob Cross (aka Bob Denny)
1950—Bob Cross (aka Bob Denny)
1951—Bob Cross (aka Bob Denny)
1952—Harry Stockman
1953—Nick Valenta
1954—Jack Gardner
1955—Nick Valenta
1956—Art Bisch

California Hot Rods Inc. Champions:
1948—Dick Vineyard
1949—Dick Vineyard

Ken Stansberry in the Duke Randall car. It went fast with a six-cylinder Plymouth engine.
(Ken Stansberry collection)

Ken Stansberry gets hit by somebody at Carrell Speedway. (Ken Stansberry collection)

Bigger is better? This car has a Model A body bolted onto a Packard chassis. Puffy Puffer drove this car at Saugus. (Al Slinker collection)

Rosie Roussel in the Miller Crankshaft V8 at Carrell. (Rosie Roussel collection)

Manual Ayulo used his track roadster as a camera car for the circa 1949 move To Please a Lady. The photo is at Arlington, Texas, where dirt champ car race was filmed. (Norris Cook collection)

These are "state of the art" track roadsters. Nick Valenta in #1 and Harry Stockman in #2. Beautiful cars! (Rod Eschenburg collection)

THE AGOURA ROAD RACE

One of the California Roadster Association's most unusual events was a race on a road course in the Agoura hills some 20 miles outside of Los Angeles. This was not the normal paved road course. Agoura was a rough two mile track fashioned with a few passes of a road grader and a shot of oil. It had right and left turns, it went up and down hills but most of all it was very rocky. Agoura was a very different race track.

This was in 1953 so both the roadsters and sprint cars of the CRA were eligible to race. President Walt James was his usual enthusiastic self about the event and talked car owners from northern California and even from Arizona into coming to Agoura. The twisty course had both fast and slow sections so track cars with no clutch and only one gear faced a stiff challenge. Scotty Cain had the right idea when he showed up with a '32 Ford highboy roadster. The car was complete with clutch and transmission—it looked like some of the 1946 CRA cars.

The fastest cars qualified at around 65mph and 50

cars lined up for a 50-lap or 100-mile race. Johnny Paulson in a roadster and Billy Cantrell in a stretched Offy midget were the early leaders but both were soon sidelined as the rough course took its toll of cars. The track was not only dusty and full of holes but the fist sized rocks were puncturing oil pans, radiators, and fuel tanks. Only luck kept drivers from being seriously injured by the flying boulders.

When the 50 laps were completed, it was Arizona driver Jay Abney the winner in the Archie Bado built sprint car. Its Ford Six engine had lots of low end torque on the slow turns and Abney was able to maintain a consistent pace. Scotty Cain in the near-street '32 Ford roadster managed a second-place finish. Conditions were so bad that there were only seven finishers. No information on the size of the purse is available but it was probably small.

Northern Californian Bill Peters was in the race until something broke. About all he remembers about Agoura is, "That was a bad place!"

Johnny Paulson in #42 and Jack Gardner in #25 dueled for the lead mid-way through the Agoura 100 miler but both went out with mechanical problems. This part of the course looks quite smooth.

Rosie Roussel storms through a dusty Agoura turn in the Bogosian Wayne Chevy. Roussel was leading the race when brake failure sent him into a gully and out of the race.

Rosie Roussel passes a competitor on the outside of a tight Agoura turn. Look at the size of those rocks! Thrown up by the sliding cars they became dangerous missiles.

Jack Gardner slides through a right hander at Agoura. Here again the rocky surface of the track is evident.

Scotty Cain in the '32 Highboy that finished second. One modification for the mostly street hot rod was an over-sized radiator.

Scotty Cain is on the inside—Cain could shift gears to pick up speed. The sprint car, with only one gear, had to slide around in the loose stuff to keep up engine rpms.

(All photos: Greg Sharp—Vintage Racing Photos)

Dirt track action at Carrell—circa 1949.
(Al Gray collection)

Balboa Stadium in 1948. These are cars from the California Hot Rods Inc. That is probably Dick Benninger in #7. The roadsters didn't run too often at Balboa—perhaps all those empty seats is the reason. (Mike Bell—Jim Chini collection)

Gilmore Stadium in 1948. The cars and drivers are from the California Hot Rods Inc. Bob Hoover is in the #6 Boydstun car from Porterville. (Boydstun collection)

It looks like slick going at Carrell Speedway in about 1955. Mike McGreevy is in the #98 sprinter. McGreevy later was a USAC Midget Champion.
(Al Gray collection—Faber-Stewart photo)

Nick Valenta at Saugus—circa 1952.
(Greg Sharp—Vintage Racing Photos)

Sprint cars and roadsters head in all directions at Carrell in about 1955. Paul Kamm is in the sprint car just going out of the photo.
(Al Gray collection—Faber-Stewart photo)

Close quarters at Saugus. Hank Henry in the #18 sprinter crowds Bob Bartlett in the roadster.
(Al Gray collection)

Carrell Speedway. Rosie Roussel in #11 and Howard Gardner in #25. (Don Gilchrest collection)

Bob Chaplin drove this nice-looking Miller Crankshaft V8.
(Greg Sharp—Vintage Racing Photos)

Sprint cars and roadsters are racing together at this Saugus race—circa 1954.
(Greg Sharp—Vintage Racing Photos)

More action at Balboa Stadium. Car #11 should be Ed Lockhart and #23 Ed Ball.
(Mike Bell—Jim Chini collection)

No identification on this car or the fate of the driver. Carrell Speedway—circa 1950. (Faber-Stewart Photo)

Ken Stansberry at Saugus in 1946. This is the car that Stansberry used to tow his house trailer from San Antonio to Los Angeles. (Ken Stansberry collection)

The beautiful Spalding Brothers Chevy at Carrell.
(Greg Sharp—Vintage Racing Photos)

Bob Cross in one of his later rides in California Roadster Association hot rods.
(Greg Sharp—Vintage Racing Photos)

A Carrell Speedway publicity shot—circa 1950. Rosie Roussel and Bob Cross and the drivers— Carol Cummings is the lady. (Rosie Roussel collection)

Bob Cross is in #45 and Rosie Roussel in the DeSoto V8-powered sprinter. The flathead V8 in Cross' car seems to be holding its own. (Rosie Roussel collection)

Ken Stansberry in action in the Duke Randall #95. This was during one of the 500-lap races at Carrell Speedway—Stansberry was out with a broken driveline. (Ken Stansberry collection)

Great action at Carrell in about 1954. No identification on the drivers.
(Greg Sharp—Vintage Racing Photos)

Action at Culver City in about 1955. That's Bob Bartlett in #11. (Al Gray collection)

Ken Stansberry with the crew of the Duke Randall car. This was one of the few West Coast cars that had the Midwest-style cut-away sides.
(Ken Stansberry collection)

Norm Hall is in the stretched Offy midget #52. He battles with Bob Bartlett in the V8-powered hot rod. (Al Gray collection)

CRA champion Jack Gardner in the Merc V8 #25 battles with an unidentified driver in the Doug Carruthers Offy. (Greg Sharp—Vintage Racing Photos)

1947
National Roadster Championship
Souvenir Program
Price 50c

Aug. 7, 1947
at The Rose Bowl
PASADENA

Saugus—circa 1954. Hank Henry in #18 just misses a spinning roadster. (Al Gray collection)

The program cover for the only roadster race held at the Rose Bowl. The midgets ran perhaps a half-dozen races there. (Greg Sharp collection)

CENTRAL CALIFORNIA

●●●●●●●●●●●●●●●●●●●●●●●●●●●●●

There was roadster racing in California's San Joaquin Valley in the early 1930s. The first races were only loosely organized and were reportedly held on a dusty oval in some farmer's field. In 1936, the roadster racers formed the Owners and Drivers Association. This group held races at Madera, Fresno and on the Shilo Grange racetrack at Modesto. Duane Carter was a regular at these races, and an entry list for a race on May 24, 1936, at Modesto lists Bill "Vucovich" as one of the drivers. (Bill Vukovich did start his racing career in the roadsters but quickly switched to the midgets.) Roadster racing continued on an intermittent basis in this area until World War II stopped all racing.

After the war, the midgets were very active in the San Joaquin Valley and this may have slowed the emergence of the roadsters. Porterville is somewhat on the fringe of the San Joaquin Valley, and it was here that roadster racing started in 1947. There was a street hot rod group called the "Porterville Wheels," the club from which the Central Valley Racing Association was formed late in 1947. The CVRA held a few races on a hastily constructed flat dirt track in 1947 but didn't really get going until the Porterville Speed Bowl was built in 1948. This was a fine quarter-mile semi-banked track that was built by Loron Bartlett on land he owned a few miles from Porterville. (The track was sometimes called the Rocky Hill Speedway for reasons that are very apparent in some of the photos.)

Porterville had a population of only around 7,000 but community support for the hot rod races was excellent. Most of the cars and drivers were from Porterville with a few from the neighboring cities of Tulare, Bakersfield and Fresno. In general the starting fields were not large and neither were the purses—usually less than $500. There was excellent roadster racing at the Porterville Speed Bowl and this went on for several years. Porterville was one of the more successful small town roadster racing operations.

Local drivers like Dick Myers, Bob Bartlett, Jack Rook, Ed Harris, Al Gray and Gene Pernu won a lot of races. Rosie Roussel lived 50 miles away in Bakersfield, but he raced at Porterville and won often. Porterville is roughly halfway between San Francisco and Los Angeles so drivers from these areas would occasionally be visitors. Ken Stansberry, Nick Valenta, Bob Hoover, Johnny Keys, Dick Vineyard and Paul Kamm were some of the drivers who enjoyed racing at the Porterville Speed Bowl.

The Porterville Speed Bowl had its biggest race on September 23, 1950, when races billed as the "Pacific Coast Championships" were held there. Promoter Arnold Brummler Jr. stuck his neck out and offered a $1,500 purse—about triple the normal payoff. Cars and drivers were invited from the Los Angeles and the San Fransisco areas and plans were made to start 33 roadsters for a 75-lap race on the quarter-mile oval. Brummler's promotional efforts paid off and a full

An early roadster race at Madera—circa 1938. Vern Gardner is in #44 and driver Smokey McCarty stands by the Andy Fanaucci owned #12. The original photo caption indicates that #12 has a very fast flathead Model A engine but what is it doing in Chevy chassis?
(Haigler-Motter collection)

This is 1947, and a basically street rod is competing in a race at Porterville's early flat track.
(Steve Larson collection)

The flat track at Porterville had no crashwalls or grandstands. This is Dutch Schultz in his flathead Model A.
(Steve Larson collection)

This is one of the first races at the Porterville Speed Bowl in April of 1948. Bob Phipps is in #8, and #1 is Gene Pernu.
(Pernu collection)

Les Cone in "The Bathtub" and Bob Phipps at the Porterville Speed Bowl in 1948. The reason the track was sometimes called Rocky Hill is obvious.
(Pernu collection)

The first race at the Porterville Speed Bowl, and a good crowd is on hand. Bob Ingrahm is in #111 and Gene Pernu in #1. Pernu won the opening race.
(Pernu collection)

Porterville—1948. The driver is unknown and so is the engine type, but there is plenty of carburetion.
(Steve Larson collection)

field of cars put on an excellent show before full grandstands. With 33 cars on a quarter-mile track a certain amount of crashing is to be expected and this did happen. A number of red flags resulted in no injuries but the race wasn't over until well after midnight. Elmer George won the long grind in Bob Shirley's Merc with Don Nickeson second and future midget racer Tommy Morrow third.

The demise of the roadsters at the Porterville Speed Bowl is the often repeated story of the stock cars taking over. Hot Rod Racing ceased around 1953 but the Porterville Speed Bowl is still in operation today.

One reason for the success of roadster racing at the Porterville Speed Bowl was the safety record—a fatality would have hit the small community very hard. Luck was with the Central Valley Racing Association drivers and other than "bumps and bruises" they enjoyed a perfect safety record.

The CVRA pretty well stuck to home at Porterville, and only a few races were sanctioned at other speedways—these were Tulare, Bakersfield and perhaps Fresno. A few roadster races were held at Fresno under the sanction of other organizations. One of these, at the half-mile Valley Speedway, was put on by the Los Angeles-based American Sports Cars Inc. This was in September of 1948, and George Seegar won the main event over a field of only 10 cars.

Over on the coast of central California there was another roadster group worthy of mention. This was the Lompoc Model T Club. Here racing began in 1936 when combination road and cross country races were held. The course wound through the countryside around Lompoc, crossed the Santa Ynez River twice and required close to six hours to finish the event. There were some fast open road sections—Laurance Cazenze remembers that his hopped up Model T roadster was clocked at 72 mph. The Lompoc Model T Club turned to track racing in 1939 with events on a horsetrack in Lompoc. After World War II the club was more active in track racing but for a couple of years the events were for trophies only and only for Model T-powered roadsters. They raced stock Ts that carried a brave passenger as well as some very potent Fronty and Rajo Ts. By about 1948 the Lompoc Model T Club was the T Club in name only and some of its members were competing along with some Porterville racers on a half-mile track at Buellton. A couple of races were held with co-sanction of the Los Angeles-based California Roadster Association. These were at the Santa Maria Fairgrounds and in one of these CRA driver Dick Bittinger was killed. The Lompoc Model T Club disbanded in 1952, and roadster racing was over in this area.

Arnold Brummler Jr. drove this neat-looking Four Port Fargo Model B at the first Porterville Speed Bowl race. Brummler later became a track announcer and promoter. *(Brummler collection)*

Les Cone leads Gene Emery in #8 and Gary Bogoshian in #404—Porterville 1948. *(Pernu collection)*

Les Cone ran a flathead Model B Ford in "The Bathtub." Cone was competitive and later won a main event. *(Rod Eschenburg collection)*

Gary Bogoshian in his #404. Along with his brother, Bogoshian later owned some very fast GMC and Chevy roadsters. *(Rod Eschenburg collection)*

Hank Henry started his racing career at Porterville in the roadsters. Henry became a star in the sprint cars and a respected car builder. Hank Henry-built sprint cars won a lot of races in the 1960s. *(Edwards Studio—Jack Rook collection)*

Porterville. Les Cone leads an unknown driver in the Ed Parker Chrysler. Art Gibson is on the outside. *(Bob Bartlett collection)*

Above—Two-time Central Valley Racing Association champion Rosie Roussel. He's in the Bob Phipps car that is powered by an early Ford V8 engine with Alexander Overheads. Rosie remembers it as "a very reliable car." *(Rosie Roussel collection)*

Left—Action at Porterville in 1949. Bob Bartlett is in #57, and the driver of #99 is unknown. *(Boydstun collection)*

Les Cone flips "The Bathtub" at Bakersfield in 1949. Cone was cut and bruised, but suffered no serious injuries. *(Edwards Studios—Al Gray collection)*

Jerry Chavest slams into a Porterville wall in this 1948 action. *(Pernu collection)*

Harold Hall was a regular at Porterville in his '28T-V8. *(Rod Eschenburg collection)*

Ed Harris in the Harris brothers #212 at Porterville. *(Rod Eschenburg collection)*

Bob Bartlett smiles after a good night at Porterville in this Chrysler-powered car. Bartlett won three heat races, the semi-main and the main event—they were short of cars that night. *(Bob Bartlett collection)*

This time it is Wyatt Harris in the Harris brothers' V8. *(Wyatt Harris collection)*

Jack Rook drove this very fast Chrysler in CVRA events. Sponsor Leo Stattle is at the left and owner John Morgan at the right. *(Jim Lusk photo—Jack Rook collection)*

Action at Porterville—circa 1949. Al Gray is in #44 and Prentice Knudsen in #3. Car #44 is one of the few track roadsters that still exists today. *(Bob Bartlett collection)*

Porterville action as Willis Dick spins and Jack Rook, with no place to go, hits him head on. (Edwards Studio—Jack Rook collection)

Porterville racers line up for a 1949 event. Jack Rook is on the pole and Sam Judy follows in the Chevy Four-powered #5. (Edwards Studio—Jack Rook collection)

Gene Emory in #12 crashes into an unidentified competitor at Porterville. (Boydstun collection)

Dick Myer has won a trophy dash at Porterville. Myer had a very promising career and quickly moved on to NASCAR stock racing before dying in a Nevada highway crash. (Bob Bartlett collection)

This is Tom Heats at Porterville—circa 1950. (Bob Bartlett collection)

The CVRA visited Bakersfield, and Harold Hall ran into trouble when he rolled his roadster. Gene Emery is in #12. (Faber-Stewart Photo—Al Gray collection)

This is probably the Santa Maria Fairgrounds—circa 1952. The Lompoc Model T Club sponsored the races, and the California Roadster Association came up from Los Angeles to race. (Boydstun collection)

Above—Al Gray, #44, and Gene Emory battle at Porterville—circa 1950. (Bob Bartlett collection)

Left—Roadsters tangle at Porterville circa 1950. Looks like a poor crowd on hand for this race. (Bob Bartlett collection)

Roaring Roadsters

Ken Stansberry visited Porterville from Los Angeles and took home a trophy. Joyce Haire is the trophy girl. Stansberry was one of the more traveled hot rod drivers and raced in many states. *(Bob Bartlett collection)*

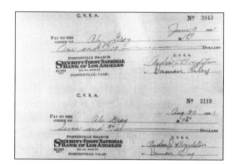

Sometimes there wasn't much money in CVRA racing as these payoff checks to Al Gray will attest. *(Al Gray collection)*

Porterville action probably in 1948. Car #7 has broken an axle and lost a wheel. Bob Bartlett in #99 and Prentice Knudsen in #3 get by OK. *(Bob Bartlett collection)*

They had a "Powder Puff Derby" at Porterville and Ed Harris talked his mother into driving his V8. Mrs. Harris looks like a real racer. *(Bob Bartlett collection)*

The Bogoshian Brothers' Chevy goes up in flames after a fuel line broke. Driver Rosie Roussel suffered burns that kept him in a Porterville hospital overnight. *(Bob Bartlett collection)*

Here is Rosie Roussel's hospital bill. Note that care at the New Porterville Hospital was all of $9 a day. *(Rosie Roussel collection)*

Spud Simkins has won a trophy dash and he and the trophy girl are all smiles. *(Rod Eschenburg collection)*

This trophy dash winner at Porterville looks very familiar. Is it Nick Valenta? *(Bob Bartlett collection)*

The Boydstun-Riley car boasted a very unusual and nice-looking 1921 Dodge roadster body. (Boydstun collection)

Bob Bartlett sends boards flying as he exits the Porterville Speed Bowl. (Boydstun collection)

This is the Santa Maria Fairgrounds. It looks like this driver has just won the main event and is being greeted by fans. (Boydstun collection)

A REAR-ENGINED ROADSTER

One of the most unusual and ungainly roasters that raced in central California was the Paul Steinhaus #26 by Tommy Morrow. Steinhaus started out with the rear engine concept for a Bonneville Speed Trials car. Midway through construction he ran out of money, but along came Tommy Morrow who wanted to be a race driver. A deal was made that if Morrow could supply an engine they'd run the car on the track and Morrow could drive. Tommy Morrow swapped his motorcycle for a Merc racing engine and the team was in the racing business—sort of.

There were a number of design faults in the 110-inch wheelbase, 2,000-pound car. The Merc engine used a '40 Ford transmission and this was linked directly to the rear end by a universal joint—there was no driveline. This arrangement might have worked OK on the smooth Utah salt flats, but it didn't work on the track. The pivot points between the power train and the radius rods were off by several feet—universal joints and radius rods broke regularly.

Tommy Morrow in his first race car ride—1948. The car had a three-inch-diameter tube frame. The back half of the body is a narrowed Model A—it was cut apart with a torch and welded back together. The liberal use of diamond plate steel is partly apparent in this photo. (Tommy Morrow collection)

Another problem was the throttle that would jam during races. Holes had been cut in the body for the carburetors, but they weren't big enough. The body would flex during races and bind up the carburetor linkage. It took a few races to find that problem. The car ran 20 races and finished only three—"something always broke," Tommy Morrow remembers today.

The handling was probably terrible but Morrow admits that, at the time, he didn't know any better. "I'd never driven anything else," he says. The car's design did save Morrow from the serious foot and leg injuries that are so common in even today's rear engined cars. Morrow crashed hard at Fresno when the steering broke, but there was lots of quarter-inch diamond plate steel up front that took the impact. Today's Indy cars are using a bit more exotic material than diamond plate steel, but they are closing in on the driver foot-leg protection that #26 had 45 years ago.

Herc Veglienzone brought his Stockton Spitfire to Porterville for this race in about 1952. The driver is probably Herb Hill. (Boydstun collection)

Tommy Morrow won the trophy dash at the "Pacific Coast Championship" race at Porterville in 1950. (Boydstun collection)

This is one of many wrecks in the "Pacific Coast Championship" race at Porterville. That is probably Reggie Asmus at the left. Car #9 was owned by Don Farmer. (Al Gray collection)

A program cover from Buellton, a small town near the coast of central California.

Scotty Cain heads for the hills at Porterville in about 1952. This was probably a California Roadster Association-sanctioned race. (Greg Sharp—Vintage Racing Photos)

A Porterville program cover. The photo caption is a bit sexist by today's standards (Boydstun collection)

Close action at Bakersfield—circa 1951.

Bob Hoover at Porterville— circa 1951. (Boydstun collection)

Porterville in 1951. Bob Hoover is in #6—the other driver is not identified. (Boydstun collection)

Northern
California

●●●●●●●●●●●●●●●●●●●●●●●●●●●●●●

Northern California roadster racing probably began in 1931 when a series of races were held at the new one-mile Oakland Speedway. These may have been some sort of speed trials rather than an actual oval track race. Whatever, it apparently wasn't a first-class affair—the promoter skipped town, leaving drivers like Freddy Agabashian holding bad checks. Despite the fact that no actual roadster organization was formed, there was quite a bit of racing throughout the 1930s. During the summers, there were races about every two weeks at San Jose, Oakland, Galt, Calistoga and probably other cities. The purses were near non-existent and a "big" crowd at Calistoga might be 150 fans. Both Freddy Agabashian and Duane Carter drove roadsters during the 1930s.

In 1939, two San Francisco Bay Area auto clubs were instrumental in forming the Bay Cities Roadster Racing Association (BCRRA). Bette

This beautiful roadster was owned by Larry Neves. It took second place as "America's Most Beautiful Roadster" at the Oakland Roadster Show in 1950. (Bob Veith collection)

Bill Steves in Bob Goux's #100 at Stockton in 1948. This car with the Model B Ford-based Moeller engine held the roadster track record at Stockton.
(Tom Motter collection)

Roadsters in action at Santa Rosa—circa 1939. Billy Franks spins and collects Buck Baker.
(Haigler-Motter collection)

Red Corbin is the driver of this nice-looking car at Belmont in 1949. (Bill Peters collection)

organized races were held on the flat half-mile dirt track at Oakland Speedway, at Santa Rosa, Calistoga and at several other tracks. By previous standards the purses were good—no promoters skipped with the cash—but a clean sweep at one of these races might net only about $20. Mauri King was crowned the BCRRA champion in 1940, and other top drivers included Gene Figone, Johnny Soares, Ed Normi, and Norm Holtkamp. Figone became the first roadster fatality in the area when he was killed at Calistoga in late 1941.

World War II brought a halt to all racing, and during this conflict the Bay Cities Roadster Racing Association changed directions. The members were more interested in midget racing, and in 1943, voted to drop "Roadster" from the group's name. They became the Bay Cities Racing Association (BCRA)—a fine organization that still sanctions West Coast midget races.

The lack of an organized group probably contributed to the fact that the roadsters were slow to resume racing after World War II. It wasn't until September of 1946 that promoter Charlie Curryer started things going. He invited five street hot rods to a sprint car race at the new five-eighths-mile Oakland Stadium. Running on the quarter-mile midget track that was part of this facility, the hot A-V8s put on a wild exhibition race that had the fans screaming for more. The roadsters were back for a full program a few weeks later and the grandstands were full. Curryer paid 19 hot rodders $75 each, and they were very happy. A few more roadster races were run in late 1946 and plans were made for a big season in 1947. A few of the roadsters running in the races were pre-war track machines, but these four bangers were outclassed by the V8s that were really street rods with minor modifications.

The Northern California Roadster Racing Association used this logo in their publicity. (Bill Peter collection)

Bob Marco spins in #10. It is probably George Pacheco in #9. Pacheco's pre-war experience helped him to win the Northern California Roadster championship in 1947. (Dana Photo by Rick—Al Slinker collection)

Gene Figone in #12 and Ellis Hough line up for the trophy dash at San Jose in 1938. (Haigler-Motter collection)

Bayshore Stadium in San Francisco in 1947. Sam Hawks is in his own #110. Number 19 is a rare Hudson roadster driven by Vince Pacheco. The driver of #99 is unknown. (Dana Photo by Rick)

Mel Senna was the driver of this neat '27T-V8.
(Rod Eschenburg collection)

Paul Kamm at Pacheco in 1947 with Chevy Six power. Kamm later destroyed this car in a crash at Sacramento's Lazy J Speedway.
(Rod Eschenburg collection)

Pacheco—circa 1948. That's Johnnie Lomonto in the GMC-powered #10. (Rod Eschenburg collection)

Bayshore Stadium in 1948. The roadsters line up for the semi-main event.
(Dana Photo by Rick—Al Slinker collection)

Johnny Key smiles at the trophy girl at Oakland. The young lady also smiles, but is probably worried about getting grease on her dress. That's Al Slinker on the right. (Dana Photo by Rick—Al Slinker collection)

By the spring of 1947, the Northern California Roadster Racing Association (NCRRA) had been formed. This group provided well-run races, reasonably well-enforced safety regulations and insurance for the drivers. During 1947, the roadsters ran five or six nights a week and drew crowds that matched those of the midgets. Purses ran up to $1,500 per race. With that kind of money available the cars quickly evolved from near-street machines to full fledged race cars. Most of the races were on the quarter-mile paved or dirt midget ovals, but the hot rods did put on several good shows on the 60-degree banks of the big track at Oakland Stadium. The NCRRA paid nearly $130,000 in purses in 1947—the roadsters were booming and the boom would continue for awhile.

This race at Stockton was the first for the Stockton Spitfire and Wayne Selser was the driver that day. It was also one of the first outings for the author's #74 in the background. (Herk Veglienzone collection)

Circa 1938 at San Jose. The engine looks like the four-cylinder Chevy with the Olds three-port head that was the hot combination in those days.
(Haigler-Motter collection)

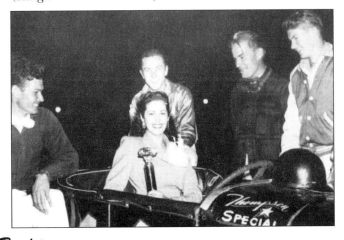

Roaring Roadsters

With all the money came dissension in the roadster ranks, and also perhaps, a bit of greed. A group of Oakland businessmen teamed with several track owners to form Racing Roadsters Incorporated (RRI). The plan was to make some money for themselves and at the same time a better deal and bigger purses for car owners and drivers. Just how this was to be accomplished was unclear then and is less clear now. Some rather grandiose promises were made to lure owners and drivers to the RRI—things like at the end of the season the top five cars and drivers would be flown to Chicago for a "National Championship Roadster Race."

The RRI did attract some good cars and drivers and somehow got the sanction to run roadster races at the high-paying Oakland Stadium. The RRI did

San Jose in early 1947. Bob Machin spins out as Eddie Bosio passes high in #101 and Ed Andrews ducks underneath. (Don Radbruch Photo)

A typical street-track roadster as raced in early 1947. This car would either evolve into a strictly track hot rod by mid-1947 or be non-competitive. (Dana Photo by Rick—Al Slinker collection)

Close quarters at Pacheco. Bob Rushing in #169, Gene Tessien in #35 and Ed Elisian in #22. (Dana Photo by Rick—Al Slinker collection)

Pacheco 1947. Bob Rushing battles with his friend Ed Elisian in the Sanders and Rowell #22. (Dana Photo—Al Slinker collection)

Chuck Harwood in 1947. Harwood managed a main event win at Oakland in this Reily Four-Port Model B. (Dana Photo by Rick—Al Slinker collection)

Action at Pacheco. Mel Senna is in #55, and that's Ed Elisian barely missing the spun-out car. (Dana Photo by Rick—Al Slinker collection)

Eddie Bosio knocks down some fence with Tony Cancilla's roadster at Pacheco in 1947. Cancilla's cars used the heavy Model A bodies for several years, and some very good engines kept them fairly competitive. (Dana Photo by Rick)

There are many photos in this book credited as "Dana Photo by Rick." "Rick" is Eric Rickman (or E. Rickman) who took thousands of racing photos in nearly a half century behind the lens of a camera. Rick got his start shooting photos of track roadsters and midgets in the San Francisco Bay Area. In the early 1950s, he moved on

to *Hot Rod Magazine* and Peterson Publications and began 41 years of snapping photos all over the country. Now retired, Rick has been honored by organizations such as the Oakland Roadster Show, the Bonneville Speed Trials and the International Drag Racing Hall of Fame. He's earned it with that special touch with a camera, which is evident in any "Dana Photo by Rick."

These 15 photos, taken at the five-eighths-mile Oakland Speedway in July of 1948, were probably the first sequential series of photos ever taken of a racing crash. Photos like these are commonplace today, but the cameras that are used now did not exist in 1948. Rick used a camera that was designed to train Japanese aerial gunners in World War II. He found it at a war surplus store in Oakland, California, and thinks he paid about $50 for it. As the photo shows, it obviously looks like a machine gun—squeeze the trigger, and it would take about 150 photos in some 40 seconds. The Japanese designers didn't provide for any adjustment of lens opening or shutter speed but, as luck would have it, both were about right for shooting auto races on a sunny day. It even had a telephoto lens. The drawback was that it weighed about 20 pounds, so when motor-driven 35mm cameras became available it was quickly discarded. Where is the camera now? Rick thinks it wound up in the trash bin at Peterson Publications many years ago.

Some of these photos appeared nationwide in *Life Magazine* in late 1948. Rick received neither credit or payment for the photos. As he now says, "Sweet, naive little me—I gave them to my friend Russ Reed at the *Oakland Tribune* to help out with roadster publicity." The *Tribune* passed them on to the Associated Press and from there the photos were probably sold to *Life Magazine*. In these pages, after 45 years, Eric Rickman finally gets full credit for a sensational series of photos..

1) Jimmy Davies in #4X breaks a tie rod, hits the crash wall and slows while partly on the 60-degree bank of the track. Bob Kelleher slams into Davies car. 2) A few seconds later, Frank Santos in #16 hits the wrecked cars. Kelleher has apparently unbuckled his seat belt and is thrown to the track surface. 3) Davies' body reacts to the force of the crash, and Kelleher appears to be almost under the still-moving wreckage. 4) Santos is stunned as Kelleher is someplace behind the wreckage. 5) Santos recovers and heads for the infield while Kelleher starts to roll out of the way. 6) A few more seconds pass, and Billy Ryan piles into the mess in #73. 7) Ryan's car starts to flip as the wreckage moves towards Kelleher. 8) Davies takes another blow. Ryan flips and Kelleher can only watch the wreck come towards him. 9) Ryan continues to flip as Kelleher has disappeared between the Davies car and his own. 10) The wreckage is still moving along the track. 11) Kelleher appears to be swallowed by the remains of his own car. 12) Ryan completes his flip as Davies appears to be checking oncoming traffic. Kelleher is laying alongside #4X. 13) Ryan sits stunned in his #73. The wreckage has come to a near standstill and Kelleher's #2 is twisted and bent in half. 14) Davies decides it is safe to leave and helps Kelleher to his feet and away from the wreck. 15) Ryan scoots a pitman out of the way as Kelleher wonders how he survived. Other than some bumps and bruises, there were no injuries. Race winner Troy Ruttman passes in #19.

OK with races at the Oakland quarter-mile track, Belmont's dirt oval, and at Salinas some 100 miles to the south. Because most of the car owners had stuck with the NCRRA, the Racing Roadsters Incorporated was sometimes short of cars for the big races on the five-eighths-mile track at Oakland. Cars were imported from Southern California for these races, and sometimes the impolite invaders took home most of the money. Even without the

Oakland races the NCRRA enjoyed a good season in 1948 with purses at places like Pacheco, Sacramento, Stockton and Modesto running from $500 to near $1,500.

Some of the best race drivers of the 1950s learned their trade in these early years of northern California roadster racing. Bob Sweigert as an Indy winner in 1955. Bob Veith was the Rookie of the Year at Indy in 1956 and raced there for 14 years.

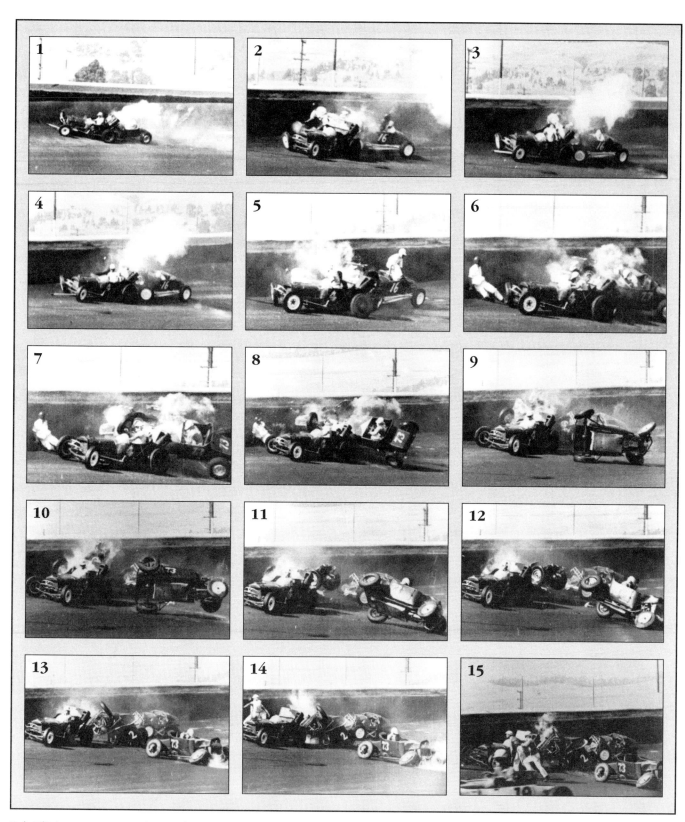

Ed Elisian ran at Indy and was a far better race driver than most people now remember. Some of the top drivers like Joe Valenta, Gene Tessien, George Pacheco and Al Slinker chose to pretty much confine their talents to the roadsters. Bob Machin moved on to the midgets and became a Bay Cities Racing Association champion.

By 1949, the boom was fading in northern California. Not only were roadster crowds falling off, but the midgets were also feeling the crunch. There had been just too much racing. The roadsters had two groups splitting the fans and the race tracks were now starting to hurt, but this wasn't the only program. Early model hardtop stock car racing had been coming on to the racing scene in other parts of the nation, and in June of 1949 promoter Bob Barkhimer brought these cars to northern California. I remember the night at San Jose

This is the remains of Merrett Carden's roadster after the throttle stuck, and he hit Oakland's hay bales and a light pole. (Dana Photo by Rick)

Tony Dutra has acquired a sponsor for this San Jose race. Dutra moved on to the midgets and was killed in one of these cars at Pacheco in 1947.
(Haigler-Motter collection)

Al Slinker at Oakland in late 1946. This was one of the first post-war roadster races, and Slinker's car is obviously a street rod.
(Photo by D'Orr Studios—Al Slinker collection)

Wild Bill Sullivan at Pacheco. Stock head, so it is probably 1947. Sullivan later won a northern California sprint car championship.
(Rod Eschenburg collection)

Bayshore Stadium in San Francisco. Author Don Radbruch tangles with #91. Number 74 was built like a tank and was not much faster. (Don Radbruch collection)

Speedway when, during the roadster intermission, a half-dozen souped up 1937ish Ford Coupes roared out on to the race-track. It was 1946 at the Oakland sprint car races all over again—only more so. The hardtops weren't all that fast, but they bounced off each other and the walls in spectacular fashion. I think most of the hardtops crashed before the exhibition was over, but the fans loved the action. Roadster racing didn't just end, but as all over the United States, the stocks were a major blow to the hot rods. Some promoters, especially Bob Barkhimer who was, and is, a class guy, did attempt to

Oakland in 1948 and Bob Sweigert gets the trophy from a pretty young lady. Sweigert quickly moved up the racing ladder on his way to an Indy win in 1955. (Dana Photo by Rick—Al Slinker collection)

George Rakatani in a "modified roadster" at San Jose. The body of this car is narrowed and the wheelbase has been shortened. The modifieds sometimes had their own races, but it looks as though Rakatani ran with the roadsters that day.
(Haigler-Motter collection)

run the roadsters, but crowds were fast dwindling. A few of the roadster drivers saw the light, raced the hardtops, and made some money. So did I, but I wasn't smart enough to take them seriously and crashed more than I won.

In 1950, the NCRRA and the RRI got together and formed the United Roadster Association, but it was too late to really do any good. There were fewer races in 1950 than in previous years, and the purses seldom exceeded $500. Over the next couple of years even fewer races were held, and the car count started to drop off as owners and drivers

Bayshore Stadium. Ed Elisian in his own #69 and Tommy Cheek in #44. That might be Ernie Reyes in #11. (Ray Hiatt collection)

Drivers signal for one more lap before the start of a heat race at Pacheco in 1947.
(Dana Photo by Rick—Al Slinker collection)

Stockton and probably 1948. This is Oscar Betts in his Chevy Six. It may or may not have had a Wayne Head. (Greg Sharp—Vintage Racing Photos)

Everybody gets in to the act at Stockton. Dave Carter is in #61 and Gene Tessien in #2.
(Dana Photo by Rick—Greg Sharp collection)

Probably opening day 1948, and this is Bob Rushing. (Greg Sharp—Vintage Racing Photos)

Number 88 spins out at Pacheco, and Bob Rushing just misses. Joe Valente takes to the outside. Valente's #16 was later shortened by about two feet. (Dana Photo by Rick—Al Slinker collection)

Night action at Pacheco. Al Germolous is in #15, but the other drivers are unknown.
(Dana Photo by Rick—Al Slinker collection)

realized that the roadsters were a dying breed. During this time, some roadsters were converted to sprint cars. The roadsters had all the expensive goodies, and these could be put on a sprint car chassis for not too many dollars. In some areas, the roadsters and sprint cars ran together in the declining years of the hot rods, but this did not happen in northern California. The last roadster race in northern California probably took place in Anderson in the summer of 1953.

THE STOCKTON SPITFIRE

When Herc Viglienzone built his #61 roadster in the spring of 1948, he didn't do it the easy way and use a Mercury V8 for power. He chose the oddball Chrysler Six. Why? "I had to be different," he says today.

Herc's car had the conventional '27 Model T body, but the frame was different. He used four-inch structural aluminum channel frame rails. (Scores of West Coast roadsters would come up with copies of this frame.) Herc's excellent workmanship was evident in the car's first outing at Stockton in April of 1948. The car ran fast, and it went even faster later on—it also went by a lot of V8s.

At the time, Herc Viglienzone was very closed-mouthed about the screaming Chrysler and all sorts of rumors floated around the northern California roadster community. Herc was firing two cylinders at once—he was running it backwards—it was over the cubic-inch displacement limit. All of the rumors were wrong. Herc was just using basic hot rodding tricks that had been around for years. No racing head was available for the Chrysler, so he built his own by filling the combustion chamber with brazing rod. This warped the head badly, and two thick beads of brass on the outside of the head were required to pull it somewhat straight. Even after some machining the head looked terrible, but it worked.

Dave Carter is greeted by a bevy of bathing beauties after a 1949 trophy dash win at San Jose. Owner Herc Viglienzone stands among the ladies at right. (Rod Eschenburg collection)

For carburetion, there were three side draft Winfields on a homemade manifold. He tried five different camshafts before an Engle cam really made the Stockton Spitfire fly. Herc tried a quarter-stroker crankshaft that gave 264 cubic inches, but the final version of the engine was a stock 252 inches. The engine gave away 40 cubic inches to some of the V8s, but you'd never know it watching the car pull the Mercs down the chutes. There is no doubt that Herc Viglienzone built the fastest Chrysler hot rod in the country.

Dave Carter grins after stacking #61 on the top of another car in a pileup at Stockton in 1948. Herc Viglienzone is at the left looking a bit disgusted about the whole thing. (Rod Eschenburg collection)

Viglienzone's drivers over the years were Wayne Selser, Bob Machin, Herb Hill, Dave Carter and Sam Hawks. All went fast but Hawks probably won the most races.

Herc liked aggressive drivers, and only recently did he reveal why Ed Elisian, who was one of the best and most aggressive drivers around, never drove the Stockton Spitfire. A few weeks before the car was finished, Herc rather timidly introduced himself to Elisian at a roadster race and asked if he was interested in driving #61. Elisian asked if he was using a Merc engine. Herc replied, "No, I'm using a Chrysler." Elisian turned and walked away without saying a word.

Viglienzone and Elisian later became good friends, but Ed never drove one of Herc's cars. Elisian was able to laugh about it and say, "Well, I guess I asked for that!"

Sam Hawks is pictured with owner Herc Viglienzone and the Stockton Spitfire in 1949. Viglienzone ran the exhaust of the back three cylinders under the car and to the left exhaust pipe. Hence there are exhaust pipes on both sides of the Chrysler Six.

(Greg Sharp—Vintage Racing Photos)

A final version of the #61 Stockton Spitfire was built in 1950. Here Sam Hawks warms it up at Oakland.

(Rod Eschenburg collection)

A huge crowd watched the runoff of what was billed as the Pacific Coast Invitational Roadster Championships at Stockton in 1948.
(Dana Photo by Rick—Al Slinker collection)

Action in the runoff at Stockton. Lemione Frey in #9, Rex McCapes in #99, Bob Veith in #32, Joe Valente in #57, Ed Huntington in #6 and George Pacheco on the outside in #92.
(Dana Photo by Rick—Al Slinker collection)

Close action at San Jose. Ed Elisian is in #7, Gene Tessien in #1 and Ernie Reyes in #42.
(Dick Liebfritz collection)

San Jose in 1950 or 1951. Number 98 is George Mebalas, Sam Hawks is in #61 and Bill Peters in #9.
(Bill Peters collection)

Bill Peters takes the short way around San Jose Speedway. (Bill Peters collection)

Probably Stockton and probably 1950. That looks like Ed Elisian in #1, Elmer George is probably in #86 and #42 is Ernie Reyes in his own Wayne Chevy. (Bob Veith collection)

Ed Elisian in Bob Rushing's V8. This is late 1946 or early 1947. (Erwin Eszlinger collection)

Lemoine Frey in Al Dickman's very fast V8 at Stockton in 1948. (Tom Motter collection)

A smiling Bob Veith collects his trophy from a pretty young lady. That's starter Les Pine behind the car. Pine lost part of his leg in a freak accident at Oakland in late 1948. (Bob Veith collection)

A relaxed Lemoine Frey waits for the start at Stockton in John Dickman's Merc. Bill Peters is on the inside. (Tom Motter collection)

San Jose in 1950, and Ed Elisian has hit something with the Ohanassian V8. From the looks of the steering Elisian had some sore ribs.
(Abrew Photo—Bob Veith collection)

Joe Gusti in his Chevy Six in 1949. Gusti built some fast Chevies, geared them low and went fast but often not for long. (Bob Veith collection)

Ernie Reyes in his Wayne Chevy. Reyes was an excellent machinist and did a lot of work for northern California roadster racers.
(Dick Liebfritz collection)

Art Armstrong in a Chevy Four at San Jose in 1938. Armstrong was a former champion in the American Racing Association big cars and later did well in the midgets. (Haigler-Motter collection)

Belmont in 1948. Al Slinker in #5 tangles with Norm Garland. (Bill Peters collection)

AAA ROADSTER RACES

In 1934, there were American Automobile Association Indy drivers taking part in "roadster" races! Great story? Unfortunately these were not track roadsters—they were late model stock cars.

The Mines Field stock car race was covered in Hot Rod Magazine in 1951. The magazine mistakenly called the cars "roadsters." (Used with permission from Hot Rod Magazine)

In 1934, a series of big-time stock car races were sanctioned by the AAA at Oakland Speedway and on road courses at Legion Ascot Speedway and Mines Field in Los Angles. The races were open to any American-made stock car, but the fields were composed almost entirely of '33 or '34 Ford V8 roadsters. The reason was simple—the Fords were the fastest stock cars and the cheapest. A few other makes, all roadsters, like Chrysler, Plymouth, Chevrolet and even a Rockne took a crack at the Fords, but they were not competitive. The races attracted some of the nation's finest drivers. At Mines Field (now Los Angeles International Airport) 20 of the 26 drivers entered had raced the Indianapolis 500.

The AAA rules at that time allowed stock cars to be stripped of unnecessary parts like fenders, bumpers and windshields. This was advertised as being undertaken in the interest of "safety." Just how this made the cars "safer" is unclear, but they sure did look like track roadsters. Since racers have been known to cheat a bit in stock car races, I had hoped that some of the roadsters had been hopped up a bit. If so, they would technically be track roadsters, and some very big names could have been added to roadster his-

Mines Field was not a true road course, and not a true oval track. Still, it was great for spectators, and an early version of stock car events. (HRM collection)

In the Mines Field stock car race, Al Gordon in a '34 Ford roadster was the winner. (HRM collection)

tory.

My hopes were dashed when I checked with historian Johnny Klann. Klann, who was active in AAA racing in the 1930s, told me that the cars were checked very carefully, and they had to be certified

Big names were part of AAA races, this is Babe Stapp and "riding mechanic" at Mines Field. (HRM collection)

Major Indy drivers at Mines Field included legendary Louis Meyer, here in a 1934 Ford (new car at the time). (HRM collection)

It was get-out-and-fix for Rex Mays at Mines Field, a time in racing when driver participation in the mechanics of things was paramount. (HRM collection)

as stock. He added, "It wasn't like today when NASCAR mechanics bend every rule that they can. Back then the guys weren't smart enough to cheat!" Darn!

Eddie Meyer was a driver at Mines Field, would go on to build a line of speed equipment for fledgling hot rod industry. (HRM collection)

Fred Frame in #10 chases Al Gordon around the Targo Florio road course at the Legion Ascot Speedway in 1934. (Erwin Eszlinger collection—Ted Wilson photo)

Fred Frame comes to grief at the Targo Florio race as a tie rod breaks. The drivers had pleaded with the AAA to be allowed to reinforce steering parts, but officials insisted that the cars be stock. Check Frame's "helmet." (Erwin Eszlinger collection—Ted Wilson photo)

THE CCRA AND PALM BEACH

The Central California Roadster Association was one of several smaller groups that operated in northern California. Starting in mid-1947, this well-organized group held races at Palm Beach Speedway a few miles from Watsonville. Despite a name that sounds like it came from a travel brochure, Palm Beach was not a pretty place. The half-mile dirt oval, which was squeezed between the ocean sand dunes and a slough, provided stark surroundings for both racer and spectator. Races started out for a guaranteed purse of $800 with $200 to the main event winner, but the crowds did not warrant this size of payoff for very long.

Many of the CCRA owners and drivers were veterans of Alemand Speedway racing. They liked the idea of a better-organized group, insurance and the possibility of a bigger payoff. In the beginning, many of the cars were the same crude and ugly ones that ran at Alemand, but in a few months at Palm Beach most had evolved into fairly nice-looking hot rods. The drivers with Alemand experience proved to be the ones to beat in 1947, as Johnnie Key, Lloyd Regan, Johnny Lomonto and Paul Kamm won most of the races. Kamm

Palm Beach Speedway program.
(Bill Peters collection)

was crowned 1947 Central California Roadster Association champion. Later, some newcomers like Bill Peters, Keith Maggini and Al Gaetano provided stiff competition for the veterans.

In 1948, races were once again held at Palm Beach Speedway, but crowds were dropping off and so was the car count. In the mid-summer of 1948, the CCRA, with help from one of the then warring San Francisco Bay Area associations, held a few races at a quarter-mile dirt track in San Jose. The races were good, but the crowds did not come. At some indeterminate date in 1948, the CCRA just quit sanctioning races and disappeared. The better drivers and the better cars found they could run with the Bay Area groups so they simply traveled farther from home to race.

Despite the high speeds and the often thick dust at Palm Beach, the CRRA's safety record was not too bad. Several drivers were badly injured, but Carl White was the only fatality. White's death came in a simple low-speed rollover at Palm Beach in June of 1948. He'd been using a common leather belt as a safety belt and was crushed by his own car when this flimsy device broke.

This 1947 race at Palm Beach looks like the trophy dash. Paul Schultz is on the pole, #76 is Keith Maggini and Johnnie Lomonto lines up his #10 GMC on the outside.
(Bill Peters collection)

Bill Wade is on the pole for this 1947 race at Palm Beach. Bill Peters is in the #4 Riley Four-Port and #36 is Ralph Lindley.
(Bill Peters collection)

Johnny Key in #2 is the only driver who can be identified in this lineup. Note that the driver of the car on the outside of the front row seems to be sitting on—not in—his hot rod.
(Rod Eschenburg collection)

Lloyd Reagen, in the dark coveralls, was the driver of this car. He usually drove the car to and from the races.
(Rod Eschenburg collection)

Bob Grossi drove this V8 at Palm Beach. The body appears to have started life as a touring car. Check the size of that fuel tank! (Rod Eschenburg collection)

Johnny Key at speed in 1947 race. (Rod Eschenburg collection)

One the five-eighths-mile dirt track at Vallejo—circa 1952. Bob Veith is in #56, but the other driver is unknown. *(Bob Veith collection)*

George Danberg (aka George Hubbard) in Dick Hubbard's car at Stockton in 1948. It looks like the first time out for the car with the newly installed aluminum channel frame rails.
(Dana Photo by Rick—Al Slinker collection)

San Jose in 1950. Car #6 is Lloyd Regan and Bob Gonzoles is in #60. The other drivers cannot be identified. *(Bob Veith collection)*

George Mehalas in the Ben Hubbard V8. This was a no-nonsense "working" roadster, and Mehalas drove it well. *(Tom Motter collection)*

Paul Kamm backs into the wall at San Jose as Lloyd Selacci watches from his #36.
(Erwin Eszlinger collection)

That looks like Al Slinker getting nailed by Jack Smyers in #46 at Oakland. Chet Richards is probably in #90.
(Dana Photo by Rick—Al Slinker collection)

Action on the dirt at Modesto. Bob Veith pitches #32 completely sideways as he tries to get by Joe Valente and Gene Tessien in #4. *(Bob Veith collection)*

Joe Valente in Cash Slayton's #57 at Stockton in 1948. It's a day race, it's hot, and that's dry ice packed in front of the radiator. The Merc V8 probably overheated anyhow.
(Greg Sharp—Vintage Racing Photos)

Bob Veith pins an orchid on the trophy girl as Joe Valente clowns and, as usual, steals the scene.
(Bob Veith collection)

OFF-ROAD ROADSTERS

In Ohio, they called it Pasture Field Racing. In Indiana, it was Steeplechase Racing. In Texas, it was Gravel Pit Racing. Today, they call it Stadium Off Road Racing and run $100,000 cars.

In the 1940s, a bit less sophisticated equipment was required. A stripped down Model A Ford roadster would do just fine. These races probably started on a more or less informal basis in some farmer's field or an abandoned gravel pit. In those simple days before lawyers and liability worries, it was an easy step to hold organized races and maybe even charge admission for spectators. Racing was on rough courses with natural and man-made obstacles like bumps, hills, gullies and streambeds. The cars spent as much time in the air as on the ground as the drivers hung on for dear life. It was wild, rough and probably dangerous racing despite the relatively low speeds.

In most areas, the off road racing didn't last too long. In some cases, the course would be improved until it became a nearly conventional oval. In other cases, the racers decided that they wanted to go faster and moved on to the local county fairgrounds track. That Model A roadster got souped up, and a track roadster racing group was born.

The Mutual Racing Association started as a Steeplechase Racing group. Out West many of the racers who competed in "Ash Can Derby" races in a San Bernardino sand pit became part of an organizations that still exists today—The California Racing Association.

This is the Steeplechases Motor Speedway at Muncie, Indiana, in 1939. The driver is unidentified, but many of these racers moved on the Mutual Racing Association track roadsters.
(Remington-Hurst collection)

It is 1946, and this Texan is flying high at "Devils Bowl" near San Antonio. (Dan Fowler collection)

A few races were held at the Oakland Baseball Park in 1950. This is the home plate turn, and Lemoine Frey is tangled with Joe Valente in the white car at left. The driver of #52 watches and waits as Bob Veith in #56 approaches.
(Bill Peters collection)

Good roadster action at Stockton in 1948 or 1949. George Pacheco is in #92, Ed Huntington in #6 and ?? in #7. (Bob Veith collection)

A number of good drivers sat in Herk Veglienzone's #61, and Bob Machin was one of them. Machin later became a top driver in BCRA and USAC midgets.
(Herc Veglienzone collection)

Johnny Key in #3 pushes Chuck Ford hard at Belmont.
(Dana Photo by Rick—Bob Barkhimer collection)

THE HUDSON THAT WASN'T

The #5 roadster driven by Al Slinker was owned and sponsored by Oakland Hudson dealer John Milton. Feeling that using anything but a Hudson for power would be bad advertising, Milton spent a lot of time and money trying to make Hudson engines competitive. The Hudson Six didn't work and the eight-cylinder engine was even worse. The Hudson Hornet, which was to dominate stock car racing, came out in 1949, but even a modified version of it would not keep up with V8s. Milton finally solved the problem by installing a very fast Ford six and telling everybody it was a Hudson. So far as driver Al Slinker remembers nobody ever caught on.

This is 1948 and there is a "real" Hudson engine in the John Milton roadster driven by Al Slinker.
(Dana Photo by Rick—Al Slinker collection)

Al Slinker gets a hot foot at Salinas as the Hudson Eight erupts in flames.
(Dana Photo by Rick—Al Slinker collection)

Perhaps the Henry Ford version of the "Hudson Hornet" is in place as Al Slinker leads at Oakland.
(Dana Photo by Rick—Al Slinker collection)

Chuck Ford flips at Belmont. Ford was painfully injured. Bud Kelleher's spin in #99 triggered the incident. (Dana Photo by Rick)

Roaring Roadsters   **57**

A pitman futilely battles a blaze at Oakland in 1948. Fire protection was minimal at most speedways in that era. (Dana Photo by Rick—Greg Sharp collection)

Dick Liebfritz at San Jose in 1951. Those pipes were LOUD! (Dick Liebfritz collection)

Joe Valente gets a trophy at Oakland in 1947. Valente was the Northern California Roadster Racing Association champion in 1948. (Dana Photo by Rick—Al Slinker collection)

Bill Peters is in the Les Marino Four-Port Riley at San Jose. Mel Senna is in the background in #9. (Bill Peters collection)

Author Don Radbruch at San Jose in 1949. Heat race and semi-main wins that day paid $32.63. (Bob Veith collection)

Ed Elisian, car owner Ben Hubbard and champion Gene Tessien show off their trophies for the 1949 NCRRA season. (Bob Veith collection)

This is either Chuck Ford or Bud White getting a thrill at Oakland. (Dana Photo by Rick—Al Slinker collection)

A roadster and a midget help promote an auto racing short at the Oakland Telenews Theater in 1949. Fred Agabashian (left) and Bob Veith are behind the roadster. (Ray Hiatt collection)

1947 and this must be Pacheco. Car #7 was probably driven by Darrell Fisher. Bob West owned #66 but somebody else drove it.
(Custom Photo—Bob Veith collection)

Budge Canty is the driver of the Hiatt Brothers' V8 in this 1949 shot at Oakland. (Dana Photo by Rick)

This is Pacheco in 1947. Bob Rushing has spun out and collected a (mad?) Vince Pacheco in his Hudson roadster. (Bob Veith collection)

THE VERY DIFFERENT ROADSTER

While most hot rodders tended to copy somebody else, Jim Smith chose to be innovative and very different. His #71 was not only front-wheel drive, but was surely the only monocoque roadster ever built. It may have been the first monocoque race car ever built! "Monocoque" means that the body sheetmetal had to carry most or all of the stresses, and the 1938 French Citroen was designed that way. Smith took the bottom part of a Citroen and welded it to a '31 Model A roadster body. This created a frameless unit that was far stiffer than the average track roadster. A full race Merc V8 was mounted backwards and fed the power to the Citroen front-wheel drive transaxle. Rear suspension was also on the Citroen, so the roadster had fully independent suspension. There was really no room for the radiator up front, so it was mounted in the cockpit alongside of the driver.

Smith put a lot of time, effort and money into his unique and good looking hot rod. In retrospect there would have been problems. The Merc would have probably overheated and surely would have torn up a lot of Citroen transaxles. Smith ran the car only once. This was at San Jose in 1949 when he spun during qualifying and lightly tapped the wall. After that both the car and Jim Smith disappeared from California roadster racing.

Jim Smith and his Citroen-A-V8. Those good looking wheels are from a '38 Citroen, and that's the radiator filler cap alongside of Smith.
(Greg Sharp-Vintage Racing Photos)

OAKLAND STADIUM

The unique design of the five-eighths-mile Oakland Stadium contributed to this crash—on a normal track it would have been a one- or at most a two-car crash. The Oakland track was steeply banked around its outer rim. One turn was banked 45-degrees—we called that the "flat turn." The other turn, where the crash took place, was banked 60-degrees and had an unusually short radius. The fast way around was right up against the concrete crash wall. This wall actually overhung the track and to hit it was just a part of racing at Oakland. A car would simply scrub off a bit of speed with little harm done. Driving the 60-degree banked turn was a little like being on the inside of a barrel—the drivers normal field of vision was only 100 feet or so ahead. With speeds in this turn near 100 mph, the drivers involved in this crash did not know there was trouble ahead until it was too late to do anything but pile into the wreckage. The crash seemed to go on forever—actually it was probably five to seven seconds.

Circa 1941. Gene Sousa in #35 at Calistoga with Johnny Soares lined up on the inside. Soares is still active as a promoter in California.
(Don Connelly collection)

Elmer George gets a kiss with his trophy at Salinas in 1948. George would soon be on his way to the AAA sprint cars and a couple of starts at Indy.
(Dana photo by Rick—Al Slinker collection)

Cars get in trouble at Oakland and go sliding up on the 60-degree bank.
(Dana Photo by Rick—Greg Sharp collection)

Sam Hawks at Stockton in 1949.
(Dana Photo by Rick—Al Slinker collection)

Jim Algers gets a trophy at Oakland. He's driving the very fast Hartman Wayne Chevy.
(Dana Photo by Rick)

Sam Hawks in the Jack Hagermann-built Pestana-George #55. While certainly one of the most beautiful track roadsters ever built, the car was not a main event winner. (Tom Motter collection)

Action at Oakland in 1949. The race is on the quarter-mile track so the cars must stay off the 60-degree bank and below the white line. The quarter-mile and the high-banked five-eighths-mile at Oakland shared this turn.
(Dana Photo by Rick—Greg Sharp collection)

Oakland action on the quarter-mile track. Identification is far from positive, but #17 might be Red Corbin, #4 Jim Alger and #6 Elmer George.
(Dana Photo by Rick—Greg Sharp collection)

George "Blondie" Pacheco was the 1947 Northern California Roadster Racing Association champion. (Dana Photo by Rick)

Gene Tessien was the 1949 Northern California Roadster Association champion. (Dana Photo by Rick)

NUMBER 119 ON ROUTE 66

In the early days of roadster racing, it wasn't unusual for a racer to drive his hot rod from home to the track. Ken Stansberry did a bit of a reverse trick on this procedure. He moved his home from track to track with his roadster.

Stansberry had been racing in San Antonio in 1946 when the time came to go home to Los Angeles. He'd acquired a 24-foot trailer, and along with his wife and two kids, was living in it. How else to get the trailer from Texas to California but to tow it with #119?

The V8 had plenty of power, but the trip was an adventure on the two-lane Route 66 of that era. The engine often overheated on the long uphill grades but Ken Stansberry, family, trailer and #119 all arrived safely in Los Angeles.

A few days later Stansberry drove #119 to Carroll Speedway and took part in one of the first California Roadster Association events.

After the races at Oakland, it was party time at Stubby's across the street from the track. Some of these racers may be gone, but they are not forgotten and most of them can be identified.
(Haigler-Motter collection)

Al Christeen at San Jose. The engine looks like the four-cylinder Chevy with the Olds three-port head that was the hot combination in those days.
(Haigler-Motter collection)

1955 Indy winner Bob Sweikert smiles from the seat of his first track roadster. Judging from its appearance the car seems aptly named, but it was typical of track roadsters in early 1947.
(Dana Photo by Rick—Al Slinker collection)

Gene Figone at San Jose in 1938. Figone was on of the few drivers to die in northern California roadsters. He was killed at Calistoga in 1941.
(Haigler-Motter collection)

Jim Algers gets a trophy at Oakland. He's driving the very fast Hartman Wayne Chevy.
(Dana Photo by Rick)

Rex McCapes was the surprise winner of the runoff after early leader Lemoine Frey broke an axle. McCapes quit while he was winning, and never raced again.
(Dana Photo by Rick—Al Slinker collection)

San Jose in 1950 or 1951. Number 98 is George Mehalas, Sam Hawks is in #61 and Bill Peters in #9.
(Bill Peters collection)

A field of roadsters lines up for a race on the five-eighths-mile track at Oakland.
(Rod Eschenburg collection)

The fast way around Oakland was up on the 60-degree band right next to the wall. Cars would often brush against the wall with little harm done.
(Dick Liebfritz collection)

Tommy Cheek seemed to be always smiling. The device on the front axle is a "skid bar" designed to provide some control should a spindle break.
(Dana Photo by Rick)

Julian Catro at Oakland in 1947. This early roadster had mechanical brakes an a Model A tie rod served as a very flimsy drag link.
(Dana Photo by Rick—Bob Veith collection)

Probably Calistoga—circa 1940. Driver and car not identified. *(Norm Holtkamp collection)*

Pacheco action. Bob Germolous in #15 and Ed Elisian in #2. Apparently Elisian has just bounced off #15. *(Dana Photo by Rick—Al Slinker collection)*

During roadster practice at the flat half-mile Oakland track, an unidentified driver spins out. This track was inside the banked one-mile track.
(Ray Hiatt collection)

Bob Machin climbs the fence at Salinas in 1949 as Don Radbruch and Joe Gusti in #22 tangle.
(Rosie Roussel collection)

This is Belmont. Bill Peters leads and is followed by Bob Veith, Gene Tessien, Lemoine Frey and Dick Liebfritz. *(Bill Peters collection)*

April 1951 at Stockton. Sam Hawks gets a trophy, as owner Herk Veglienzone looks on. That's 1947 roadster champ Joe Valente in the cowboy hat. *(Tom Motter collection)*

John Barlow in Don Kolb's V8 in 1947. The frame appears to be very stout. *(Dana Photo by Rick—Bob Barkhimer collection)*

Future AAA Midwest Sprint Car Champion Elmer George at Oakland in about 1949. *(Dana Photo by Rick—Al Slinker collection)*

Johnny Key was the Racing Roadsters Inc. champion in 1948 and 1949. He was well on his way to speedway stardom when he was killed in a midget at Cincinnati in about 1954. (Greg Sharp— Vintage Racing Photos)

This is Mario Banchero at San Jose. Banchero drove under the rather unflattering name of "Fat Mario." (Haigler Motter collection)

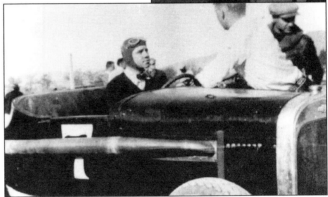

John Timmons in his Chevy at San Jose. Note that Timmons wears only a cloth helmet. *(Haigler-Motter collection)*

Rollie Smith is pictured at San Jose in 1938. *(Haigler-Motter collection)*

Ed Elisian spins out in the Ben Hubbard Merc at Belmont. *(Rod Eschenburg collection)*

THE OUTLAWS AT ALEMAND

The first post World War II roadster racing in northern California was at Alemand Speedway a few miles east of Gilroy. The track was in a former stock watering pond

Alemand Speedway had a fatality early in its history. The accident took place in practice before a race. The car is only slightly damaged and odds are that the driver, and passenger had neither helmets nor seat belts. *(Rod Eschenburg collection)*

on John Alemand's cattle ranch. A narrow valley and the pond's dam provided a natural bowl for the odd-shaped, and anything but level, half-mile track. There was no racing organization formed, so it was strictly a case of show up and race, and often a spectator in a hot rod would find himself recruited as a racer. There was no insurance for the drivers, and probably none for the spectators. Helmets were not required in the

early races, and it is doubtful if Alemand ever had a seat belt rule. There weren't even any grandstands, but large crowds happily sat on the hillsides or parked around the edge of the track. Beer often flowed freely and sometimes the crowds were rougher than the races.

A few nice-looking street rods competed at Alemand, but most of the cars were crude and primitive track roadsters. The track's odd shape made shifting gears a necessity, so most cars retained the clutch and transmission. Alemand was fast and on the long downhill main straightaway some cars hit near 90 mph. Alemand offered lots of action as drivers scrubbed off speed by sliding sideways through the banked first turn.

The crowds were good at

Johnnie Lomonto dominated most of the Alemand races. This is one of his early cars— a cutdown GMC pickup. *(Rod Eschenburg collection)*

Alemand Speedway in 1947. The cars are on the downhill main straightaway. Lloyd Ragon leads with Johnny Key and Johnnie Lamonto close behind. *(Rod Eschenburg collection)*

Action as the cars come out of turn two. They are in second gear and heading uphill on the backstretch. Bob Bailey is in #5. *(Rod Eschenburg collection)*

receipts. Paul Kamm raced there and thinks that, at first, the winner of the main received about $200. Only a few places were paid and most of the racers went home with no prize money. Kamm and Lloyd Ragon won a few races, for the most part, Alemand was dominated by Johnnie Lomonto and his GMC-powered roadsters.

As might be expected, Alemand's safety record was not very good. In one of the early events, Model T races were held, and a driver was killed when he was tossed out of his errant T. There were a number of serious injuries in the roadster races and two fatalities. The last one in mid-

Alemand in 1946, but dropped off rapidly in 1947 as enthusiasm for the races faded. Nobody seems to remember just how much the purses were at Alemand or if they were a set percentage of the gate receipts. Paul Kamm raced there and thinks that, at first,

A typical Alemand hot rod: crude and anything but pretty. The roll bar is sturdier than most but lacks bracing. *(Rod Eschenburg collection)*

Action in Alemand's first turn. Johnnie Lomonto has spun out in #10. Bob Kelly is in #7-11 and Paul Kamm in #00. The elbow hooked over the door is to keep drivers from sliding around in the seat. Most cars did not have safety belts.

1947, led to the closing of Alemand Speedway a few weeks later. Peace and quiet returned to the little valley and the cows had their watering hole back.

Norm Garland's A-V8 was neater than most Alemand cars. Garland is pictured on the stock pond dam that formed the end of the main straightaway. *(Rod Eschenburg collection)*

COLORADO

The distinction of being the first track roadsters to race on a paved track goes to the Colorado racers. In 1932, they raced on the five-eighths-mile Dupont Speedway—a rare paved oval in those dirt track days. The Dupont track was about 10 miles north of Denver and the roadsters, as well as the big cars, raced there on a fairly regular basis from 1932 until 1941.

The Dupont roadsters were billed as "stock car races" for at least the first few years. Future Indy and Pikes Peak driver, Johnny Mauro, got his start at Dupont in 1932 by stripping the lights, windshield and fenders off of his '32 Ford V8 roadster. Mauro later ran a '34 Ford roadster and,

during one season, won 11 of 12 feature races at Dupont. Another winner at Dupont was Bill Ketz in his Cragar Model A roadster—this car survived to race until about 1950. Dupont Speedway appears to have been a successful operation but it was torn down during World War II.

After World War II, the first roadster race in Colorado was held on a rough rodeo grounds track at Table Mountain, near Golden. Other than a few leftover pre-war Dupont cars, the roadsters were street machines. The drivers passed the hat after races to collect whatever purse there was. A few races were held on a five-eighths-mile horse track at Brighton later that same year. During the winter of 1946-47, the Colorado Auto Racing Club was formed—a group that still exists today. Under the sanction and promotion of the CARC, racing resumed at

(Unless otherwise noted, all Colorado photos are by Lynn Day or Leroy Byers, from the Leroy Byers collection.

Glen "Babe" Bunyard in his Fronty T at Brighton in 1946. The car is basically a 1917 Model T. Note that there is no rocker arm cover on the engine—it was run this way. (Sonny Coleman collection)

Action at the Arapahoe Fairgrounds in 1949. T.E. Russell is in #3, and Red Dutton is on the pole in #73. It is dusty!

Sonny Coleman at Brighton in 1946 or 1947. Check that Snell DISAPPROVED helmet! Coleman was later a three-time Rocky Mountain Midget Champion.
(Sonny Coleman collection)

Willy Young flipped the Kenz-Leslie V8—probably at Brighton. Young was OK, but it was reported that Roy Leslie was very angry at him.

Brighton—circa 1947. Keith Andrews in his own V8 roadster. Although this is but a slightly modified street rod, the talented Andrews drove it to many victories.

Willy Young wins a trophy at Brighton. Young drove many of the Kenz-Leslie cars, including a 270 mph streamliner at Bonneville in the 1950s.

Pappy Hendricks in the Syers Studebaker Eight leads the field at Brighton in 1946. The flagman is Harry Schmidt.

Wild action at the Gage Ranch track just east of Denver in 1946-47. The track was in a natural bowl and had no grandstands.

Brighton in the spring of 1947, and soon the 1,200-seat grandstands were overflowing with race fans. As is very evident in some of the photos, spectator protection at Brighton was nonexistent. It appears that racing at Brighton was discontinued in mid-1947—fortunately before a major disaster took place.

After Brighton, most of the Colorado Auto Racing Club activity was at Englewood Speedway, a third-mile oval just south of Denver. The track was dirt at first but was later paved—probably in

T.E. Russell drove the Ed Murray Riley Four Port. This is Brighton around 1947.

The roadsters line up at Brighton. Fred Massey drove #1, and #15 was Forrest Fisher's ride.

Harry Yost flipped his car at Brighton. Yost was OK after crewmen lifted the car off him.

Johnny Tolan spins out in the Kenz-Leslie V8 at Brighton in 1946.

1948. The roadsters continued to race at Englewood through the 1950 season. Despite the fact they were competing with the midgets for the fan's dollars, the crowds at Englewood were good. Not too much data on the size of the purses is available, but it is probable that most of the payoffs were between $1,000 and $1,500. Future Rocky Mountain Midget Champion, Sonny Coleman, was one of the roadster racers who competed at Englewood. Coleman readily admits that the hot rod he drove was far from a first-class car, but he remembers winning as much as $150 at Englewood—he also remembers winning as little as $4.54.

For much of the time during the roadster era Lafe Ellsworth was president of the Colorado Auto

Red Johnson in #14X and Ralph Iacovetta in action at the Gage Ranch track around 1947. The track was located near Stapleton International Airport.

Brighton-1946-47. Keith Andrews in the Syers' Studebaker gets a trophy. Andrews had a brilliant racing career that was cut short when he died in a crash during practice at Indianapolis in 1957.

Keith Andrews proves that he doesn't need four wheels to win a race. Gage Ranch track in 1947.

The car looks OK, but Tony Rice was severely injured in this crash at Brighton in 1946.

Action at the Gage Ranch track. No identification on #89, but that's Buck Russell in #3 and Red Johnson in #14X.

A REVERSE CAM CRAGAR

A Colorado roadster with a long history was the #7 Cragar-Model A owned by Bob Conrad. This car was unusual because it used a "Reverse Cam" Cragar engine.

From Joe Gemsa in El Monte, California, comes to the story of just what in the heck a "Reverse Cam" engine is. The Cragar overhead valve head for the Model A or Model B Ford was designed so that the stock two-port intake and four-port exhaust manifolds could be used. This made installing the Cragar head a simple matter, as the only other modification required was to weld a four-inch extension on the manifold side of the exhaust pipe. The Cragar head sold for $92 and came complete with valves, springs, push rods and a plate to cover the stock Ford ports. One drawback of the Cragar was the two-port intake system—it would not perform like the Riley or other heads that had four intake ports.

One solution to this drawback reversing the camshaft in the engine block. With a bit of machine work, the timing gear could be put on the back end of the camshaft. The cam was then installed in the block backwards—this changed the valve action so that intake ports became exhaust ports and vice-versa. With four intake ports the engine could breathe a lot better and, even though the exhaust was choked up somewhat, the performance was much better than with stock Cragar head. As Joe Gemsa says, "Reversing the cam really woke up a Cragar engine."

Car #7 was built by Bill Kenz around 1935, and it ran in Colorado roadster races. Kenz also ran the car in the Pikes Peak Hillclimb and with the big cars at a two-day event at Sterling in 1937. Kenz got Lloyd Axel to drive at Sterling, and he finished second to a D.O. Fronty big car on both days. On another occasion, Kenz's Cragar was running in a roadster race at Dupont Speedway when a California visitor, Joel Thorne, showed up at the race track.

Thorne was on his way to Indianapolis and had his race car in tow. One of Thorne's pitmen had a '32 V8 roadster and figured he'd pick up some easy money running in the roadster races. With the Reverse Cam Cragar running strong this was easier said than done. Joe Thorne unloaded the Indy car to see if it could handle the Kenz roadster. A match race was held and, with the crowd screaming encouragement, Bill Kenz's Cragar beat Joel Thorne and his Indy car!

Kenz sold the Cragar around 1940, and the car spent the World War II years in Detroit. After the war, Bob Conrad brought the car back to Colorado where it resumed its winning ways with Dick Isaac at the wheel. Isaac won races at Brighton and Englewood, but tragedy struck during a race at the Arapahoe Fairgrounds mid-1947. Dick Isaac tangled with another car, the Cragar flipped several times, and Isaac was fatally injured.

Dick Isaac in the Conrad Reverse Cam Cragar at Brighton in 1946. Owner Bob Conrad is at the left. The car is essentially unchanged from the way it raced in the 1930s.
(Leroy Byers collection)

The remains of the Bob Conrad Cragar after Dick Isaac's fatal crash at the Arapahoe Fairgrounds, Littleton, Colorado, in 1947. It is not known if the car ever raced again
(Leroy Byers collection)

Racing Club. His ambitious promotion resulted in the Colorado racers traveling to Kansas for several races, to Rapid City, South Dakota, and to Ord, Nebraska. A number of races were also held at other Colorado tracks: the Arapahoe County Fairground at Littleton, Fort Collins and the Pikes Peak Speedway in Colorado Springs. The roadsters also raced at the Gage Ranch track just west of Stapleton International Airport. Although the summers are short in Colorado, the Colorado Auto Racing Club kept busy.

A number of drivers did well in Colorado roadster racing. Red Fitzwater was probably the most consistent winner—he was a two-time CARC champion. Keith Andrews was the 1946 champion and won a lot of roadster races before turning most of his attention to other types of racing. Slim Roberts, Tom Rice, T.E. Russell, Fred Massey and veteran driver, Pappy Hendricks were all race winners. Willy Young did OK in the hot rods, but most of his fame would come later at Bonneville as the driver of the 270 mph Kenz-Leslie Streamliner.

Most of the roadster racing in Colorado was sanctioned by the Colorado Auto Racing Association and, in general, centered around the Denver area. In southern Colorado, the Durango

Tom Clark drove this unsafe-looking hot rod at Englewood. Owner Rocky LaFant is standing at the right.

Brighton—circa 1947. No identification on the driver but ex-big car and midget driver, Mat Pulver, owned #52.

Auto Racing Association ran a mixture of roadsters and home-built sprint cars. Durango is on the other side of the Rocky Mountains from Denver and, especially in the late 1940s, was just about inaccessible to the CARC racers.

Hub Cook made the long haul to Durango for a "roadster race" in about 1950 and found, to his surprise, he was up against a near full field of sprint cars. Cook wound up second in the main, so the trip was a success. Roadster racers from New Mexico and Arizona raced at Durango, and drivers like Earl Emmons and Pappy Noe won races there. Purses at Durango were almost surely less than $500.

There were three known fatalities in Colorado roadster racing. Dick Isaacs died at the Arapahoe Fairgrounds half-mile dirt track in 1947. Buck Russell was killed at Englewood Speedway on May 21, 1948, and later that same year Ralph Icovetta was also killed at Englewood.

The Colorado Auto Racing Club Champions were:

1946 Keith Andrews in his own '32 Ford roadster
1947 Fred Massey
1948 Red Fitzwater in the Charlie Codner V8
1949 Red Fitzwater in the Charlie Codner V8
1950 Don Padia in the Charlie Codner V8

Herb Hessling drove his own lightweight Miller-Schofield T at Brighton.

Action at the Arapahoe Fairgrounds half miler in 1949. Don Padia is driving #73 and Frank Carter is in his own Studebaker Six.

A field of Colorado Auto Racing Club roadsters lines up at the Arapahoe Fairgrounds around 1949. Glen Masters is on the pole in #23.

T.E. Russell gets a trophy from Lafe Ellsworth at Englewood. Ellsworth was president of the Colorado Auto Racing Club and was instrumental in the successful promotion of roadster racing in Colorado.

Buck Russell was fatally injured in this 1948 crash at Englewood.

Far Left—The hot rods climbed a mountain at Georgetown, west of Denver, in 1954. These cars were closer to street rods than track roadsters. (Jeff Sharp collection)

Center—The advertising writer for the Durango roadster group used some rather lurid terms. (Bob Noe collection)

Left—A program cover for "The Roaring Hotrods" at Durango. Durango had a separate roadster group that raced in southern Colorado and New Mexico. (Bob Noe collection)

Jim Roberts knocked down the two-story judge's stand at Englewood. Lots of bumps and bruises but no serious injuries.

Don Codner drove this Nash-powered hot rod at Englewood. Codner was primarily a car owner and left the driving to others.

One of the early Colorado roadsters—the Ed Vickers Chevy Four at Brighton.

A little thing like a Denver snowstorm didn't stop the Colorado Auto Racing Club from taking this publicity shot. Jack Smith looks warm enough in his Riley two-port, but the lady at the left looks COLD.

AN INDY CAR MYSTERY

One of the Colorado track roadsters ran a Studebaker straight eight engine. This is unusual in a roadster, but even more unusual is that this engine almost certainly ran at Indianapolis in the 1930s.

The history of this Studebaker's participation in the Indianapolis 500 is a tale worth telling. In 1930, rules for the Indianapolis race were changed radically from those in effect in 1929. Not only was a riding mechanic required for the first time since the early 1920s, but the use of semi-stock motors was encouraged. This rule change has acquired the rather unflattering name of "Junk Formula" and that's exactly what some of the cars were. Slightly modified passenger automobiles, such as Buick, Hudson, Chrysler, Stutz, Oakland and Reo, were fitted with two-man racing bodies, and with semi-stock engines they became "Indy Cars." Most of these cars were private entries but the Studebaker effort had factory backing. Studebaker did it right and the cars were built by professional racing people such as Tony Guletta and Russ Snowberger. The cars used a racing version of the 336-cubic-inch Studebaker straight eight. While not fully competitive with the Miller or Duesenburg racing engines, the Studebakers gave a creditable account of themselves. Russ Snowberger put one of the Studebaker factory cars on the pole for the 1931 500 mile race and finished fifth. In 1932, Cliff Bergere drove one of the Studebakers to a third-place finish.

Colorado historian, Leroy Byers, has documented that one of the Studebaker Indy cars came to the Denver area in the mid- to late 1930s. Under the ownership of George and Harry Syers, the Studebaker ran in big car races in the Denver area. Whether it was modified for the dirt track races is not known.

After World War II, the Syers brothers put a '27 Model T body on the car and ran it as a track roadster. As the photos indicate, many changes have been made in the car. The original Studebaker Indy car four-spring suspension is gone, and the car has been shortened. There are resemblances between the Syers' (later Voorhies) roadster and the Studebaker Indy cars. The wheels and hubs appear to be same, and the rods that brace the radiator indicate that perhaps the original firewall is still in place under that T body. The frame rails may or may not be the same as the Indy cars.

Do enough parts from the original car remain so that the Syers-Voorhies roadster can be called an ex-Indy car? Perhaps a Studebaker historian could help solve the mystery.

Brighton in 1947. Dick Isaac stopped #1X just before it hit that wire fence.

Ralph Iacovetta starts to flip his #55 at Englewood. Joe Garrone is in #17. Iacovetta was fatally injured at Englewood—this may be the fatal crash.

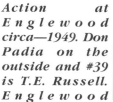

No identification on either of these Englewood drivers. Number 6 appears to be in deep trouble.

Action at Englewood circa—1949. Don Padia on the outside and #39 is T.E. Russell. Englewood Speedway's racing surface was changed from dirt to pavement and back several times.

Babe Bunyard in his Fronty T battles with Bob Russell in the #14 blown Ford Six. This engine was banned after the 1949 season.

Englewood action. Keith Andrew is in #72, T.E. Russell is in #74, and Slim Roberts is in #1X.

Early hot rod action at Englewood. Ray Dutton is in the Doc Burns Miller-Schofield #73. He is getting a push from an unknown driver in the #44 Chevy.

Action on the dirt at Englewood in 1946. T.E. Russell is in #74, Willy Young is in #6, and Sonny Coleman is in his own #21.

T.E. Russell gets a trophy at Englewood. The Colorado Auto Racing Club cooperated with a modeling agency, so that professional models appeared as trophy girls.

Ruth Penn was one of the professional models. Here she gives a trophy to Harry Yost.

FLORIDA

● ●

There was some roadster racing in Florida, but the sport never really did take off as it did in other areas. Even while the roadsters were running, the modified stock car was king in Florida.

There were two known roadster organizations in Florida, which operated from about 1948 until about 1950—both groups were in south Florida. The South Florida Racing Association ran roadster races on the one-mile dirt horse track at Pompano in 1949 and 1950. It is probable that there were races at other tracks in that area, but no records have been found.

The other group, the Greater Miami Racing Association, sanctioned roadster races before switching over to stock cars. It is probable that the roadster races were in conjunction with stock car races. The races were held at the Opa-Locka Naval Air Station on a track located in a baseball field complex. The track started as a half-mile dirt oval but wound up as a half-paved/half-dirt third miler. Racing started in 1948, and so far as is known, the roadsters ran until 1950 when the Naval base was re-activated for the Korean War and racing ceased.

There was also roadster racing in central and north Florida, but probably no actual organizations were formed there. On the east coast of Florida races were definitely held at Cocoa and possibly at Melbourne. There was also roadster racing at Jacksonville in north Florida. The only evidence of this racing comes from a few photos that appeared in *Speed Age Magazine* and in *National Speed Sport News*. No other details have been found. Strangely, some of the Cocoa cars very closely resemble the "Barrel Hoop" cars that ran in Pennsylvania, Maryland and Virginia in the early 1940s.

The most thoroughly documented roadster racing event in Florida was the NASCAR-sanctioned race at Davie in February in 1949. So far as Florida roadster racing goes "documented" means one article that appeared in *Speed Age Magazine*. This race was on part of an abandoned World War II air training facility. The course, named the New Broward Speedway, was a two-mile circle—flat and with very abrasive paving. As related elsewhere the entry list was probably not what NASCAR hoped for, but there were a few good cars and drivers on hand. Jim Rathmann in the California-built ex-Yam Oka car, then owned by Andy Granatelli, was fast qualifier at 126 mph. During the 50-lap, 100-mile race, the high-speed track took its toll of engines and the rough pavement wore out tires in a hurry. The "documentation" in *Speed Age Magazine* does not mention Buddy Schuman, who

Jim Casey is pictured in his Florida track roadster, which was cut down from a coupe.
(Marty Little collection)

This is the Red Vogt '37 T driven by Bob Flock to a win at Davie. The car is a Modified Ford Coupe with a Model T body bolted on. The frame rails look like Model A.
(Art Powell photo)

according to historian Art Powell, dominated the race until he had trouble. Art Powell's memory is probably more accurate than the text of the *Speed Age* article but, at any rate, Schuman was not among the top finishers. The finishing order was:

1. Bob Flock
2. Jim Rathmann
3. Ray Erickson
4. Howard Mowell
5. Ronnie Cash
6. Paul Hooper
7. Hank Pollard
8. Emil Reutimann Jr.
9. Harold Sneed
10. James Hodgcs

Drivers Hank Pollard, Emil Reutimann Jr., Harold Sneed and James Hodges were Florida entrants.

As I indicated previously, information on Florida hot rod racing is very sparse, but there were no known fatalities.

NASCAR AND THE ROADSTERS

When it was founded by Bill France in the late 1940s, NASCAR not only sanctioned stock car racing but also modified stock car racing. The modified stock cars were mostly souped up pre-war Ford coupes. Roadsters were, after all, a form of modified stock cars so it is logical that NASCAR would be interested in the hot rods.

In 1948, this interest somehow resulted in agreement by NASCAR to co-sanction roadster races in Ohio. This probably came about through Russ Catlin who was a noted automotive writer and a sometimes racing official. The roadster group was the Ohio Speedway Association and Catlin's by-line appears on articles about this eastern Ohio racing organization throughout most of 1948. Perhaps this was to be the forerunner of NASCAR involvement with roadster racing in other areas.

The Ohio Speedway Association—NASCAR roadster racers suffered dreadful racing luck in early 1948. They lost three drivers in the first four races and had another fatality a few months later. The races were on the deadly half-mile county fair horse tracks, but the casualty rate should not have been that high. NASCAR's involvement with the Ohio Speedway Association seems to have been quietly dropped sometime mid-1948.

Bill France wasn't finished with the roadsters. He advertised that a NASCAR-sanctioned roadster race would be held in Florida in February of 1949. The distance was to be 200 miles, and it would be held on the famed four-mile Dayton Beach course. (This course was used for racing up until 1958 and consisted of two miles of beach and two miles of narrow roadway connected by "U" turns at each end.) A little later another race was set for a week after the Daytona Beach event. This one was at Davie, near Miami, and it would be 100 miles on a two-mile circular course at an abandoned World War II airport. With two races and a total purse of $7,100 Bill France obviously hoped to attract an excellent field of hot rods to Florida.

The expected entries must not have materialized as the Daytona Beach race was abruptly cancelled because of "tidal conditions." The race at Davie was held on February 20, 1949. There were 28 entries, but only a handful could be considered top-ranked drivers and cars. Jim Rathmann in an Andy Granatelli entry ran strong as did Willy Stormquist and Ray Erickson, but it was stock car ace Buddy Schuman who had a big lead until a rock punctured the oil pan of his roadster. Bob Flock took over the lead and won by a lap over Jim Rathmann. Flock drove a car that looked suspiciously like a modified coupe with roadster body stuck on it. The purse was probably $2,100, and from what few photos are available it appears that the crowd was small.

No record of any further NASCAR involvement in roadster racing has been found.

This advertisement appeared on the back cover of Speed Age Magazine in the summer of 1948. (Jim Penney collection)

Another Speed Age advertisement in 1948. The race advertised for the New Broward Speedway at Fort Lauderdale is the Davie race.
(Glenn McGlonie collection)

Walter Young drove this car at Pompano Beach in 1949. The roadster was cut down from a coupe. *(Marty Little collection)*

Another Ohio car, this one driven by Chicago's Willy Sternquist. The car ran on methanol fuel and for a hundred miler a special tank was required. That's it beside the driver's seat. *(Art Powell photo)*

A Florida roadster at Pompano Beach Speedway in 1949. The driver might be Jim Mallard. Note the use of inverted fenders as a belly pan.
(Marty Little collection)

NASCAR official Bill Tuthill (left), looks over one of the entries for the Davie race.
(Marty Little collection)

There is a lot of racing history in this photo. Jim Rathmann drove the car to a second place finish at Davie despite breaking an oil line during the race. In the center at the rear of the car is Andy Granatelli who owned the #8 roadster. Granatelli is flanked by Duane and Arza Carter. Carter was in Florida racing midgets. Arza Carter is the mother of current Indy driver Pancho Carter—she later married Johnny Parsons and gave birth to Johnny Parsons Jr. *(Art Powell photo—Jim Casey collection)*

Daytona Beach—circa 1951. Francis Morse drove this track roadster. Here he is running in NASCAR speed trials.
(Jim Casey collection)

The start of a roadster race at Pompano Beach Speedway in 1949. This was a one-mile horse track. That is probably Opie Clayton in #7.
(Marty Little collection)

Far Left—A roadster program from Pompano Beach Speedway in 1950. The winner of the race would be champion of south Florida, but nobody remembers who won. *(Jim Casey collection)*

Center—The entry list for the Championship Roadster Races at Pompano. Rags Carter is a name that later became familiar. *(Jim Casey collection)*

Left—These are the NASCAR "National Championship Roadster Specifications" that NASCAR issued for the Daytona Beach race that was cancelled. They were probably in effect for the Davie race.
(Art Powell collection)

This is the car Fred Frame drove to second place in the 1931 Indianapolis 500. The Duesenburg engine has been replaced by a V8. George Huntoon drove the car at Davie in a preliminary sports car race and perhaps in the 100-mile roadster race.
(Art Powell photo)

Stock car ace, Buddy Schuman, drove this Ohio car at the Davie race. (Art Powell photo)

Local driver Bill Jordan (aka Jordon Klein) drove this '34 Ford roadster in the Davie race. He was running in the top 10 when the engine scattered. (Jim Casey collection)

The early stages of the Davie race on the two-mile circular course. That looks like Bob Flock in the lead. (Marty Little collection)

ROADSTERS ON THE BOARDS

The Board Track era was a great part of American racing history. This racing was primarily for American Automobile Association Indy cars, and the time period was a decade or more before the roadsters. Logically, there was never a roadster race on a board track—yet there was!

The race was held on the mile-and-one-quarter high-banked board speedway at Charlotte, North Carolina, in 1927. From Ted Brown in Elkins, North Carolina, comes some information on this race—a race that he drove in, and darn near won!

The roadsters ran in a support race for one of the major AAA events. It was probably billed, not as a roadster race, but as a Model T race. The Model T Fords were all roadsters and modifications were allowed so, technically, it was a track roadster race. The fenders and windshields were removed and, apparently, engine regulations were wide open. Ted Brown's '27 T was fitted with a four-cylinder Buick engine—an odd combination considering the T speed equipment that was available. Brown remembers that there were 10 to 15 cars in the race and that speeds averaged around 70 mph. The race was for about 10 laps and Brown, in his T-Buick, was leading by a large margin when the engine seized up. He'd had the Buick engine rebuilt for the race and the pistons were fitted too tight.

Someplace more information and photos of this race must exist—the board track races were well documented. Dick Wallen in his fine book, *Board Track—Guts, Gold, Glory*, does not mention the roadster race at Charlotte. Personal communication with Dick indicates that his research was primarily concerned with the AAA races and did not extend to possible support events. Thanks to 85-year-old Ted Brown, we know that the roadster race did take place and an amazing bit of roadster history has been preserved.

Does anybody out there know anything more about this race?

New Broward Speedway at Davie in 1949. Curley Cotner brought his Cee Bee hot rod from Ohio for the 100-mile race. The car ran fast, but did not finish. (Art Powell photo)

ILLINOIS

● ●

Very little is known about early roadster racing in Illinois. The only information available is that there was roadster racing at Sterling in 1941. No doubt there were other races run at various county fair tracks, but almost certainly there was no organization formed.

Most Illinois hot rod racing is centered around the Hurricane Hot Rod Association formed by Andy Granatelli in 1947. Granatelli organized Hurricane primarily to race roadsters at Solider Field in Chicago, and the group did race there in 1947. No race results are available, but it is known that Willy Stromquist was crowned the champion of Hurricane in that year. The big season for Hurricane, especially at Solider Field, was 1948, and the races drew huge crowds. People's memories of just how big the crowds were vary considerably but there are documented crowds of up to 21,000 in *National Speed Sport News* articles and of 38,853 in paid advertisements. Whatever number is correct there is little doubt that the Solider Field crowds were the biggest in the history of roadster racing.

One reason that the Soldier Field hot rod races drew big crowds was that Andy Granatelli was a showman—and a good one! In his book, *They Call Me Mr. 500,* Granatelli readily admits to some strange happenings in the stock car races at Soldier Field that came after the roadsters. He employed "Booger Artists" who would deliberately cause crashes. Such tactics would be too dangerous for the roadsters, but was definitely some showmanship tossed in occasionally. Granatelli remembers that, at times, he paid the first six finishers in the main event all the same. Whoever was leading at the white flag lap had better not win the race or he wouldn't get paid—this made for some wild finishes. Driver Al Swenson remembers that he was on Granatelli's payroll to "put on a show." Swenson would start at the tail end of the semi-main event, even though he had qualified for the feature. Swenson would then come through the field in spectacular fashion and win the race by a few feet. Most of these shenanigans were probably in the first roadster races in 1947. As the cars and drivers got better, such "showmanship" tactics would be hard to hide.

Hurricane had some good drivers like Willy Sternquist, Ray Erickson and Al Swenson. Drivers from Indiana's Mutual Racing Association also raced with Hurricane as often as their schedules permitted—these included Smokey Stover, Red Renner, Sam Skinner and Dick Frazier. California drivers heard about the big purses and came east to race. Dick and Jim Rathmann, Pat Flaherty and Don Freeland ran well with Hurricane. Dick Frazier and Jim Rathmann were probably the most successful at Soldier Field.

During most of the 1948 season, Hurricane ran

Al Swenson scatters a hay bale and heads for photographer Bob Sheldon. That's Vince Granatelli in #59.
(Bob Sheldon photo)

Joe Granatelli lands upside-down at Soldier Field in 1947. Granatelli was OK. *(Bob Sheldon photo)*

Soldier Field in 1948. Nick Karles in #2 climbs all over Wally Edmunds. (Bob Sheldon photo)

Crewmen wheel away Joe Granatelli's wrecked hot rod. Joe and Vince Granatelli drove roadsters for awhile. Andy Granatelli did not drive roadsters but did attempt to qualify at Indianapolis in 1948. (Bob Sheldon photo)

five nights a week. Races were at Soldier Field as well as Rockford, Illinois, the South Bend and 16th Street Speedway in Indiana, and in Milwaukee, Wisconsin. There were also spot races on Sundays. These included events at Harvard, Illinois, and on the famous trotting horse track at Aurora Downs. Oh, how the horsemen must have loved this! A season-ending 50-lap championship race was held in October at Soldier Field and Dick Frazier was the winner.

In 1949, the Hurricane Hot Rod Racing Association announced a race schedule that was as follows:

Every Thursday night: St Louis Missouri, Walsh Stadium

Every Friday night: Springfield, Illinois

Every Saturday night: Rockford, Illinois

Every Sunday night: Soldier Field

Every Tuesday night: Milwaukee, Wisconsin

Alternating Wednesday nights: Peoria, Illinois and Cincinnati, Ohio

Purses were to be a guaranteed $1,500 per race or 40 percent of the gate. Any car making the entire circuit was guaranteed $150 per week. It is not likely that this very ambitious schedule lasted very long. By about June of 1949, Andy Granatelli started promoting stock car races at Soldier Field. These races attracted huge crowds and soon Hurricane virtually forgot about roadster racing.

In early 1949, a midget organization, Tri-States Auto Racing Alliance, announced plans to sanction roadster races at four of their tracks in Illinois, Indiana and Kentucky. Curley Cotner was the Racing Director of this group and his announcement as reported in *National Speed Sport News* read,

The field gets the green flag at De Kolb in 1948. There is no identification on the drivers, and no information on the sanctioning group. (Bob Sheldon photo)

Paul Ambrose at Soldier Field. The car looks like it is from the Mutual Racing Association in Indiana. (Bob Sheldon collection)

Soldier Field action in 1948. There is a big crowd/ field on hand (Bob Sheldon photo)

Early 1949 action, as Tilford Ashe hits a chain link fence. it looks as though he is about to be hit by the car's roll bar.
(Bob Sheldon photo)

Soldier Field workers tend to the injured Tilford Ashe. Ashe was OK, but his #50 hot rod was thoroughly bent.
(Bob Sheldon photo)

George McKendy gets ready to race his '34 Ford roadster at Sterling, Illinois in 1941.
(Hal Ullrich collection)

Action at Raceway Park in the Chicago suburb of Blue Island. No identification on the drivers. Check those headers on #26!
(Bob Sheldon photo)

A HISTORY LESSON

The older readers of *The Roaring Roadsters* remember World War II and the effect it had, not only on their lives, but on auto racing. For the younger readers, however, some background on what happened to racing during this conflict is probably in order.

Most professional sports continued during the war, but auto racing was halted by the a United States Government order on July 31, 1942. The reason was that gasoline was being rationed and tires were almost impossible to obtain. The government reasoned that it would set a poor example for the public to see these critical materials used on race cars. Actually, the amount of rubber and gas that would have been used in racing was miniscule, and both items were used indirectly in other sports.

Perhaps if racing had friends in high places the order would not have been issued. Nobody really protested very much, and all racing was halted for three years.

The main event lineup at De Kolb in 1948. It is a safe bet the dust got worse as the race went on. (Bob Sheldon photo)

No identification on these drivers, and even the track location is uncertain. It may be someplace in Illinois or perhaps Crown Point, Indiana. (Bob Sheldon photo)

in part: "In my opinion, it is better to create a place in organized racing for hot rods, where activities can be controlled and regulated, rather than let them go on their unhappy way and create dissension within the sport."

Just what "unhappy way" and "dissension" meant was not clear, and so far as is known Tri-State's plans to race roadsters never materialized.

It appears that in Illinois there was very little roadster racing after 1949—the stock cars had taken over. There were a few races at Raceway Park and at Willow Springs. The roadsters ran as late as 1952 at Willow Springs in mixed races with sprint cars.

Illinois roadster racing had one known fatality. Tony Marinck was killed during a Hurricane Hot Rod Association race at Rockford on September 25, 1948.

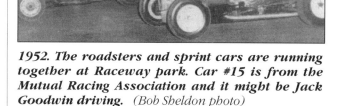

1952. The roadsters and sprint cars are running together at Raceway park. Car #15 is from the Mutual Racing Association and it might be Jack Goodwin driving. (Bob Sheldon photo)

More Soldier Field action as #2 slams the wall. Note that there is no "wheel fence" to protect spectators. On at least a couple of occasions, wheels sailed into the grandstands, but there were no serious injuries. (Bob Sheldon photo)

Andy Granatelli takes time out from his Soldier Field promotional duties to go for a ride in Hal Ullrich's Duesenburg-powered street roadster. That's Granatelli in the middle with Hal Ullrich (right) and Bill Ullrich (left). (Bob Blake collection)

Raceway Park action in 1949. These cars are probably from St. Louis, Missouri. (Bob Sheldon photo)

Raceway Park in 1952. There is a mixed field of roadsters and sprintcars Number 2 looks more like a modified. (Bob Sheldon photo)

INDIANA

The first known roadster racing in Indiana was at Jungle Park Speedway in the summer of 1938, when there was a 200-lap race for "stock cars" on this half-mile oval. Throughout most of the Midwest then, roadsters were called "stock cars" so it was probably a roadster race, but who knows, there may have been coupes and sedans in this race as well. This same group of cars and drivers held a few more events at Fort Wayne and Montpilier during 1938.

During the winter of 1938-39, a group of young men from the Muncie-New Castle area, who were interested in racing roadsters, met and formed the Mutual Stock Car Racing Association. The man who was behind Mutual was Harold "Dutch" Hurst who would remain pretty much in control of Mutual throughout its existence. Other roadster groups would be formed, but in general, a history of Mutual is a history of roadster racing in Indiana.

The first Mutual-sanctioned races were held in 1939 at the Muncie Steeplechase course. This was not an oval but rather an "off road" track that

This is Sun Valley Speedway in 1949. Only the three drivers at the rear of the field can be identified. They are, in order, Sam Skinner, Red Amick and Smokey Stover.
(Remington-Hurst collection)

Jack Goodwin in Edgar Beste's V8. Check that roll bar! (Remington-Hurst collection)

The crew of #12 poses for a photo at Mt. Lawn in 1940. Driver Howard Ice is second from the right.
(George Tichenor collection)

Probably the same day at Mt. Lawn. Howard Ice has hit something very solid—like maybe a tree? Ice was severely injured but recovered to race again. Number 12 did not.
(George Tichenor collection)

The start of a heat race at Winchester—circa 1950. Bob Stokes is on the pole in #95, and #66 is probably Roy Prosser.
(Remington-Hurst collection)

Ralph "Smokey" Stover in the Joe Walls Hudson-Terraplane-powered roadster. This was probably the first Walls car to use this potent six-cylinder flathead engine.
(Don Anderson collection)

featured mud holes, bumps and gullies. Most of the cars were Model A Ford roadsters, and most were near stock. The races were popular with drivers and spectators alike—the admission charge was all of 35 cents. The races went on all summer and Eddie Ripon was crowned the first Mutual champion. It is unclear why racing was not resumed at the Muncie track in 1940, but instead, the Mutual roadsters took to dirt track racing. Races were held at Lake Placed, at Montplier and on the banked five-eighths-mile track at Fort Wayne. In the summer of 1940, a group of Mutual racers used farm equipment and built the odd-shaped Mt. Lawn Speedway near New Castle. This became Mutual's "home track," and for many years and the roadsters always drew good crowds. (With but a few changes, the track is still the same today.)

Mutual ran a few other tracks in 1941 and 1942, but most of their races were at Mt. Lawn. Drivers

This is one of the first events sanctioned by the Mutual Stock Car Racing Association. It is at the Steeplechase Motor Speedway in Muncie.
(Remington-Hurst collection)

George Tichenor is in the Model A Ford-powered Walt Stabler #39. This is the first of a series of #39 cars fielded by Stabler. His Merc-powered #39 won the 1949 Little 500 with Sam Skinner driving, and it may have used the same body. (George Tichenor collection)

A good crowd at Sun Valley in 1949. Mickey Potter leads in the Muterpaugh Chevy Six. Red Amick is in the white #25.
(Remington-Hurst collection)

George Tichenor tried a Buick roadster in 1940 but it was too heavy to be competitive.
(George Tichenor collection)

This is 1941, and Harry Modlin has a V8 in his roadster. Modlin became the starter for the Mutual Stock Car Racing Association in 1945.
(Don Anderson collection)

The same turn at Mt. Lawn and this time #11 is collected by the spinning car.
(Remington-Hurst collection)

Ray Brown's #24 arrives at Mt. Lawn—circa 1941. Narrow roads in those days called for narrow trailers—it looks unstable.
(George Tichenor collection)

Buzzy Henline is in the Isaac Bennett Merc in this 1951 photo.
(Zane Howell collection)

Floyd Bowyer was Mutual's second fatality at the McMillen track near Logansport in 1942. These are the remains of his car.
(George Tichenor collection)

Tom Cherry, Kenny Eaton and Dick Frazier were race winners. The majority of the cars were slightly modified Model A roadsters, generally with flathead Model A or B Ford engines. Joe Walls was starting to work with six-cylinder Hudson-Terraplane engines, and his car won a few races with Smokey Stover at the wheel. The purses at Mt. Lawn, and for a few races at Winchester, were a guaranteed $500, which would pay $90 to the winner of a main event. Drivers usually got a one-third share in those days, but that $30 was still a couple weeks' salary for most people. Dick Frazier was the 1942 champion as racing was halted by government order in July of that year.

Since Mutual was well organized, they quickly resumed when World War II was ended in 1945. Dick Frazier was out of the Army, and he started where he left off by winning the 1945 championship in Roger Cox's flathead Model A. The first post-war race at Mt. Lawn drew a turn-away crowd of 10,000 starved fans. Was the purse that day the guaranteed $500 or a percentage of the gate?

In 1946, the Mutual Stock Car Racing Association voted to drop "stock car" from its name and became the Mutual Racing

Association. Mutual rode the crest of the post-war racing boom and had a very active schedule for the next several years. Mt. Lawn was still home, but races were also held on a regular basis at Dayton, Ohio, Winchester, Fort Wayne, South Bend, the Cincinnati Speedbowl and a bit later at Sun Valley Speedway in Anderson. Purses averaged about $1,200. With more cars competing, the payoff was spread around more, but a main event win with the $1,200 purse would pay $138. Cars that qualified

This is Mt. Lawn in 1939, and car #10 belongs to Joe Walls. It still has the Model A Ford engine and Smokey Stover is probably the driver. That looks like a '32 Ford V8 trailing.
(Remington-Hurst collection)

Leon Waltz was the first Mutual driver to lose his life in a roadster. His fatal accident was at Mt. Lawn on September 21, 1941. (Don Anderson collection)

Mt. Lawn in 1940 and a Lee Izor (at left) Chevy. Izor always fielded neat-appearing cars—note the covered wheel wall. The driver is not identified. (Izor collection)

A large crowd turned out to pay final respects to Leon Waltz at this special Mt. Lawn race in October of 1941. (Remington-Hurst collection)

Hack Winniger later owned some very fast Mutual roadsters and a "Little 500" winner, but in this 1947 photo he is driving the "Greyhound." (Tom Cherry—Joe Walls collection)

A 1939 photo at Mt. Lawn Speedway. The driver with the leather football helmet is unidentified. (Remington-Hurst collection)

Mt. Lawn 1939 or 1940. Bob Beeson spins out the McCormack Model A Ford as Harry Modlin ducks to the inside. (Remington-Hurst collection)

Bill Watkins in his Chevy Four-powered Model A Ford at Mt. Lawn. Watkins must have been a dedicated Chevy man—the Ford medallion seems to have been forcibly removed from the radiator shell. (Remington-Hurst collection)

Jocko Wise is tossed out as his car rolls during a 1939 race at the Muncie Steeplechase track.
(Remington-Hurst collection)

Roy Prosser in Isaac Bennett's Merc. This car once ran a few races with an automatic transmission. It probably didn't work. (Remington-Hurst collection)

were guaranteed 1 percent of the purse. Drivers such as George Tichinor, Dick Frazier, Wayne Alspaugh, Avery McAdams, Tom Cherry, Red Renner and Smokey Stover won their share of this money, as did visiting Californians Red Amick and Jim Rathmann.

The V8 Ford and Mercury engines dominated roadster racing in other areas, but this was not true in Mutual. Even by late 1947, the V8s were rare and the longer-stroke engines like Hudson (especially those built by Joe Walls), Ford Six, Chevy Six and even some leftover pre-war four bangers were the race winners. In 1948, along came Dick Frazier with his #32 Mercury, and the Mutual racers learned that the V8s would go fast and stay cool. Tom Cherry took note of this and began building engines in his Muncie speed

Smokey Stover models the latest style in 1940 driving uniforms.
Dale Fairfax collection)

Red Renner (left) and Smokey Stover get their trophies from Dutch Hurst at Mt. Lawn.
(Remington-Hurst collection)

shop. There is a rumor that a Californian with a very fast Mercury roadster stopped to visit Cherry at his shop. Cherry took the owner out on a two-day drinking binge while his shop foreman very carefully took the Mercury engine apart and put it back together again. At any rate, Tom Cherry's Mercs went fast from the beginning and won races.

The glory years were over by 1950, but Mutual survived the invasion of the stock cars better than most roadster groups. They managed to maintain a near-full schedule of roadster racing through the 1951 season. Mutual had some races in 1952 and 1953, a few for good purses, but car shortages were becoming common. The better drivers had moved on to sprint cars, and some cars had been converted to sprinters. As related elsewhere, the Mutual

Harry Modlin spins out at Mt. Lawn. Looks like there was plenty of action on this turn. (Remington-Hurst collection)

Ray Kriegler is aboard Lee Izor's Chevy Six in this Mt. Lawn photo. (Izor collection)

That is the #41 "Greyhound" on the pole, but who is the driver? The Greyhound sponsor was the local gasoline company, not the bus company. (Remington-Hurst collection)

A group of top Mutual drivers pose for the cameraman—circa 1942. (Don Anderson collection)

Dick Frazier smiles from the seat of the #2 car, in which he won the 1942 Mutual Stock Car Racing Association championship. That is probably a V8 under the hood. (Don Anderson collection)

This is Curly Boyd—circa 1949. Boyd did well in the Mutual roadsters and later went very fast in the sprint cars.
(Remington-Hurst collection)

Smokey Stover at Mt. Lawn in 1946. This is one of Joe Walls' potent six-cylinder Hudsons. The body is from Bantam (American Austin)—circa 1935. (George Tichenor collection)

This is George Tichenor in the other Walls' Hudson. Tichenor moved on to the midgets and sprints and made it to Indy. (George Tichenor collection)

DICK FRAZIER, #32 AND THE SMITHSONIAN

In the Midwest, one combination of car and driver stood head and shoulders above the rest. This was Dick Frazier and the #32 Mercury roadster that owned just about everything in both the Mutual and Hurricane racing associations in 1948. Frazier's record is unmatched by any hot rodder anywhere.

Frazier had been a Mutual Racing Association regular ever since the group formed in 1939. He was always a winner and was the Mutual champion in 1942. For the most part, he drove four-cylinder Ford-powered cars with only an occasional ride in a V8. For some reason, the Ford or Merc V8s were not popular in the Mutual Racing Association—the longer-stroke engines like Hudson, Ford Six or Chevy were the race winners. In 1948, Frazier changed a few minds. Using $2,500 borrowed from his mother, Dick teamed with Floyd Johnson and Hack Winninger

The restored #32 at Don Anderson's Dayton, Ohio, shop in 1991. Dick Frazier is at the left and Anderson on the right.
(Don Anderson collection)

The cockpit of the restored #32. The exhaust pipes from the Merc engine run through the drivers compartment but are well insulated.
(Don Anderson collection)

and built the soon to be famous #32. With V8 technology lagging in the Midwest, Frazier went to California and had Clay Smith build him an engine for $900. The Mercury was a relatively small 267-cubic-inches and Frazier remembers Clay Smith telling him to "turn it tight." Most hot rodders probably turned the V8s at little more than 4,000 rpm. Smith recommended that Frazier run the Merc between 4,500 and 5,600 rpm. He assured Dick that the engine would survive—it did, and the rest is history.

With the high rpm, excellent handling and Dick Frazier's skill, #32 was a winner almost from the start. During the 1948 season, the car racked up 72 feature wins in 96 starts. A lot of publicity was generated on June 20, 1948, when Frazier broke the AAA sprint car record on the high-banked, lightning-fast Winchester Speedway. Since he was using a percentage of his race winnings to repay the loan from his mother, Frazier kept accurate records of the payoffs for most of the 1948 season. In the first 60 or so races, #32 won $9,866 so the total for the season must have approached $15,000. When his mom was paid off in early August, records were no longer kept. The biggest payoff

The end of #32 at Sun Valley in 1950. Driver Everett Burton was thrown from the car and suffered only minor injuries.
(Don Anderson collection)

April 1992 and #32 is on display at the Smithsonian Museum in Washington, D.C. The car is in the transportation section.
(Don Anderson collection)

came at Soldier Field in Chicago where a heat race and main event win was worth $751.

There are those, mostly Californians, who said, and will still say, that Dick Frazier had no real competition in Mutual and Hurricane. While it is true that there were more good cars and good drivers on the West Coast, it is also true that Midwest racers went quite fast. Visiting California drivers, such as Jim and Dick Rathmann, Pat Flaherty and Red Amick, found this out in a hurry. While these drivers did well and usually ran up front, they did not dominate as they might have expected. Mostly, they did not dominate Dick Frazier and #32.

Frazier drove #32 a few times in 1949, but for the most part he had moved on to the AAA with an eye on Indy. Everett Burton took over the control of #32 and did nearly as well as Frazier had. No detailed records are available, but apparently the car was not raced very often as it appears that Burton also drove other cars. Burton brought about the rather undignified end of #32 in May of 1950, when he flipped into the third row of the grandstands at Sun Valley in Anderson. Burton escaped serious harm and no spectators were injured. Judging from a photograph of the wreck the damage to #32 was certainly not terminal, but for some reason the car was never raced again. It virtually disappeared for some 30 years.

Historian and race

car restorer Don Anderson stumbled across what was left of #32 at a Midwest swap meet in September of 1981. He bought the stack of bent metal and some assorted parts only when he learned the car's history—Dick Frazier was Don Anderson's boyhood hero. At the time, Anderson wasn't really thinking about a restoration—he now kicks

Dick Frazier warms up #32 at Winchester. His qualifying lap of 21.37 seconds on June 20, 1948, broke the track record. The previous record was held by Ted Horn in an Offy sprint car. (Don Anderson collection)

himself for not taking photos. The restoration came later when Anderson learned how few roadsters still existed and what a gem he had acquired. With help from Frazier, Don Anderson tenderly restored #32 to perfection. In 1992, the Smithsonian Institute asked for and received the car. As Don Anderson says, "This was the Mother of all Ego Trips, believe me!"

Dick Frazier smiles after setting the Winchester track record. Frazier won a 10-lap heat race and the 30-lap main event that day and took home $350. (Bill Hill collection)

The Smithsonian displayed the car for about one year and then loaned #32 to the Eastern Museum of Motor Racing in Williams Grove, Pennsylvania. Currently, plans are for the car to be exhibited at other museums. Ultimately, the roadster will find its way to exhibits all over the country.

Another view of the Smithsonian exhibit. Number 32 sits proudly alongside a recent Indy car. (Don Anderson collection)

Sun Valley Speedway in 1949. Dick Frazier in #32 battles with Howard Mowell in the Lee Izor Chevy. (Remington-Hurst collection)

A driver flips at Mt. Lawn. He was probably considerably battered, but his identification has been forgotten. (Remington-Hurst collection)

Roadster drivers Sam Skinner (left) and Chuck Farquer pose with their trophies at Mt. Lawn. Note the midgets on the trophies. (Remington-Hurst collection)

Racing Association's showcase event, the "Little 500" was a roadster race until 1954.

Mutual was doubtless the premier roadster organization in Indiana, but there were other groups formed and a lot of hot rod racing was unsanctioned and "outlaw." Andy Granatelli's Hurricane Racing Association ran a number of races at the 16th Street Speedway in Indianapolis. The Mid West Hot Rod Association operated partly in northern Indiana and in Michigan. The Southern Indiana Racing Association was another organization. Journeyman big car driver, Billy Earl, was a three-time champion with this group. Pat O'Conner began his racing career with the Southern Indiana racers in 1948 and learned a lot before he moved on to Mutual in 1950.

Of interest is the Universal Racing Association. This group obviously challenged Mutual in 1948. Whoever was behind Universal managed to attract 1947 Mutual champion Avery McAdams and a few other good drivers like Mickey Potter and Joe Nestor. They even had the nerve to promote races at the New Castle Fairgrounds a few miles from Mt. Lawn. Most people don't even remember Universal, and for some reason the group ran only a few races. Only some diligent research by Jon Gullihier of Anderson, Indiana, turned up any mention of

HOT RODDERS AND THE AAA

During the roadster era, the American Automobile Association, also known as AAA or "Three A," ruled major league racing with an iron hand. (The American Automobile Association still exists, but only as an auto club—the racing has been passed on to the USAC and CART.) Around 1950, the AAA sanctioned not only the Indianapolis 500, but also sprint, midget and even stock car racing all over the United States. If a driver competed in AAA events, he was not allowed to race with any other organization.

It didn't take long for some of the hot rod racers to move into AAA. Jack McGrath competed at Indianapolis in 1948, but a few weeks later he was back at the wheel of a roadster in a Mutual Racing Association event at Winchester, Indiana. Troy Ruttman had run with the AAA on the West Coast when he raced in the "Pacific Coast Invitational Hot Rod Championships" at Stockton, California, on Labor Day, 1948. Ruttman's appearance was heavily advertised, and I'm sure he and car owner Reg Schlemmer had some sort of a deal with the

promoter. I remember talking to Ruttman at the race and asking him what the AAA thought about him racing roadsters. He grinned and said, "The Three A doesn't consider the hot rods real race cars."

Further evidence of the AAA's attitude towards the roadsters surfaced a few years later in an article in *The Wall Street Journal*. The article was primarily about the fact that auto racing had become a popular sport and that it was now a big business. There were a number of quotes from AAA official Russ Catlin. Catlin had this to say about the roadsters in the April 29, 1952 issue of *The Wall Street Journal*:

"We do not sanction or condone hot rod racing," says Catlin of AAA. "It is not professional auto racing. The hot rod is a menace not only on the highway, but the speedway."

In the 1952 Indianapolis 500, about half the drivers in the starting field had begun their racing careers in the roadsters—including the winner, Troy Ruttman.

Universal.

Indiana roadster racing was dangerous, and the hot rods claimed their toll. Leon Waltz was the first to die in 1941 at Mt. Lawn. Floyd Bowyer lost his life at McMillin Speedway in 1942. In the late 1940s, Freddie Wingate died at Winchester, and Al Cobb died at Greenville in an unsanctioned race. In 1951, Everett Burton was killed at Kokomo and Lloyd Stanbrook at Greensburg. On July 4, 1952, Robert "Deacon" Jones died in a roadster race at Salem. Unfortunately, this sad list is probably not complete.

They had night racing at Mt. Lawn in 1940. George Tichenor spins out in his own Model A #K9 and is nailed by Bobby Beeson. (George Tichenor collection)

Circa 1946. Jim Morrison goes flying off into space at Winchester. Another driver tries to stop to go to Morrison's aid. (Jack Hathaway collection)

Jim Morrison is OK after his trip over the wall at Winchester, but the body panels on the repaired #39 don't line up very well. (Jim Hathaway collection)

It is 1947, and Dick Frazier is in a McCormack car. The original photo caption says Sun Valley Speedway, but that track wasn't built until 1948. (Don Anderson collection)

Another spin on that same turn at Mt. Lawn. This time there is no identification on the drivers or cars. (Remington-Hurst collection)

This is 1942 and according to the original photo caption there is a Chevy Six in the Buick now. That's Freddie Wingate taking part in a "pie race." (Izor collection)

Tom Cherry in the "Greyhound" in 1942. Cherry was the 1941 Mutual champion. (Tom Cherry collection)

The Beautiful New
Sun Valley Speedway
(New $250,000.00 Track)
Pendleton Pike (State Road 9) and 29th Street
Anderson, Indiana

GRAND OPENING!
The event all Indiana has been waiting for!
INDIANA'S FINEST TRACK!!!

ROARING ROADSTER

AUTO RACES
FRIDAY NIGHT—JUNE 25

9:30 P. M.

Featuring ★ MUTUAL ★ Racing Association
"Fastest in the World"

"DUTCH HURST" at the Mike

—INVERTED MAIN EVENT—
"See Them Go on the High Banks!"

This newspaper ad implies that the Mutual roadsters will be the opening event at Sun Valley Speedway. According to other information, the AAA midgets had already been racing there for a couple of months.

Souvenir Program 25¢   N⁰ 1945
SUN VALLEY SPEEDWAY
(Div. HELPLING OIL COMPANY, Inc.)
Sun Valley • Anderson, Indiana

JOHNNY ARNOLD
MAIN EVENT WINNER — J
ROARING ROAD
MUTUAL RACING AS

A program cover for a Mutual Racing Association event at Sun Valley Speedway. (Zane Howell collection)

Mutual drivers in late 1941 or 1942. Mutual mentor Dutch Hurst is at the far right. Surprisingly most of these drivers can be identified. (Remington-Hurst collection)

The date written on this Mt. Lawn program cover is rather cryptic. It must be a 1946 race as Mutual is still calling the roadsters stock cars. (Zane Howell collection)

MOUNT LAWN
FIVE MILES WEST NEW CASTLE
Every Sunday
SANCTIONED BY MUTUAL
STOCK CAR RACES
.OFFICIAL PROGRAM
17 PHOTOS AND NEWS 17

DICK FRAZIER   JIM MORRISON   RED RENNER

FOR SUGGESTIONS—INFORMATION—ADVERTISING
"CHILTON'S"
AMERICA'S BEST PROGRAMS

This montage of photos was used to advertise the Muncie Steeplechase races. The racing looks rough, but there is no record of any serious injuries. (Remington-Hurst collection)

Jim Rigsby in the California-built Reg Schlemmer car. Rigsby later raced at Indy and starred in the sprint cars before dying in a crash at Winchester.
(Izor collection)

Winchester—circa 1948. Mutual Racing Association officials were always neatly dressed. Starter Harry Modlin is at left and next to him is Mutual boss-man Dutch Hurst.
(Remington-Hurst collection—Thompson photo)

Bob King in the Frank Brown Merc that won two Little 500 races at Sun Valley Speedway. King won in 1953 and with Tom Cherry as the driver and with Howard Hall as the owner the car won in 1952. *(Remington-Hurst collection)*

EVERETT BURTON AND THE VACANT POLE POSITION

Everett Burton won a lot of roadster races with the Mutual Racing Association, but his biggest honor may have been capturing the pole for the 1951 Little 500. His time of 14.59 in the Anderson Brothers' Mercury was the fastest of the 33-car starting field.

In 1951, qualifying events were held a full week before the 50-lap race, and Mutual had several other events scheduled during that period. One of these races was at Kokomo. The owners of the pole-winning car, Don and John Anderson, would have preferred to skip Kokomo and save the car for the big race. However, Everett Burton was the president of Mutual, and he knew there would be a car shortage at Kokomo. He also felt obligated to support the organization, so he insisted that the Andersons take #54 to this race. During the main event at Kokomo, Burton tangled with another car and flipped down the main straightaway. Burton was thrown out of the car and suffered fatal injuries when he was slammed against the grandstand. (Don Anderson believes that Burton may have unfastened his seat belt during the race as he felt more comfortable racing without one.)

At Sun Valley Speedway a week later, the Little 500 crowd stood in silent respect to Everett Burton, and the field of 33 cars lined up with the pole position vacant.

Ironically the Anderson #54 did come very close to winning that Little 500. Even though saddened by Burton's death, Don and John Anderson fixed the car and took it to the race. With Wayne Alspaugh at the wheel, they were cruising with a several-lap lead late in the race when a pin snapped in the gear box, sidelining the car.

John (left) and Don Anderson with the roadster they built in 1950. Don Anderson cheerfully and unashamedly admits that he and his brother

copied Dick Frazier's #32 as closely as possible.
(Don Anderson collection)

Everett Burton in the Anderson Brothers #54 Merc V8. This photo was taken at the Cincinnati Speed Bowl shortly before Burton's death.
(Don Anderson collection)

Jungle Park—circa 1948. Bill Cassidy is the driver of the #26 V8. *(Hobson collection)*

The long and short of it with Mutual drivers: Roy Prosser is the short, and Mickey Potter is the long, with Dutch Hurst in the middle. Prosser must have gotten tired of posing for similar photos wherever he raced. *(Remington-Hurst collection)*

The remains of a wrecked hot rod at Jungle Park. The identification and fate of the driver are unknown.
(Hobson collection)

1949 action at Sun Valley Speedway. Sam Skinner in the second car is the only driver who can be identified.
(Remington-Hurst collection)

This is Mutual driver Bob Beeson. *(Remington-Hurst collection)*

This is allegedly 1950 and the Reg Schlemmer #2 is being unloaded after it was flown in from California for the Little 500. This same photo appeared in 1948 publicity for Soldier Field hot rod races. Did the car ever really fly?
(Remington-Hurst collection)

This is Charlie Holloway's Merc with Bob King at the wheel. The photo is probably taken at Sun Valley Speedway in Anderson.
(Zane Howell collection)

George Tichenor was home on leave from the Army when he flipped this A-V8 at the New Castle Fairgrounds in 1942. He's wearing his GI khakis.
(George Tichenor collection)

Charles Black (left) was a Mutual regular and towed his car from Dayton, Ohio, for this 1947 Mt. Lawn race. The driver might be Ray Krieger.
(Zane Howell collection)

Action at Mt. Lawn in 1949. Wayne Alspaugh leads in #88, and that's Dick Frazier up against the fence. (Remington-Hurst collection)

Bob King is in L. Hudson's Studebaker in this circa 1949 photo. No clue as to whether it is a six or an eight. (Zane Howell collection)

Wayne Alspaugh was one of the top Mutual Racing Association roadster drivers. He won the Little 500 in 1958, but that was after the roadster era.
(Bud Williams photo—Wayne Alspaugh collection)

Some nice trophies for Roy Prosser (left) and Red Renner. That's Dutch Hurst at the mike.
(Remington-Hurst collection)

Mickey Potter is in the Art Rhonemus Merc in this 1949 photo. *(Remington-Hurst collection)*

Mickey Potter went through the steel pipe guard rail at Winchester and down the steep bank. There was very little left of the Meterpaugh Chevy. Somehow, Potter survived, although he was severely injured. *(Wayne Alspaugh collection)*

ROADSTER DRIVERS AT INDIANAPOLIS

The roadsters were a great training ground for race drivers, and many roadster racers made it to the pinnacle of their sport: the Indianapolis 500. Most of the drivers listed made the starting field for the 500-mile race, some failed to qualify and a few had rides that did not materialize. All are listed in the official records of the Indianapolis Motor Speedway. A few drivers on the list did not start in the roadsters but did drive these cars during their early careers.

Some drivers who started in the roadsters won the ultimate prize in racing: the 500.

These are:

Jimmy Bryan	Floyd Roberts
Pat Flaherty	Troy Ruttman
Jim Rathmann	Bob Sweikert
	Bill Vukovich

These names appear on the "Driver Performance Records" in the *Illustrated History of the Indianapolis 500* by Jack Fox:

Fred Agabashian	Keith Andrews	Art Bisch
Red Amick	Manual Ayulo	Jimmy Bryan
Les Anderson	Bobby Ball	Bill Cantrell

Duane Carter	Johnny Mantz	Bob Scott
Bill Cheeseburg	Johnny Mauro	Colby Scroggin
Larry Crockett	Rex Mays	Wayne Seltzer
Jimmy Davies	Roger McCluskey	Len Sutton
Donnie Davis	Jack McGrath	Bob Swanson
Ed Elisian	Johnny McDowell	Bob Sweikert
Pat Flaherty	Al Miller	Shorty Templeman
Dick Frazier	Jim McWithey	George Tichinor
Don Freeland	Pat O'Connor	Johnny Tolan
Elmer George	Ray Pixley	Bob Veith
Bob Gregg	Dick Rathmann	Bill Vukovich
Mel Hansen	Jimmy Reece	Leroy Warringer
Chuck Hulse	Gordon Ried	Wayne Weiler
Joe James	Jim Rigsby	Dempsey Wilson
Van Johnson	Floyd Roberts	
Al Keller	George Robson	Rex Mays was the
Jud Larson	Hal Robson	first roadster driver to
Chuck Leighton	Bud Rose	race at Indianapolis
Bayliss Levrett	Roy Russing	in 1934, Bob Veith
Andy Linden	Troy Ruttman	was the last in 1969.
George Lynch	Eddie Sachs	
Bill Mackey	Bill Schindler	

Kenny Eaton in the Huddleson-Cox #42 "Greyhound." The Model A Ford-powered roadster was one of the first to use the '27 Model T body. (Remington-Hurst collection)

Larry Crockett is pictured in the Erickson Merc V8. (Izor collection)

Sun Valley Speedway. Larry Crockett spins as Tom Cherry in #38 and Red Amick in #25 get by safely. The early model (circa 1925) Model T bodies were rare in Midwest racing—car #25 was built in California. (Remington-Hurst collection)

Mutual cars line up for a 50-lap championship race at Logansport in late 1941. (George Tichenor collection)

This is Mellot, Indiana, and it is probably 1949. It is a Mid West Racing Association event. (Dale Swain collection)

This is Gene Pyle in his own #85. The engine was listed as a Studebaker but was it a six or an eight? (Zane Howell collection)

A wreck at Jungle Park—circa 1950. Note the famous "stepped" grandstand. The main straightaway at Jungle Park was downhill. (Hobson collection)

THE LITTLE 500

The Little 500 at Anderson, Indiana, has been a fixture on the American racing scene for more than 40 years. Relatively few fans who watch this great sprint car race realize that the Little 500 was originally a roadster race. It was the brainchild of Joe Helping, the owner of the Anderson track, which was then called Sun Valley Speedway.

The track was originally built for midget racing in 1948, but Helping was soon dissatisfied with the way the AAA ran things—the races were parades. Helping brought in the Mutual Racing Association roadsters, and they were an instant success. Purses for the hot rods at Sun Valley ranged up to $3,800.

Early in 1949, Helping dreamed up the idea of a 500-lap roadster race to be held the night before the Indy 500. He presented his idea at a Mutual Racing Association meeting by unveiling a big sign which read, "The First Annual Little 500—Starting 33 Cars—500 Laps to Go." The MRA owners, drivers and officials reacted with considerable enthusiasm; they all thought Helping was nuts! They were convinced that 500 laps was too far saying, "No cars will finish," and "How about 200 or 300 laps?" Joe Helping insisted it would be a 500-lap race if it took all night or they had to come back the next day to get somebody to run 500 laps. It took a special meeting of Mutual members to grudgingly agree to run what has become the greatest short track race in the country. Eighteen cars finished the long grind and to Sam Skinner went the honor of winning the first Little 500. The purse was around $6,000 and Skinner took home about $1,200.

The biggest purse was probably in 1950, when it was $9,578. In 1955 the roadsters were gone, and the "Little 500" became a sprint car race.

LITTLE "500"

200 LAP   100 MILE   HOT ROD

AUTO RACES

JUNGLE PARK
SPEEDWAY

8 Miles North of Rockville on U. S. 41
Sunday May, 21, 2:00 P. M., D. S. T.
33—Fastest Qualifiers Starting—33

Time trials all day Saturday, May 20, and Sunday morning, May 21. Advance tickets on sale at Rust Bros Recreation.

LITTLE 500 WINNERS IN THE ROADSTER ERA

YEAR	DRIVER	OWNER	ENGINE MAKE
1949	Sam Skinner	Walt Stabler	Mercury V8
1950	Tom Cherry	Hack Winnigear	Mercury V8
1951	Red Renner	Carl Reynolds	Mercury V8
1952	Tom Cherry	Howard Hall	Mercury V8
1953	Bob King	Frank Brown	Mercury V8
1954	Tom Cherry	Howard Hall	Mercury V8

A typical roadster race hazard in 1940. Later owners would learn how to reinforce wheels so both spectators and racers were safer. (Remington-Hurst collection)

This is Zane Howell in the ex-Andy Granatelli-Jim Rathmann car. It looks as though it has been bent a few times since Rathmann drove it at Davie, Florida, in early 1949 (Zane Howell collection)

Here Freddie Wingate is driving the Dan Walls Ford Six. Wingate was killed in a roadster at Winchester in 1946. (Zane Howell collection)

Zane Howell is on the pole for this 1949 race at Sun Valley Speedway. Others are Wayne Alspaugh in #88, outside of him is Sam Skinner, and Tom Cherry lined up last in #38.
(Remington-Hurst collection)

Dutch Hurst and Avery McAdams are all smiles as McAdams gets his championship trophy. Mutual did not have a point fund—just trophies.
(Remington-Hurst collection)

Circa 1950. Dale Swain in the Cassidy V8. Swain drove this car to main event wins in 13 starts with the Mid West Racing Association.
(Dale Swain collection)

Dale Swain drove this nice-looking Dan Hobson Merc in the Little 500 (or "Baby 500") at Jungle Park. This was in 1950 or 1951, and Swain looked like a winner until he had trouble late in the race. (Hobson collection)

A fine shot of Everett Burton in the Zimmerman #85. Burton served as president of the Mutual Racing Association in 1951.

Nub Wysong is shown in this circa 1948 photo. (Zane Howell collection)

Everett Burton in a DeSoto-powered car. The flathead six soon came out and was replaced by a Merc.
(Remington-Hurst collection)

The McCormack brothers flank Bob Beeson in their first track roadster. The McCormacks were active Mutual car owners for years. (Remington-Hurst collection)

Roy Prosser aims for the cameraman at Sun Valley Speedway in 1950. This car, with Sam Skinne, driving, won the 1949 Little 500. (Remington-Hurst collection)

THE OTHER LITTLE 500

About 100 miles west of the Anderson, Indiana, home of the Little 500, are the remains of a legendary racetrack—Jungle Park Speedway. Starting in about 1925, Jungle Park was home to some great race drivers and great races. It even looked like a jungle, as there were no crash walls to keep cars from hurdling off its banks into the trees that surrounded the track. In 1950, Jungle Park advertised its own Little 500 for hot rods. Joe Helping had already run a Little 500 in 1949 and had another scheduled for May 27, 1950. Two Little 500s?

It appears that Charlie Foxworthy who ran Jungle Park had an ace up his sleeve and may have had more rights to the name Little 500 than did Joe Helping. Thanks to the Rockville (Indiana) Public Library, I obtained a copy of a *History of Jungle Park* written by an anonymous author in about 1970. Quoting from this history:

"One race that proved very popular was what was

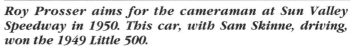

SECOND ANNUAL
"BABY 500"
HOT ROD RACE
JUNGLE PARK
SUN. AFTERNOON
May 20, 2:00 P.M.
200 — Laps — 200
33 Cars Starting
Time Trials May 19th
Rain Date May 27th
—PACE CAR—
Chrysler Firepower 8—
Furnished by Dahl
Motors— Terre Haute,
Ind.

called the Little 500, run on the order of the Indianapolis 500, but only for 300 miles. The name 'Little 500' was even registered with the secretary of the State for the exclusive use of Jungle Park."

According to ads in *National Speed Sport News,* Jungle Park's first annual Little 500 would be sanctioned by the Mid West Hot Rod Association. A 200-lap (100-mile) hot rod race was to be held on May 20, 1950. For some reason, local ads referred to the Little "500" but, whatever, the race was held and Larry Weaver was the winner. The purse was reported to be $2,000. Jungle Park was back with a big roadster race again in 1951. Local newspaper articles refer to the race as the "Little 500," but paid advertisements called it the "Baby 500."

Just what went on between Joe Helping and Charlie Foxworthy in 1950 and 1951 has been lost to history. So has the winner of the 1951 Baby 500. This was the last "500" of any kind ever held at Jungle Park.

Winchester in 1947. The deadly steel "guard rails" are clearly visible. George Tichenor is on the pole, and right behind him is Al Cobb who eventually died in a Salem roadster crash.
(Zane Howell collection)

The track looks like Jungle Park. The driver is not identified. (Hobson collection)

Zane Howell is pictured in 1947. Howell was a winner in Mutual Racing Association roadsters for many years and finished fourth in the 1951 Little 500.
(Zane Howell collection)

Chuck Farquer usually ran in Ohio, but here he is racing with Mutual. Note how far forward the rear wheel is. Mutual allowed cars a minimum of a 90-inch wheel base—six inches shorter than most roadster groups. (Tom Cherry—Joe Walls collection)

Joe Nester with the Dan Walls Ford Six.
(Zane Howell collection)

In 1949, Red Amick brought this Ford Six from California and ran up front in Mutual. (Don Anderson collection)

Red Amick went over the wall at Winchester in 1949. Car #25 was destroyed but Amick was OK.
(Wayne Alspaugh collection)

This is Jim McWithey. He raced in four Mutual Racing Association Little 500 races and later made it to the Indy 500.
(Remington-Hurst collection)

Avery McAdams. His 1947 Mutual championship came in Walt Stabler's Ford Six.
(Remington-Hurst collection)

Red Crammer was a Mutual competitor for many years.
(Remington-Hurst collection)

This is Buck Teal circa 1948.
(Don Anderson collection)

Red Amick started in the Southern California roadsters and raced with Mutual and many other roadster groups. He made it to the Indy 500 in 1959.
(Remington-Hurst collection)

From the Southern Indiana Racing Association to Mutual came Larry "Crash" Crockett. Crockett was a standout in the AAA sprint cars and raced at Indy.
(Don Anderson collection)

Joe Walls (right), who built fast Hudsons for years, finally built a Merc in 1950. Pat O'Conner drove it and won a lot of races.
(Jack Hathaway collection)

This is 16th Street Speedway in Indianapolis. Pat Kirkland is in the Ralph Potter V8.
(Dale Fairfax collection)

THE RETURN OF THE ROADSTER?

In 1959, the track roadsters were all but forgotten, and hardtop stock car racing was the rage everywhere. Joe Helpling had been running these stock cars at his Sun Valley Speedway in Anderson but noted that the crowds were dropping off. Probably the main reason was over-racing, but Helping, always the innovator, decided to try something different.

He reasoned that it would be better if the fans could see the drivers in action as they did in the "old days" of roadster racing and in other forms of open cockpit racing. He talked the Sun Valley racers into cutting the tops off of their coupes and, presto, to an extent roadsters were reborn! The cars did resemble some of the early track roadsters. Most of them were '36 to '39 Fords, and some cars of this vintage, including coupes, had been cut down into hot rods a decade earlier. (*As examples see the Harley Gunkle and Bruce Byers cars in the North Dakota chapter.*)

Joe Helping called his new group of cars Y.O.U.R. Racing. Today, nobody is sure whether these letters really meant anything. Perhaps it was just "Your Racing" and meant "for the fans." The new roadsters didn't last very long. The Anderson fans apparently wanted *lots* of action and drifted away to the Figure 8 races.

Claude Coles was a main event winner at Sun Valley Speedway in this "new roadster." The engine appears stock but perhaps hidden modifications were allowed.
(Sam Liesure collection)

This is Bill Rumbler at Sun Valley in 1959. The bumper and roll bar are a lot huskier than a "real" track roadster would use, but otherwise this car is quite similar. (Bill Rumbler collection)

IOWA

wo known organizations sanctioned roadster racing in Iowa: the Central Iowa Racing Association and an un-named group from Marengo, a small town in eastern Iowa. There was also racing at Playland Speedway in Council Bluffs, but racers there were mostly from the Kansas City area.

The Central Iowa Racing Association began racing in 1948 and was quite active for about four years. As was the norm, the cars started out as street hot rods and evolved into track roadsters. Almost all of the group's races were on county fair half-mile horse tracks. Many of the races were in conjunction with county fairs, and occasionally there would be a two- or three-race series at a fair. Races were held at Cedar Rapids, Central City, Chariton, Greenfield, Webster City and several other Iowa towns. The CIRA also raced at Des Moines, but this race was surely not a fair date—the then mighty IMCA sprint cars had these prime state fair dates.

Nate Grassfield was one of the drivers who ran the circuit, and he remembers that despite low purses he managed to break even—rare for a roadster racer anyplace. Grassfield's payoffs ranged from around $75 to win a main event to $3 and a steak dinner at Des Moines. Most of the Central Iowa Racing Association drivers pretty much stuck close to home, so they gained little recognition outside of Iowa. Besides Grassfield, the top drivers were Speed Lyman, Jimmy Maddox, Kenny Cook and a driver who did quite well with NASCAR later on—Johnny Beauchamp. Another NASCAR star, Tiny Lund, started in the Iowa roadsters and probably ran with this group.

Some of the Central Iowa Racing Association events were promoted by Russ Carne and his partners. Carne remembers, "We set out to make a million dollars promoting hot rod races." In 1948, several successful races were held at Chariton and in Knoxville at the now famous home of the Knoxville Nationals sprint car races. Carne bought out his partners late in 1948 and expected big things in 1949. He lined up what he hoped to be a series of weekly races at Cedar Rapids, Waterloo, Davenport and Des Moines. He anticipated "lots of cars and lots of action"—six cars showed up at Cedar Rapids—seven at Davenport and that was

HOT ROD RACES
PLAYLAND PARK STADIUM

PICTURES - ENTRIES - NEWS

15c

Ainsworth Printing & Office Supplies

Broadway at 4th

Phone 5519   **Council Bluffs, Iowa**

There were many fine roadster races held at Playland Stadium in Council Bluffs. Sadly, no photos of these races were found.
(Ray Boyles collection)

Bob Roggentien drove this neat Chevy roadster in races at Marengo and Vinton. (Dean Roggentien collection)

This is Kenny Cook at a Central Iowa Racing Association event in 1950. (Nate Grassfield collection)

Jimmy Maddox at a fairgrounds track in Iowa—circa 1950. (Nate Grassfield collection)

that. There just weren't enough roadsters in the area for such an ambitious program. Russ Carne came up a bit short of making a million dollars on his hot rod racing promotions.

The Marengo roadster racing was technically jalopy racing as the cars were allegedly stock. The rules did limit engines to 1931 models or earlier, so Ford V8s were ruled out. Racing started in 1949, and it was really a small town operation—even today Marengo has a population of only 2,300. The Marengo racers somehow combined with a group of drivers from Vinton, another small town 40 miles to the north, and races were held in both towns on alternate Sundays. The races drew crowds of up to 2,000 and the payoffs weren't bad. Dean

Roggention won a number of races and got checks for up to $70.70. Some of the other drivers who did well were Bob Roggention, Donald Danskin and Les Gunzenhauser.

There was a serious accident in one of the early races when Bill Hobbs in a stripped down 1929 LaSalle roadster crashed through the fence at Marengo. A two-by-eight-inch plank went through the LaSalle but missed Hobbs. Several spectators

No identification on this driver. The Central Iowa Racing Association ran a few quarter-mile midget tracks—this looks like one of them. (Nate Grassfield collection)

Bill Bone drove #62. The engine appears to be some sort of straight eight.

Only the driver's first name is known—Larry. He went to considerable trouble to build that padded headrest. (Nate Grassfield collection)

Wayne Snyder Jr. is pictured someplace in Iowa—possibly Webster City?

Shorty Martin was one of the drivers who raced on Iowa fairgrounds tracks. (Nate Grassfield collection)

Bob Roggentien in his Chevy roadster. It is good advertising when sponsor Sherman Body Shop could use their phone number as the car number. (Dean Roggentien collection)

Dean Farmer and his Iowa hot rod—circa 1950. (Nate Grassfield collection)

Dean Roggentien also won some Marengo and Vinton races in a Dodge roadster. H.R. Fox was the mechanic on the car. (Dean Roggentien collection)

were painfully injured when the Hobbs car struck their parked Oldsmobile. The Marengo-Vinton racers began the transition to hot rods in 1951 when engine restrictions were removed. This did not last long as tragedy struck when Ronald Worell was killed at Marengo. The newspaper accounts of the crash indicate that Worell was struck by parts of the wooden fence. This ended roadster racing in Morengo and Vinton.

There were roadster races at Council Bluffs for several years around 1950. There were at Playland Park on a quarter-mile dirt track owned by Abe Slusky. Kansas City drivers like Junior Hower and Scotty Scoville competed there as well as some of the Nebraska racers. Abe Slusky kept detailed records of the races, as well as many photos but, unfortunately, these have disappeared over the years. A thorough search by Slusky's son, Jerry, turned up nothing. There were two roadster fatalities at Playland. Black driver, Cyclone Ross,

The Winner! Dean Roggentien celebrates after a win at Marengo in 1950. (Dean Roggentien collection)

Below—Nate Grassfield prepares for a race at Chariton, Iowa—circa 1949. (Nate Grassfield collection)

and California visitor, Bill Pettit died during successive races in 1951.

THE FRIENDLY INFIELD FENCE

Probably 50 percent of all roadster racing took place on county fair tracks, which were designed for horse racing—not auto racing. As is apparent in some of the photos in this book, these tracks often had wooden rails running along both the inside and outside of the track. These fences varied from flimsy to stout, but in general, consisted of upright wooden posts with horizontal rails running about two and four feet above the ground. Both the inside and outside fences were potential deadly, but the inside (infield) fence was the most dangerous. The cars normally ran close to the inside, and that upper rail seemed poised like a spear ready to impale an unlucky racer. All too often, it did.

A field of roadsters line up at the Arapahoe County Fairgrounds, Littleton, Colorado, in 1949. The fence is typical of most fairgrounds all over the country. The potential danger to the drivers is obvious. (Leroy Byers collection)

Ideally the upper rail was removed from at least the infield fence, and removing much of the hazard. Most of the time this did not happen. It seems impossible that so little concern was given to safety, but county fair officials were hesitant to supply the necessary labor for what was often a one-time auto race. On the other hand, the racers were happy to remove the top rails with whatever tools they had available, but they never bothered to replace

them after the races. The top rail usually stayed in place.

The rails were more of a danger to roadster drivers than to sprint car drivers who also raced on the county fair ovals. Sprint cars of the roadster era usually had a cowl that provided a bit of protection, and the drivers sat fairly low in their cars. Most roadster drivers sat high and very exposed. They just tried not to think about what could happen if they tangled with that infield fence.

The fences had other uses as well. County fairground tracks often had another delightful feature— thick and blinding dust! On the straightaway, a driver might be able to see both the infield and outside fence and use them as navigational aids. The dust was always worst in the turns and visibility could be near zero. The only way to keep from getting lost in the dust was to follow the infield fence. Perhaps drivers were being a bit cynical and tongue in cheek, but we called it "the friendly infield fence." Things really got rough if somebody knocked down a section of that fence. You'd find yourself flying blind across the gap until the "friendly infield fence" was once again in view.

KANSAS

● ●

Roadster racing in Kansas started in the mid-1930s when 25- to 100-mile races were held on half-mile fairgrounds tracks. Just where these races were held has, unfortunately, been lost to history. Historian and ex-*National Speed Sport News* writer, Emmett Carpenter, remembers driving a Model A Ford roadster in these races as early at 1935. Carpenter did OK and, along with Harold Forrest, won what must have been some very dusty races.

After World War II, in about 1948, roadster racing got started at Cejay Stadium in Wichita. A Wichita Hot Rod Association was formed, and this group sanctioned the races at Cejay as well as spot races at other Kansas cities. Races were held at Hutchinson, Newton, Dodge City and no doubt other cities. In June of 1948, plans were announced to organize a Kansas-Oklahoma Association so that roadster races could be sanctioned in both states. Whether or not this venture succeeded is uncertain, but plans to race in Tulsa and Oklahoma City apparently never materialized. Some of the top drivers in the Wichita area were Harold and Will Forrest, Frank Lies, Dale Reed, Harold Leep and Charlie Lutkie.

Another group that ran some races in Kansas was the Mid West Roadster Racing Association. Mid West was apparently located in the Kansas City area and raced in both Kansas and Missouri. Some very good drivers like Junior Hower, Hi Fashing, Herschel Wagner and Jay Sears raced with this group.

In north-central Kansas, most of the roadster racing was under the sanction of the Nebraska Hot Rod Racing Association. The high banks of Belleville were the center of this racing, and these events drew good fields and paid good purses. There were also hot rod races at Concordia and further west in the small towns of Norton, Stockton and Wakeeney. Most of the cars and drivers that supported these races were from Nebraska. Kansas-Missouri racers, Hi Fashing and Jay Sears did make a few trips to Concordia to race against Nebraska hot-shots like Andy Anderson, Gordy Schuck and Gaylor Higer.

An interesting race was held at Great Bend in May of 1951. The race was on a triangular two-mile course on the runways of a World War II airbase. Pre-race publicity sounds like the race was to be open competition, and that it was not sanctioned by any roadster group. The promoters of the race hoped to attract a large field and even announced that sprint cars would be welcome to run for the $1,400 purse. Thirteen hot rods and one sprint car showed up as well as a reported 3,000 fans. Frank Lies won the race in a roadster, made $350

Belleville in 1950. Frank Brennfoerder is in #96. That is Fred "Pop" Goodrich checking the engine.
(Frank Brennfoerder collection)

These are the picturesque grandstands at the North Central Kansas Fairgrounds at Belleville. The stands were usually full for an auto race. This is about 1952, and there are sprint cars running with the roadsters.

Andy Anderson in the "Belle of Belleville." Anderson won many Nebraska and Kansas races in this car. It was built and owned by Ray Goodrich of Belleville.
(Republican County Historical Society collection)

and averaged 76 mph.

Kansas roadster racing went on from 1948 through 1952 with about 20 races a year under various sanctions. In general, starting fields were sparse with the exception of the early races at Cejay Stadium in Wichita and some of the Belleville events. Almost no data on purses is available, but odds are the average was about $500. Belleville attracted crowds of up to 3,000 and the purse may have approached $1,500. Andy Anderson remembers winning $350 at Belleville, but that was probably for a clean sweep of the program.

While most of the Kansas roadster activity took place on the dangerous half-mile horse tracks the only two known fatalities took place on "real" race tracks. Darrell Wilkerson was killed on the quarter-

mile dirt Cejay track in 1948. At Belleville, Jim Vineyard died during a race on these deadly high banks in 1951.

The pits at Belleville in about 1950. Most of these cars are from the Nebraska Hot Rod Association. The high banks of Belleville are visible in the background—the actual racing groove was very narrow.
(Republican County Historical Society collection)

Above left—This is from Lorene Goodrich's scrapbook—her husband, Ray, owned the "Belle of Belleville." With George "Andy" Anderson at the wheel, the Goodrich car had fast time, won the trophy dash, won a heat race, and won the feature. Above right—Belleville was fast and dangerous. As reported by the Belleville Telescope *there was lots of action in this hot rod race.*
(Lorene Goodrich collection)

Roadsters at Belleville. That's Andy Anderson in second place.
(Republican County Historical Society collection)

Roadsters in action on the half-mile Belleville track—circa 1951. A good crowd is on hand.
(Republican County Historical Society collection)

A combination sprint-roadster race at Concordia on October 16, 1955. Frank Brennfoerder gets ready to drive the #39 car that raced as the Belond Special in Southern California in 1948. The car spent some time in Colorado before migrating to Kansas.
(Frank Brennfoerder collection)

MICHIGAN

oadster racing in Michigan began in about 1940 when a series of races were held on county fairground tracks. These races were organized by Pete Spencer, a name that would be prominent in Michigan racing for decades. Races were held at Standish, as well as at the Carrolton Fairgrounds, and they were strictly for fun with no purses paid. Pete Spencer did race his street roadster, but who drove it, who won the races and who lost have all been forgotten.

After World War II, Spencer began a long career of race promotion by leasing the Saginaw Fairgrounds half-mile track. The first really organized roadster races were held there in late 1946. Roadster racing soon spread to other groups such as the Michigan Racing Association and the Michigan Modified Stock Car Racing Association. There may have been other groups as well, and certainly there were outlaw hot rod races held in many smaller Michigan cities. In addition, a

"Michigan Racing Association" was formed by southern Michigan and Indiana racers.

As elsewhere, the heyday of the roadsters in Michigan was from 1947 to about 1951. Even though Saginaw was basically a horse track there were some excellent races held there under Pete Spencer's leadership. At Owasso, some 50 miles to the south, a high-banked dirt track opened in September of 1946. The roadsters were soon running there and going very fast. The early years of Michigan hot rod racing saw events being held at Kalamazoo, Grand Rapids, Marne, Muskegon and at Jones Speedway in Allegan. In 1949, a series of excellent races were held at Parkington's Pastures near Detroit. Also in 1949, the roadsters made a rare appearance at Detroit's Motor City Speedway and enjoyed what was most likely their biggest Michigan payoff. Promoter Andy Barto was faced with a shortage of midgets that night and ran the hot rods instead. The purse was $3,240 and Hod Preston won the main and about $800.

Michigan roadster racing did produce some good drivers and Al Miller was one of the best. It is not

Probably 1947 at Saginaw. Joe Quinn is on the pole, and Ken Miles is in #48. (Larry McClosky photo—Marion Spencer collection)

This car is obviously from Standish, Michigan, but other than that nothing is known about it. (Marion Spencer collection)

This is the "Mad Russian," Gervasse Imek. Imek won a lot of races at Partington's Pasture near Detroit. (Greg Sharp—Vintage Racing Photos)

The driver of the Janson Special is unknown. That pitman arm will provide quick steering, but it looks scary. *(Marion Spencer collection)*

Saginaw—circa 1947. Nothing is known about the car or the driver other than his nickname is probably "Tiny." *(Marion Spencer collection)*

This is Marne in 1948 or 1949. That's probably Ray Hubble sitting very exposed in #30. *(Paul Weisner collection)*

Emory Alderton is in Pete Spencer's first track roadster. The engine is a Model B Ford, but what is the body? Perhaps a rare special version of an Essex roadster? *(Marion Spencer collection)*

certain that Miller started in the hot rods but he is recorded as winning a main event at Motor City Speedway in 1951. Miller raced at Indianapolis from 1962 until 1969, putting in his best performance during a fourth place finish in 1965. At Saginaw and Owasso, drivers like Joe Quinn, Matt Heid and Tommy Lane were the stars. Around Detroit, it was "The Mad Russian," Gervasise Umek, who seemed to own Parkington's Pastures. Probably the most famous Michigan hot rodder was future stock car racing great, Iggy Katona, who got his start at Marne.

There were three known fatalities in the roadsters in Michigan, and all took place on the high banks of Owasso. During a night race on July 17, 1947, two drivers died in a multi-car crash. It all started when George Keenan blew a tire and hit a light pole at the end of the backstretch. Joe Quinn

Joe Quinn at an unknown Michigan track in 1947. Joe's dog, Duke, is serving as pit crew on this day. *(Paul Weisner collection)*

1948 at Saginaw. This is a faster roadster, and apparently Duke is now the driver. Quinn looks a bit jealous. *(Paul Weisner collection)*

was close behind and either hit the Keenan car or flipped trying to avoid it. Quinn's seat belt snapped and he was thrown to the track. Newspaper accounts of the wreck indicate that most of what happened next was obscured by thick dust and perhaps the lack of light. About five cars piled into the wreckage, and at least one of them struck and killed Joe Quinn. Nick Lazzaro hit wreckage and a concrete wall and he died a few days later in an Owasso hospital. Tragedy struck again at Owasso on June 29, 1948, when popular Matt Heid died in a single car crash. Heid's car hurdled off the bank at the wet end of the track in what was either a mechanical failure or driver error. Tom Cherry was a visitor from Indiana that night and had been trouncing the Owasso regulars. An eye-witness remembers that Heid had vowed to beat Tom Cherry and thinks he may have been trying just too hard.

The early model stock cars arrived on Michigan tracks in 1950, and the roadsters just sort of disappeared. Some roadsters did run with the sprint cars, but this didn't last long. Where and when the last roadster race was held in Michigan is not known.

Saginaw in 1947. The driver is unknown; the Chevy is probably a four banger.
(Marion Spencer collection)

Action at Saginaw. Cliff Wright is in the #2 Pete Spencer car. The other drivers are unidentified.
(Larry McClosky photo—Marion Spencer collection)

Trouble at Saginaw. Just who was driving #XIX is unknown, but since that rather flimsy roll bar held up, he was probably OK.
(Paul Weisner collection)

Tom Cherry came from the Mutual Racing Association in Indiana to race at Saginaw.
(Paul Weisner collection)

Nick Lazzero is pictured at a county fair track someplace in Michigan. Along with Joe Quinn, Lazzero died in a tragic 1948 crash at Owasso.
(Paul Weisner collection)

Leo Kosecki drove this neat-looking hot rod at Saginaw.
(Larry McClosky photo—Marion Spencer collection)

Future stock car great Iggy Katona is on the pole as Glen Rockey follows closely in #1. (Paul Weisner collection)

Matt Heid is the driver of this neat-looking Ford Six. Heid was killed in this car at Owasso in 1949. (Paul Weisner collection)

Marne in 1948. Gene Farber is on the pole in a Cadillac V8, and Tom Suspenski is in #10. Joe Quinn lines up third with Glen Rockey on the outside, and Tommy Lane fights the dust from fifth starting position. (Paul Weisner collection)

Saginaw action. No identification of drivers is available for this 1948 photo. (Paul Weisner collection)

A fixed field of cars lines up at Saginaw in 1947. Gene Farber is on the pole in a car that defies description. (Paul Weisner collection)

Hod Preston drove the Brown Dog roadster to many wins in Michigan roadster racing. (Paul Weisner collection)

A large crowd at Saginaw waits as the roadsters line up for a race. (Marion Spencer collection)

The sprints and roadsters sometimes ran together at Saginaw. Harry King is in #2A with roadster legend Tom Cherry in #38. (Larry McClosky photo—Marion Spencer collection)

Action at Saginaw. Emory Alderton is leading in #2. Leo Kosicki is second and Joe Quinn is running fourth in a Buick. (Paul Weisner collection)

Iggy Katona looks over his #T-3 prior to a race. This is probably Owasso.
(Marion Spencer collection)

Detroit's Al Miller made it from the Michigan hot rods to the Indy 500. He's pictured at Sun Valley Speedway in Anderson, Indiana.
(Zane Howell collection)

PENNEY-ROYAL SPEEDWAY
LEON, N.Y.

Emory Alderton in #2 goes wheel to wheel with Joe Quinn at Saginaw. (Paul Weisner collection)

The field takes the green flag at Saginaw in 1947. *(Marion Spencer collection)*

Marne in 1947. Tommy Lane is in a very slightly modified street rod. Lane later did very well in the midgets. *(Ray Hubble collection)*

Saginaw, 1947. The engine type is unknown and so is the driver. The back of the body appears to be made from the hood of some 1942ish car. *(Marion Spencer collection)*

Another view of the same car. That hood fits the chassis just fine but leaves a lot to be desired so far as driver protection goes. (Marion Spencer collection)

Although the Brown Dog name is not in place, this is the car. Hod Preston was probably the driver who hit something solid at Saginaw.
(Marion Spencer collection)

Joe Quinn is on the pole in Pete Spencer's Chevy Six sprint car, and Tom Cherry lines up on the outside. Saginaw in 1948. (Marion Spencer collection)

Glen Rockey at Whiskey Ridge in Joe Bisocky's V8. (Paul Weisner collection)

Gervaise Umek uses a strong right arm to keep his roadster from turning over on him as track attendants rush to his aid. This action took place at Motor City Speedway in about 1950.
(Illustrated Speedway News Photo)

A WONDERFUL NAME: WHISKEY RIDGE

It is likely that the name of the remote ridge in Western Michigan came from certain illegal activities that took place there during prohibition. At any rate, when Jack Fiske carved out a race track in the apple orchards on this hilltop, he named it Whiskey Ridge Speedway. While a remote location is an advantage for making moonshine it is hardly desirable for a race track. Whiskey Ridge was 20 miles from the nearest big town, Muskegon, and was accessible only over gravel roads. Despite these two handicaps racers and fans alike found their way to Whiskey Ridge, and the

The crowd sometimes shared the hazards of racing at Whiskey Ridge. Here Gene Farber loses his steering and heads for the spectators. Fortunately there were no serious injuries. (Joe Bisocky collection)

track was a successful operation for a number of years.

The first races were advertised as "Jalopy Races" and that's exactly what the cars were—it would take a lot of imagination to call an early Whiskey Ridge car a track roadster. Harry Connell raced there in the remains of a Model A Ford that had only a cowl and a seat for the driver. The track was a half-miler that had "natural obstacles" such as hills, gullies and bumps. Speeds did get up to 60 mph, but despite this, Connell remembers that the safety record was good. "After awhile," Connell recalls, "they did want us to have a helmet and a roll bar or a high-backed seat." Harry Connell managed a second place finish in 1946 race and took home $22.

The track gradually smoothed out, the cars became faster and more like true track roadsters. It is not known if full bodies became a requirement or if racers just thought they looked better. By mid-1947, Whiskey Ridge was running a mixture of hot rods and home-built sprint cars, and the track had become a rather odd-shaped oval. With a name like Whiskey

Ridge there just had to be a "Hell's Turn" and there was. On the outside of "Hell's Turn" was an unprotected 30-foot drop off. Drivers who had sailed over this baby cliff swore it was a 300-foot drop.

Roadster racing went on until about 1950. For some reason, most of the Whiskey Ridge cars remained rather crude, but there were some fast roadsters. Gene Farber drove a flathead Cadillac V8 that ran very well. As elsewhere, the Ford and Merc V8s were hard to beat and Joe Quinn, Glen Rockey, Roger Joneson, and Joe Biscoki won races with these engines. Apparently nobody ever bothered to keep point standing,s so the honor of being crowned track champion at Whiskey Ridge Speedway went unclaimed.

Jack Fiske's advertising for Whiskey Ridge used lots of colorful adjectives and a bit of "blood and thunder," but it attracted the fans. Check the very complicated rules under "Entries." (Harry Connell collection)

Bill Murray is in for a wild ride, as he slides off "Hell's Turn" at Whiskey Ridge. Murray escaped serious harm. (Paul Weisner collection)

Jack Fiske, who managed Whiskey Ridge Speedway, did a good job with publicity. Jalopy News was printed weekly and distributed all over the Muskegon area. (Harry Connell collection)

In 1949, the "Whiskey" seems to have disappeared from the speedway's name. The track now measured about three-eighths of a mile so Joneson's 19.2 second lap was a creditable time. (Ralph Mapes collection)

Whiskey Ridge—circa 1950. The track appears smooth, there is no dust and even the spectators are out of harm's way. Looks like a nice place to race.

It is 1948, and Jalopy News has become Speedway News at Whiskey Ridge. The race cars were now a mixture of roadsters and home-built sprint cars. (Ralph Mapes collection)

Vern Johnson's 1946 Whiskey Ridge car. Hardly a track road-ster, but it does have a V8 engine in what is left of that Model A chassis. (Harry Connell collection)

Early action at Whiskey Ridge. No helmets and probably no seat belts. That should be Dick Peoples in #6. He went on to become a fine race driver. (Harry Connell collection)

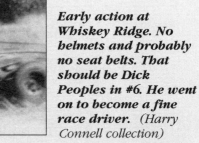

MINNESOTA

Roadster racing in Minnesota began on May 27, 1947, on a three-eighths-mile dirt track at Farmington, a few miles south of Minneapolis. The cars were fresh off the street and most had stock motors, but a crowd of more than 4,000 turned out to see the action. Howie Hoffman and Jerry McCormick raced neat A-V8s with the usual speed equipment, and they should have run up front. Unfortunately, the winner of the first hot rod race in Minnesota is unknown.

The roadsters ran at various Minnesota tracks in the summer of 1947 and were loosely organized under the Mid West Roadster Racing Association and something called the Minneapolis 50th Street Racing Association. In October, a race was scheduled for the Minnesota State Fairgrounds at Minneapolis. The race was backed by the State Fair Board of Directors and was heavily advertised. It was a chance for the fledgling roadster racers to gain a lot of publicity and prestige. This didn't happen as the hot rodders just were not ready for such a big time event. Newspaper accounts of the race

★ MIDWEST ★

"HOT ROD"

RACING CHAMPIONSHIP

On the Minnesota State Fair

★ SPEEDWAY ★

SOUVENIR PROGRAM

SUNDAY, SEPTEMBER 28, 1947

SUNDAY, OCTOBER 5, 1947

Price ★ 25c

This "Midwest Hot Rod Racing Championship" at the Minnesota State Fairgrounds turned out to be a very poor show. Pictured are Howie Hoffman in #77 and Jerry McCormick who drove two of the better cars that competed. (Dave Norgaarden collection)

indicate that poor officiating and overheating cars resulted in a very poor show. Tom Adelmann nursed a sick and overheated V8 to a win in the 50-lap main event—he may have been the only finisher. The State Fair Officials, who were used to the smoothly run IMCA sprint car races, announced that the hot rods would not be back.

At some point, probably in early 1948, the Minnesota Roadster Racing Association was formed, and it was apparently the dominant roadster group in the state. During the next couple of years, races were held on county fair ovals at towns like Albert Lea, Austin and Hibbing. Races were also held on dirt tracks in the Minneapolis area at Rex, Farmington and Crystal Speedways. The Minnesota racers also helped roadster groups in adjacent states of Wisconsin, Iowa and South Dakota. Very little information is available on just what sort of purses were paid in Minnesota roadster racing, but the odds are that most purses were under $1,000. During the 1948 season, Harvey Benedict, who

Farmington—circa 1949. Car #13 has a flathead Model B Ford engine, but there is no identification on the driver. (Bonnie Bailey collection)

Twin Cities Speedway in 1949. Tommy Adelmann is in a later version of #111. That's probably a barbed wire fence between the track and the cornfield.
(Dave Norgaarden collection)

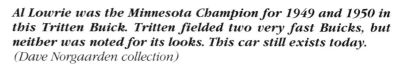

Art Bailey won a lot of races in the GMC-powered #33 "Flying Disk." (Bonnie Bailey collection)

This is the final and fastest version of Harvey Benedict's string of #4R hot rods. Harvey Porter drove it well and won a lot of races. (Bonnie Bailey collection)

This is Rex Speedway and Neal Arendt is at the wheel of a Tritten Buick. (Dave Norgaarden collection)

Art Bailey in the "Flying Disk" #33 leads an unidentified driver at Farmington in 1949. (Bonnie Bailey collection)

owned the very fast number 4R Mercury, did keep track of his winnings. In 26 races, some of them out of state, the car won a little over $2,400. Driver Harvey Porter probably won most of the races.

Like elsewhere, the Merc and Ford V8 engines were used in most Minnesota hot rods. There were some Model A or Model B engines with various speed equipment and also a four-cylinder Essex with some sort of overhead valve conversion. There was even a supercharged Cord V8—a very rare and interesting combination, but odds are it did not run all that fast.

Crystal Springs Speedway near Minneapolis was well promoted and was successful for a few years. That is a Hudson engine in the #72 driven by Roy Smith, but what kind of chassis is that? Jerry Stageburg is in his #66 A-V8. (Bonnie Bailey collection)

The Minnesota Roadster Racing Association had no cubic-inch-displacement limit, so some cars used the big Buick Eights. With 320 cubic inches, these big brutes put out a lot of power and were easier to cool than the V8s.

The Minnesota roadster champions were as follows: (This is probably the Minnesota Roadster Racing Association)

1947: Tommy Adelmann. Car #111, Ford.

1948: Al Lowrie. Car #1 1/2, Buick Eight.

1949: Al Lowrie. Car #1 1/2, Buick Eight.

1950—Harvey Porter. Car #4R, Mercury.

Other top drivers were Harold Burns, Art Bailey, Speed Chamberland and Neal Arendt.

The Minnesota roadsters had a reasonably good safety record, but one driver was fatally injured. Veteran sprint car and midget driver, Art Bailey, was killed at Rex Speedway on June 22, 1950.

Harvey leads Howie Hoffman at Rex Speedway.
(Dave Norgaarden collection)

In 1950, Art Bailey drove one of the Tritten Buicks. He was killed in this car at the Rex Speedway.

Art Bailey spins at Farmington. The original photo caption indicates that Jerry Stageburg in #66 missed Bailey. *(Bonnie Bailey collection)*

Neal Arendt probably didn't realize how brave he had to be to drive this Tritten Buick.
(Dave Norgaarden collection)

A Tritten Buick after Neal Arndt wrecked it someplace in Minnesota.
(Dave Norgaarden collection)

Car #47 uses an unusual Nash engine—no driver identification. Jerry Stageburg is in #66, Art Bailey in #33 and the driver of #13 is unknown. *(Bonnie Bailey collection)*

Tommy Adelmann gets #111 crossed up at Rex Speedway near Minneapolis in 1948. (Dave Norgaarden collection)

Rex Speedway. Tommy Adelmann is in #111 and Harvey Porter in #4R. Porter is driving the first of Harvey Benedict's successful string of #4R cars. (Dave Norgaarden collection)

1948 Rex Speedway. Car #7 is Sterling Stageburg, #4R Harvey Porter, #44 Jerry McCormick and #111 Tommy Adelmann. Car #7 has a supercharged Cord V8 engine. (Dave Norgaarden collection)

Above left—Groups like the American Legion often put on roadster races like this one at Albert Lea in 1950. Above right—The entry list for a race at Albert Lea in 1950. (Bonnie Bailey collection)

Right—Rex Speedway in 1948. Tommy Adelmann is in #111, and Howie Hoffmann in what is described as a "California Car." It sure looks like a street rod. (Dave Norgaarden collection)

Excellent action at Rex Speedway in 1949. Jerry McCormick is in #44, but the other drivers cannot be identified. (Bonnie Bailey collection)

Missouri

The earliest information on roadster racing in Missouri comes from a booklet entitled "Building a 100 mph Model A Ford" by George Riley. Data in the booklet reports that Vic Damon, in a Riley-equipped Model A roadster, "set a new state record at Smithville on May 24, 1931." This was an exhibition run at a big car race, and the photo is of a street roadster. It is logical that there would be some sort of roadster activity, at least in Smithville, in the next 10 years, but no information has been found.

Roadster racing started in Springfield, Missouri, in early 1947. Not much is known about this first race other than future Missouri great, Junior Hower, finished last. Hower, along with Johnny Tatlock, drove his street rod from Kansas City to Springfield to race and was totally surprised to find that most of the cars were lightweight and stripped track cars. Hower returned to Kansas City, built a Merc powered T-bodied car and didn't lose too many more races.

Racing started at Smithville, a few miles north of Kansas City, in May of 1947, and continued there

Here is an ad for races at Independence in 1949. Lots of adjectives are used. Were those of us who drove roadsters really "speed crazed" and "death defying"?
(Ray Boyles collection)

throughout the summer. The Mid West Hot Rod Association was soon formed, and this group sanctioned additional races at Hopkins, Bolivar, St. Joseph and Kansas City. Later, in the summer of 1947, a new speedway, The Heart of America, opened a few miles east of Kansas City and the roadsters had plenty of places to race.

In 1948, there was even more roadster racing when promoter, Bud Wilson, liked what he saw and formed the Pony Express Racing Association. Wilson promoted roadster races in half a dozen Missouri cities, so 1948 was a busy season for the hot rod racers. Wilson employed some questionable tactics in his promotions and apparently made some people angry with him. At one point, the track roadster he owned was barred from entering a Mid West-sanctioned race even though the group was short of cars that day.

At some point, probably in mid-1948, another group was formed someplace in Missouri. This was the Tri-States Hot Rod Circuit. Not much is known about this organization other than that Jay Howard of Maryville was the champion.

By 1948, most of the cars had completed the

Junior Hower (left) had a nice-looking rig to tow his track roadster. Ray Boyles (right) supplied information and photos for this chapter.
(Ray Boyles collection)

Below—Herschel Wagner drove this car at Savannah in 1950. The car still exists and is owned by Ray Boyles of Blue Spring, Missouri. The car originally came from California, and Boyles is trying to trace its history.
(Ray Boyles collection)

transition from street rods to full-fledged race cars with all the usual equipment, and there was intense competition in Missouri roadster racing for the next few years. Missouri drivers like Junior Hower, Hi Fashing, Herschel Wagner, Pat Cunningham, Tom DeVolter, Johnny Tatlock and Scotty Scoville were all winners. The Kansas City area seemed to attract visiting drivers from all over the country and some of them were able to run wheel to wheel with the locals. Ray Boyles of Blue Spring, Missouri, has documented 120 drivers that raced in the Kansas City area hot rods. On the visitor list are names like Tiny Lund, Stan Kross, Cyclone Ross, Ken Stansberry, Oklahoma champion Bill Flintchem and St. Louis Roadster Association champion Don Hill. Junior Hower won more races than anybody and also won the Mid West Hot Rod Association championship several times.

Herschel Wagner at Heart of America Speedway in 1947 or 1948. The car looks like a converted street rod. Wagner later went very fast in IMCA Offies— he always "wore" that cigar. (Ray Boyles collection)

Junior Hower at his best—on dirt and all crossed up. This is Kansas City's Olympic Stadium. This was primarily a midget track, but the hot rods ran there a few times. (Ray Boyles collection)

Circa 1950. Junior Hower crowds somebody. Photo location is uncertain—possibly Savannah, Missouri. (Scotty Scoville collection)

A lineup of Missouri roadsters. Car #20 was driven by Herschel Wagner, #6 by Tommy DeVolter, and #24 is the Junior Hower car. (Ray Boyles collection)

Howard Token drove this car at Hopkins on August 15, 1948. The car is crude, but it looks STRONG! (Ray Boyles collection)

Smithville on May 16, 1947. This was one of the first roadster races held in the Kansas City area. There is no identification on the drivers—note the spectators right up against the fence.
(Howdy Williams collection)

This is Fred Bowers with his Riley Four Port. Scotty Scoville drove it on this day.
(Scotty Scoville collection)

Scotty Scoville in the Bowers Four-Port Riley. The car featured an unusual tail section—Bowers made it from two 1946 Pontiac door caps.
(Scotty Scoville collection)

Because Hower was so successful with a Merc-powered car, many of the other racers probably copied him, also using the Merc V8. One exception was a nice-looking Riley Four-Port owned by Fred Bowers and driven by Scotty Scoville and Herschel Wagner. An engine type that got considerable space in pre-race publicity was a Lincoln V12 that was being built by Junior Welder of St. Joseph. Welder was several times reported to be "working day and night on the Lincoln." Apparently he never finished the car as there is no record of it actually racing.

Purses for most Missouri races were small—usually around $500, sometimes less than that. Documentation of crowd size and purses is rare. Data was reported for a race at Hopkins in September of 1947. The purse was reported to be a guaranteed $400, plus, "prizes from local merchants." Junior Hower no doubt made money racing roadsters, but only because he won almost everything. On April 10, 1948, Hower swept the program at Bethany and took home $175.

There was one known fatality in Missouri roadster racing. George Warren was killed at Smithville on August 13, 1948. A benefit was held the next week at Smithville and this netted $400 for Warren's family.

Bethany, Missouri in 1947. It is a cold and miserable day, but 1,200 fans showed up to see Junior Hower in his #24 sweep the program. Only eight cars were on hand that day.
(Ray Boyles collection)

The field comes down for a start at Smithville in 1947. The cars appear to be basically street rods.
(Howdy Williams collection)

Tom DeVolter drove this nice looking car in Missouri roadster races. (Ray Boyles collection)

Herschel Wagner in action at Olympic Stadium in Kansas City—1950. (Ray Boyles collection)

Circa 1949. The Mid West Hot Rod Association journeyed to Topeka to race on the fairgrounds track. Junior Hower leads Bill Reynolds.
(Ray Boyles collection)

THE WILSON-HOWER-CUNNINGHAM SHOW

Bud Wilson's Pony Express Racing Association had an active schedule of hot rod races in Missouri for several years. Wilson was a talented showman and not all of the races he presented were really races—some were best classified as entertainment.

Some of the details of Wilson's operation have been lost over the years, but he would apparently sell a "show" to officials of various county fairs. This would include roadster races, stock car races, tractor races, motorcycle stunts and anything else that came to mind. Wilson sometimes promoted two or three of these shows a week. The hot rods were the star attraction, and Wilson had about half a dozen drivers on his payroll at $100 per "race." The object was to put on "hippodromed" (fake) races that would look good to a crowd that may not be completely race-wise.

On at least a few occasions, the feature of the evening's entertainment was a take-off on the old "drunken farmer" routine that was used uncounted times at airshows in the 1920s and 1930s. Pat Cunningham was Wilson's "drunken farmer." Cunningham was a top-ranked midget driver at California's Gilmore Stadium during the 1930s. He also won a 100-mile race at Oakland in 1936 driving an Offy

midget against a full field of big cars. Cunningham drove roadsters in the Kansas City area and was still a very capable race driver. His job at some of the Wilson shows was to sit in the grandstands, pretend to drink a lot of beer and to heckle the roadster drivers. His target was sometimes Junior Hower; Cunningham would loudly proclaim, "I can beat that bum!"

The track announcer and Hower would go along with the act and soon Cunningham was told to "put up or shut up." He'd stagger out of the stands, beer bottle in hand and accept Hower's challenge of a match race. Wilson's roadster was wheeled out, and Cunningham climbed aboard. The starter gestured and hollered, "Hey, you can't take your beer in a race car!" Cunningham finished off the "beer" in the bottle, and tossed it aside.

The race was run at near normal speeds, the lead changed hands, and Cunningham nearly spun out. As per the script, Cunningham won by inches and the crowd went wild.

The Bud Wilson-Junior Hower-Pat Cunningham show was good entertainment and a crowd pleaser. It probably wasn't used too often, as Hower and Cunningham preferred to battle legitimately on the speedway.

This was taken at the Smithville race on May 16, 1947. No identification on the driver, but his car is far more a track roadster than his competitor's cars. (Howdy Williams collection)

Tom DeVolter must have won a race someplace as he sure is all smiles. The crew is, left to right, car owner Jess Eaton, unknown, sponsor Bill Durfee and Nate Montgomery. (Ray Boyles collection)

Scotty Scoville in the Bowers Four-Port Riley. (Scotty Scoville collection)

A Model T Derby was held at Smithville in 1938. One of the drivers was William Hower—the father of Junior Hower. (Ray Boyles collection)

Henderson Tonnes somehow escaped from this mangled hot rod without serious injury. (Photo from the Kansas City Times—Scotty Scoville collection)

MUD GOES WITH THE GLORY—Hot rod racing on a wet track can be anything but pleasant. Scotty Scovill, 24-year-old Kansas City driver, won the second heat race at the Heart of America track Sunday afternoon, but ended up looking like this. Scovill, who lives at 3625 Pennsylvania avenue, has lowered his goggles, but a handkerchief around the lower part of his face still is in place. "I couldn't see where I was going most of the race...

The surface of the Heart of America Speedway was HEAVY as Scotty Scoville can attest. (Scotty Scoville collection)

Someplace in Missouri in 1949. Driver Eddie Fairman came from Des Moines, Iowa, to race. (Ray Boyles collection)

Left—Late 1947 at Heart of America Speedway just east of Kansas City. Junior Hower in #24 battles with Johnny Tatlock. (Ray Boyles collection)

Above—Later that same day Hower's car has collected more mud. Here he passes an unidentified competitor.

Left—More muddy cars at Heart of America. Scotty Scoville goes around Roy Conklin who sits high and exposed in his V8. (Ray Boyles collection)

Lyle Fine drove this Lincoln V12-powered car at Hopkins in 1948. Can anybody identify that "body"? (Ray Boyles collection)

This is the Lucien Bean car at Hopkins in 1948. It looks as though he used only the top half of the '29 Model A body. (Ray Boyles collection)

Junior Hower at Savannah in 1951. The #24 is still there, but a '27 T body has replaced the T body used previously. (Ray Boyles collection)

NEBRASKA

This is Gordy Shuck's first track roadster. He built it himself out of what is mostly a '32 Ford. That's a '27 Studebaker hood and the back part of the body is the hood from a Studebaker Champion. The cockpit area is built out of upside-down fender wells from something—Schuck doesn't remember what. (Gordy Schuck photo)

Street hot rods were few and far between in Nebraska, but a group of owners from the Hastings area did get together in 1948 to form the Nebraska Hot Rod Racing Association. A few exhibition races were held that year—these were probably part of sprint car racing programs. In 1949, the NHRRA began its first full season of racing with an event at Hastings in June. There were about 15 cars on hand and most were crude and anything but attractive. The cars had been "constructed" (mostly with a cutting torch) from whatever was available and some were cut down coupes. An exception was Gordy Schuck who had a very neat street rod he'd built from a '32 Ford roadster. The car was the class of the field, Schuck drove it well, and he was a main event winner that day.

During 1949, races were held at Hastings, Beatrice, Fairbury, North Platte, Broken Bow and several other small Nebraska towns. The tracks were all half-mile county fair horse tracks, and the almost ever-present dust made for dangerous and unpleasant racing conditions. The Nebraska Hot Rod Racing Association did venture into the big city of Omaha for one race on a quarter-mile track. The track was built at a drive-in movie theater. It ran around the movie screen, and spectators sat in their cars in the normal drive-in spaces. Gordy Schuck was the 1949 NHRRA champion.

In 1950, the Nebraska hot rodders ran almost every Sunday all around the state. The group also sanctioned races at Belleville, Kansas, and some racers towed to Missouri and Iowa for races. Gordy Schuck won a lot of races, and he would be champion again in 1950, but competition was getting tougher. The Merc-powered #69 "Belle of Belleville" was on the scene with Cliff Clapper at the wheel. Built by the racewise Goodrich

brothers in Belleville this was the car of the future in Nebraska racing.

Clapper was unlucky enough to get drafted because of the Korean war, and Andy Anderson stepped into the Belle of Belleville for the 1951 season. Anderson preceded to dominate Nebraska roadster racing for the next two years. In 1951, he won 17 of 33 main events, and in 1952 Anderson went 18 for 29. Not all of the wins were easy, as some good roadsters from California had found their way east by then. Local builders were quick to copy these more advanced machines, and there were some good looking fast hot rods racing in Nebraska. Gordy Schuck was still winning and other drivers who did well included Chuck Sears, Bob Rager, Gaylord Higer, Frank Brennfoerder and Curly Wadsworth.

So far as engines go, the Merc and Ford V8s won most of the Nebraska roadster races. An exception was the Ranger-powered roadster driven by Bob Rager. These huge aircraft engines were relatively common in Midwest sprint car racing but were way over the cubic inch displacement allowed by most roadster groups. The Nebraska group had no limit on displacement so Rager fitted a roadster body on a Ranger sprinter and usually ran up front.

Much of the information on Nebraska roadster racing came from Bill Smith who drove a few races with the NHRRA and then owned a car for a couple of years. Smith is now president of Speedway Motors in Lincoln. His firm is one of the leading manufacturers and distributors of auto racing parts in the United States. Bill Smith remembers some of the "technology" used by Nebraska racers around 1950. He recalls that keeping the V8 Fords and Mercs cool was a real problem—all of

Someplace in Nebraska in 1949. Donald Gunn is at left and driver Gordy Schuck at right. Car is powered by a V8. Check Schuck's helmet.
(Gordy Schuck collection)

the races were in the daytime and Nebraska summers are very hot. Water would sometimes be circulated through the roll bar or there would be an extra radiator in the trunk—none of this helped much. So far as safety goes Smith was concerned when there were two roadster fatalities at nearby Council Bluffs in Iowa. He made a roll bar for his roadster out of a tubular bedstead and fastened it to the car with muffler clamps! Fortunately for Bill and for his driver this device was not tested.

Over the years, the purses in Nebraska Hot Rod Racing Associations were not high—probably averaging around $500. (Purses at Belleville, Kansas, were far above this figure.) Despite the low purses Andy Anderson may have won more money than any other roadster racer in 1951 and 1952. (By then roadster racing was in sad shape in most areas.) The payoffs were heavy towards the front, and Anderson usually took home around $100 per race.

By mid-1952, roadster racing was in trouble in Nebraska. There was a car shortage and sometimes only eight or 10 cars would appear for a race. The sparse fields were supplemented by sprint cars and on a few occasions by midgets, but this really didn't work. Soon the stock cars took over. In about 1953, the Nebraska Hot Rod Racing Association was disbanded (formally or informally?) and a new racing group, the United Motor Contest Association, was formed. Although it was primarily for sprint cars, the roadsters were allowed to run until 1956. It is believed that a roadster, with Roy Stills at the wheel, won the championship of this group in 1954.

Despite the very dangerous racing conditions the NHRRA suffered only two driver deaths. Francis Schulze died at Wayne in 1951 and Jim Vineyard was killed in a Nebraska Hot Rod Racing Association-sanctioned event at Belleville, Kansas. A tragic accident at Beatrice took the life of starter Roy Boggs. Boggs was struck by an out-of-control roadster, and the popular 1920s racer and local rancher died of his injuries.

Bill Smith at Hastings in 1949. His #4 is an A-V8. This car was the first of the one hundred race cars that Bill Smith has built or owned in the last 40 years. (Bill Smith collection)

Bill Smith is in #4 at Hastings. It is a nice-looking '30 Model A with a very stock '40 Ford V8 engine. Harry Hoff is at right—his car sports a REAL roll bar. (Bill Smith collection)

Chick Byers owned this great-looking hot rod. The car had an engine that was identified as a Horning GMC that ran 126 mph at Indianapolis. The engine was probably in the Motor Trend car driven by Bill Cantrell that failed to qualify for the 1951 race. (Gordy Schuck collection)

Lyle and Mike Cotter fielded this Ford V8 roadster in 1950 Nebraska races. What kind of car did that radiator shell come from? (Gordy Schuck collection)

This is one of the latest Nebraska roadster photos. It is July 1, 1956, at Nelson, and Frank Brennfoerder is driving the Jack Skinner Chevy. This was a combined roadster-sprint race under the sanction of the United Motor Contest Association.
(L.A. Ward photo)

THE RACES AT ORD
A SEMI-MYSTERY

There were roadster races at Ord in central Nebraska on July 4 and 5, 1948. The races were sanctioned by the Colorado Auto Racing Club so most of the cars and drivers were from the Denver area.

The track at Ord was not the typical county fair horse track. The half-mile track was built in 1927, and banked in the 1930s. The IMCA big cars ran there on a fairly regular basis, and there were even a few AAA races. The track was very similar to Belleville—steeply banked, narrow and lightning fast. It was advertised as the fastest track in Nebraska and there is little doubt about this.

The hot rod races were well advertised and drew reported crowd of 2,000 on July 4. Newspaper reports indicate that the roadster put on a show that was far short of crowd pleasing. The *Ord Quiz* quoted one spectator as saying, "You can see more speed on the highways these days!" Could it be that the Colorado hot rodders were intimidated by Ord's high banks? This seems highly unlikely as racers back then didn't even know such a word existed. The probable reason for a poor show was a dusty track and a stiff north wind that blew the dust into the grandstands. On July 5, the crowd numbered only 830, but the racing was excellent according to the *Ord Quiz's* reporter. He didn't bother to get drivers' names but wrote about a great battle between White 2, Yellow 99, White 8 and Black 77. White 2 was the

winner, and from the Colorado photos we learn that this was Keith Andrews.

Research has turned up a few people who saw the roadster races at Ord. About all these people remember is that, "There were two California cars at the races and they won everything." One version of the story has the car owner showing up in a Cadillac and the drivers in a pickup with a double-decker trailer for the roadsters. It could be that these California cars and drivers were on their way to race further east, but nothing on Ord has turned up from some of the logical California racers. California hot rods enjoyed a certain mystique in 1948. "California" seemed to mean "fast" so perhaps a couple of the regular Colorado cars were billed as being from California? If this is so, it is likely that there would have been publicity in the *Ord Quiz*, but in stories both before and after the races there is no mention of California cars. However, the fact remains that to this day racing fans in Ord remember, "Two California cars." It seems a bit like the end of most episodes of "The Lone Ranger." Who were those Californians?

Mysterious Californians or not, the promoters at Ord apparently did not like the hot rods. The roadsters never raced there again.

Note: Most of the information for this story came from Ray Valasck of Lincoln, Nebraska, who is working on a book about the history of racing at Ord.

Gordy Schuck in the Chick Byers GMC at Fairbury in 1952. Byers paid $3,000 for the ex-Indy engine only to have it throw a rod through the block in its third race.

Mark Clausen is pictured with his low-slung roadster at a Nebraska race in 1950. It is not known who drove the car.

Bob Rager wrecked this car at Hastings in 1950. The six cylinder, 450-cubic-inch Ranger aircraft engine was unusual for a roadster.

Bob Rager later had a Merc in his #620 roadster. Rager's son, Roger, ran Indy cars in the 1980s.

Tom Egan and Frank Brennfoerder drove this neat-looking Madson and Grove V8.

Dale Dalle was obviously a Chrysler fan, but he used a Ford V8-60 for power. Want to bet that it ran hot? *(Gordy Schuck collection)*

Gordy Schuck works on his Merc roadster at a Nebraska race in about 1949. Note the driver in the background who wears a football helmet.

York, 1950. Frank Brennfoerder in #96 on his way to a trophy dash win over Don Biltoft.

A pit scene at Nelson in 1950. Jerry Adams drove #7-11 and Frank Brennfoerder handled #96.

Frank Brennfoerder is pictured at York in 1950. Brennfoerder missed a lot of Nebraska roadster racing when he was drafted into the army in 1951.

These two cars were from Superior. The sleek appearing #208 is unusual, but other than this photo, nothing is known about the car.

Gordy Schuck from Edgar, Nebraska— rough and tough on the track, but a nice guy off the speedway. *(Bill Smith collection)*

FRANCIS SCHULZE—INNOVATOR

Most of us who built track roadsters copied from someone else and/or had help from material in *Hot Rod Magazine.* Where did Francis Schulze get the idea for his totallly different car? Probably he'd seen roadster races in Kansas or neighboring Nebraska, but most of those cars were basically modified street rods. Maybe an issue of *Hot Rod Magazine* had found it's way to his home in Norton, Kansas, by early 1951, but there was nothing like Schulze's creation in those pages. "Kansas Farm Boy" is a well worn and overused phrase, but that is exactly what Schulze was. However, he created a car that was, in many ways, years ahead of its time. Francis Schulze was an innovator.

Using mostly Ford parts, Schulze built a rear-engined car. The front suspension wasn't standard Ford, but rather cantilevered transverse springs that gave a semi-independent action. On the rear, the car was really unusual. The entire engine and in-and-out box were bolted solid to the rear end. A sub-frame supported this unit and this was pivoted at a point just behind the driver. This was all unsprung weight. A single center-mounted coil spring supported the main frame of the car at the rear. The radiator was also at the rear, which apparently came from a Ford truck. Although the radiator barely stuck up in the airstream, the car probably didn't run any hotter than other V8s of that era. Power came from a very potent bored and stroked Mercury V8. The body was fashioned from part of a Word War II aircraft belly tank. Technically, it was a sprint car, but it ran only with the Nebraska Roadster Racing Association.

The car probably weighed less than 1,200 pounds and

Francis Schulze works on his car at a Nebraska roadster race in 1951. The sub-frame that supported the motor and rear end is visible behind the main frame of the car. This unit pivoted at a point just in front of the Mercury engine.

with about 75 percent of the weight on the rear wheels it had "bite" that would be the envy of today's cars. It was brutally fast, and nothing could touch it on the straightaways. Handling was another matter—it was terrible.

Schulze would have preferred leaving the driving of his car to others and some drivers did try the car. It scared most of them. Buddy Quick drove it a few times and was brave enough to earn a trophy dash win at Hastings, Nebraska. At other races Schulze drove it himself and managed a heat race victory at Broken Bow, Nebraska.

On September 16, 1951, Schulze brought the car to a race at Wayne, Nebraska. Top driver, and present day Indianpolis Speedway official, Andy Anderson's ride did not show up so Schulze offered him the seat in #81. Anderson turned it down as did a couple of other drivers. Even today, Anderson wonders if he could have prevented what happened at Wayne that day. Francis Schulze died in an end-over-end flip down the backstretch. The design of the car cannot be completely faulted as the crash was an "accident" all too common in 1951. Blinded by thick dust Schulze rammed into the rear of another car at high speed. The car was torn in two by the force of the crash, and he died a few hours later. Perhaps Schulze would have survived in a conventional car—perhaps not.

One wonders what would have happened if Francis Schulze had had time to work on his rear-engined design—he was 10 years ahead of everybody else.

(Thanks to Glenn Schulze of Norton, Kansas, for most of the details of his brother's story and for the photos.)

Hastings, Nebraska, in 1951. Francis Schulze at left with Buddy Quick, who has just won the trophy dash with the rear-engined car.

Francis Schulze's #81 at a race in Hasting, Nebraska. Rear suspension for the main frame of the car was the single coil spring with enclosed shock.

Schulze sits in his creation at his shop in Norton, Kansas. Just how the steering gear operated is not evident but it certainly wasn't a conventional roadster unit.

Nebraska Hot Rod Racing Association flagman, Harold Gardner, takes time out to have his photo taken in the car normally driven by Don Biltoft.

Jim Guessfort is shown with the nice-looking roadster that he owned. Gordy Schuck drove it to a number of wins in 1951.

This is Fairbury in 1952 and Tony Echomeyer smiles from the cockpit of the car owned by Clarence Lucking.

Gaylord Higer drove this GMC-powered roadster, which was owned by Bob Rager and Ross Garber.

Dick Richardson loses a wheel at Hastings in 1950. His #77 appears to be a cut-down coupe.
(Hastings Tribune photo)

Chuck Sears is pictured in Jim Guessford's "Ace" at Fairbury in 1952.

Don Elliot drove this nice-looking roadster in Nebraska Hot Rod Racing Association events. Engine type unknown.
(Andy Anderson collection)

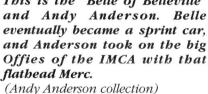
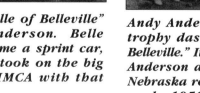

This is the "Belle of Belleville" and Andy Anderson. Belle eventually became a sprint car, and Anderson took on the big Offies of the IMCA with that flathead Merc.
(Andy Anderson collection)

Andy Anderson wins another trophy dash with the "Belle of Belleville." It is 1951 at Hastings. Anderson and Belle dominated Nebraska roadster racing in the early 1950s. (Andy Anderson collection)

A STAR-STUDDED FIELD

Would you believe that two Daytona 500 winners and a prominent modern-day manufacturer of racing equipment were all in the same field at one Nebraska roadster race? This was a Hastings in 1949. The future NASCAR greats were Johnny Beauchamp and Tiny Lund. Bill Smith would go on to run the multi-million dollar Speedway Motors operation in Lincoln, Nebraska.

Tiny Lund won the Daytona 500 in 1961. Many historians now believe that Johnny Beauchamp won the first Daytona 500, even though Lee Petty was declared the winner of that 1959 race. (It was several days before a winner of that race was officially announced. Who knows what went on to make sure that Petty, a southern hero, won over a virtually unknown outsider from Iowa.)

The purse was $717.23 for that roadster race at Hastings, and Johnny Beauchamp did OK. He won the trophy dash, won the fast car heat race and took second in the main event. He earned $200.81. Tiny Lund was not so lucky and must have had problems after qualifying midway in the field—he went home to Iowa empty handed. "Billy" Smith in his own A-V8 took second in the consolation race and sixth in the main for total winnings of $39.44.

NEW MEXICO

New Mexico's rugged terrain pretty well divides the state into two parts, and in general, roadster racing was divided in the same manner. In the southeastern part of the state, adjacent to Texas, two roadster groups were formed. These were the Pecos Valley Racing association and the South West Roadster Association (SWRA). The SWRA was formed in 1947, and it appears to have been the dominate group. The SWRA had rules similar to other roadster organizations, but did specifically ban "fish tails" or "pointed backs." This rule was obviously designed to keep sprint cars from running, but as is obvious in the photos, the rule was seldom enforced. With an average of eight or 10 cars appearing at races, anything remotely resembling a roadster was welcome to run. Engine rules were completely open except for banning double overhead cam engines. Most of the cars used V8 engines with a scattering of other makes.

The South West Roadster Association reportedly demanded a guaranteed purse of $400—this would pay a bit less than $100 to win the main event. On November 9, 1947, a "Southwest Modified Roadster Championship" race was held at Hobbs, and this race may or may not have paid more than the $400 minimum. Races were also held at Clovis, Artisia and Carlsbad.

Earl Emmons in the Faulk's Salvage V8 won most of the races, and had a champion been crowned, it would have been Emmons. Other top drivers were Paul Pearson, Elton Green and from Texas, A.M. Farris. Future Indy driver, Jud Larson, occasionally came over from Texas to race in New Mexico. In a 1948 race at Clovis, Larson won a heat race and finished fourth in the main event. The car earned $20 that day, so Larson probably took home $8.

In northwestern New Mexico, most of the roadster racing was at Gallup. There may have been a few races at Albuquerque, and later on there was racing at Aztec. There was no actual roadster organization formed, but races were held on a intermittent basis from 1947 until about 1955. There were only five roadsters in

1948 action at the Ceremonial Grounds in Gallup.
(Bob Noe collection)

Pappy Noe with Bob Noe in a Miller Schofield Model B—circa 1948. (Bob Noe collection)

Charlie Montgomery in his #11 "Box Car." The engine is a 252-cubic-inch Chrysler Six, and the chassis is probably the same make. Is the body plywood or metal? (Bob Noe collection)

SEE THESE CARS
IN ACTION EVERY
RACE DAY

LOCAL AND OUT-OF-TOWN
CARS RACE AT
CARLSBAD SPEEDWAY

Jud Larson drove this car at Clovis in 1948, but it doesn't look like him in this program photo. (Dixie Emmons collection)

This advertisement shows some typical southeastern New Mexico cars. Note the mixture of roadsters and sprint cars. (Dixie Emmons collection)

Not Responsible for Accidents

Presenting Hot Rod Auto Races

CARLSBAD SPEEDWAY

OFFICIAL PROGRAM

OFFICIALS

Bill Ross — Announcer

TTY HARE—Starter	JERRY ROHL — Referee Scorer
N BEASLEY — Timer	"TOOTER" MORRISON — Judge
GRIMES — Timer	GEORGE GILL — Judge
COX — Pit Manager	RAY V. DAVIS — Photographer

EEDWAY LOCATED 2 MILES EAST ON HOBBS HIGHWAY

Gallup, so help was needed from cars that came from Holbrook, Arizona and Pueblo, Colorado. For the first few year,s there were apparently two different classes of cars running at the races—jalopies and roadsters. Jalopies were cars stripped of everything except the cowl and perhaps stock engines were required. The two classes competed in separate races but were combined in the main event as fields were always short. The track roadsters varied from some rather crude street rod conversions to well-built and nice-looking cars. For the most part the engines were modified Model A or B Fords. There were some sixes and straight eights, but for some reason the V8s were rare.

Southwest legend, Pappy Noe, was the big winner, and he often swept the program to take home about $120. The race-wise Noe had competed before World War II, and his roadster was a Model B Ford Miller-Schofield sprint car with a narrowed and sectioned Model A body. Noe raced until he was well into his 50s, and he won in the sprints and modifieds after the roadsters died out.

An unusual car that ran at Gallup

This is 1947 at Hobbs Speedway. A.M. Farris' Chevy is on the pole with Earl Emmons winning in #562. Why #562? That was the street address of the sponsor. (Dixie Emmons collection)

Hobbs Speedway in 1947. Earl Emmons leads the #48 Buick of Bob Sparks. (Dixie Emmons collection)

THE LOST "SUPER SPEEDWAY"

There were a few roadster races held in New Mexico in the 1930s. Most of these were on half-mile horse tracks in eastern New Mexico, and most of the racers were from Texas. Lee Wick of San Antonio remembers one race track near Clovis that was very different. He recalls that it was a mile or more in length, that it was "high banked," and it was built around a dry lake bed. Wick's Cragar-Model A roadster was fully capable of 105 mph, and he says that it was "wide open all the way around." Even though the track was dirt, it sounds like an early version of today's super speedways.

The track's name, location and everything about it have been forgotten. Research in the Clovis area turned up nothing.

was the #11 "Box Car" owned and driven by Charlie Montgomery. The rules were somewhat lax regarding body type, and some owners fashioned bodies that resembled sprint cars, but Montgomery chose to build a body that looked like a box. Depending on who tells the story after 40 years had passed, the body was built out of either metal or plywood. Pappy Noe's son, Bob, remembers Montgomery and the "Box Car" ran well and consistently, and that if point standings had been kept it may have been a championship car.

Despite the fast half-mile tracks and the often primitive equipment, the New Mexico roadsters had a good safety record. The only known fatality was a driver named Krammer, who was killed someplace in southeastern New Mexico.

It is easy to spot Charlie Montgomery in #11, but the other drivers are unidentified.
(Bob Noe collection)

Pappy Noe's roadster had a Model A body narrowed and chopped to fit on his 1941 sprint car. Noe was a winner everyplace he raced. (Bob Noe collection)

Aztec, New Mexico—circa 1955. Wayne Martin is the driver of this car, which is probably from the Phoenix area. (Bob Noe collection)

The field lines up for the start of the main event at Gallup in 1948. Pappy Noe is on the pole, and Charlie Montgomery's "Box Car" is easily identified back in the field.
(Bob Noe collection)

SWRA Drivers
"BULLET BILL" DISBROW

ROLAND HAYES, JR.

L. J. "DUFFY" FRAUENDORFER

SWRA Drivers
RONALD HELLAND

FRANK PILLSBURY

SAM FABICK

NO. 2 IN THE PITS

These photos are copied from the 1947 Southwest Modified Roaster Championship program. The race was held at Hobbs Speedway, Hobbs, New Mexico, on November 9, 1947.

BILLIE O'NEIL, WINNER OF WOMAN'S SPECIAL EVENT, ROSWELL, N. M.

Right— Earl Emmons in the Faulk's Salvage Merc V8. The chassis type is unknown, but it is certainly no Ford. (Dixie Emmons collection)

Left—Circa 1953. A mixed field of roadsters and sprint cars takes the starter's flag at Gallup. Floyd Reynolds is in car #8.
(Bob Noe collection)

NEW YORK

Roadster racing in New York was apparently limited to the western part of the state—New Yorkers would call this "Upstate New York." Racing in this area started in 1940 at a track called "Satan's Playground" near Bethany Center, south of Batavia. The races were on a half-mile steeplechase track, and the cars were a mixed field of Ford or Chevy roadster and jalopies that were stripped to the point that little more than a seat for the driver remained. The same cars and drivers also raced at Le Roy on a dirt oval in a wheat field called Circle Hill Speedway. Racing at Circle Hill ended in 1941 when a spectator was fatally injured by an out-of-control racer. This accident resulted in all racing being banned in Genesee County for a number of years. The most notable thing about this early New York roadster racing was that future Indy driver and stock car ace Al Keller got his start at Satan's Playground.

After World War II, the Rochester Roadster Racing Association was formed, and it was this group that sanctioned most of the hot rod racing in New York. This organization had about 20 cars

Action at the Hemlock Fairground in about 1949. The half-mile track was often dusty.
(Lou Campagno—Bob Chaddock collection)

and drivers, and from 1948 to 1951 put on races at perhaps a dozen different tracks in western New York. Most of the tracks were the typical half-mile county fairgrounds horse tracks, and most were located in the smaller towns. The RRRA ran only one exhibition race on the fine midget speedway at the Buffalo Municipal Stadium. The purses were usually under $500. Bob Chaddock, who was a car owner and a Rochester Roadster Association officer, remembers, "We were sometimes supposed to get more money, but it never seemed to happen." The Rochester hot rodders finally rebuilt a half-mile track at the Hemlock Fairgrounds, removed the normal horsetrack hazards, and promoted their own races.

One unusual thing about the Rochester Roadster Racing Association was the rule prohibiting any motors later than 1936. Nobody remembers just why this odd cutoff date was chosen—perhaps to

A drivers' meeting at Penney-Royal. Looks like there was a small field that day. *(Lloyd Moore collection)*

Bud Fanale drove this car in the Penney-Royal roadster races. Fanale also campaigned the car in western New York sprint car races. (Lou Ensworth collection)

Carl Pintagero and his Buick Eight in action at Penney-Royal. (Lou Ensworth collection)

Bud Fanale relaxes after a race. A top driver for many years, Fanale began racing at Penney-Royal in 1949 and competed on western New York tracks until 1963.
(Lou Ensworth collection)

Some of the Penney-Royal drivers in 1949. Left to right—Carl Pintagero, Al Fanale, not identified, and Carl Conta. Note the strange location of the roll bar.
(Lloyd Moore collection)

Lucky 7 wasn't so lucky for George Ott, who was killed in this car at Penney-Royal. Ott cut the top off a coupe to create this "roadster."
(Lou Ensworth collection)

keep out the later 24 stud Ford and Merc V8 engines?

The top RRRA drivers were Jerry Earll who drove a Wayne Chevy, Irv Morrison in a flathead Model B and Danny Daniels who also drove a Model B powered roadster. The group did suffer one fatality as John Morrison died at Caladonia when his steering gear failed and the car flipped end-over-end.

Aside from the Rochester Roadster Racing Association the only specific information on roadster racing in New York that has surfaced is at Penney-Royal Speedway. Although it sported a rather auspicious name Penney-Royal was a primitive oval scraped out of a pasture near the tiny town of Leon, some 20 miles north of Jamestown. The races were sponsored by the Leon Volunteer

Jerry Earl in action at Hemlock in 1949. The Rochester Roadster Racing Association ran at Hemlock quite often, and later they removed some of the obvious hazards shown in this photo.
(Lou Campagno—Bob Chaddock collection)

Fire Department and no actual roadster organization was formed. The events were billed as "Jalopy Races," and that is exactly what some of the

Jerry Earl at the Hemlock Fairgrounds in about 1949. The engine was a Wayne Chevy. (Lou Campagno—Bob Chaddock collection)

Bill Chick takes the checkered flag in Jerry Earl's Chevy at the Hemlock Fairgrounds in Hemlock, New York.
(Lou Campagno—Bob Chaddock collection)

Bill Chick drove this Dodge Six-powered Model A at Hemlock. Co-owner, Bob Chaddock, is leaning against car #36 at the left.
(Lou Campagno—Bob Chaddock collection)

A FINGER LAKES MYSTERY

New York's Finger Lakes District is located about 100 miles east of where any known roadster racing took place in that state. According to *National Speed Sport News* in May, 1951, there was a race at Chemung, New York, that was sanctioned by the Finger Lakes Roadster Association. Very little information was given on the race other than Dutch Hoag was the winner.

The known roadster racing in New York was all over by May of 1951. Dutch Hoag won hundreds of modified stock car races but claims that he never drove a roadster.

What was the Finger Lakes Roadster Association? Had they earlier sanctioned roadster races and is all that information missing?

cars were. Others were fairly nice-looking street-track roadsters, and still other cars were actually sprint cars. About the only obvious rule was that coupes were not allowed.

The racing at Penney-Royal began in 1949, and continued on a regular basis until mid-1950. The half-mile dirt oval attracted fields from 15 to 20 cars and crowds of 400 to 1,500 fans. Purses were usually small, but Lloyd Moore took home $75 for winning a main event in July of 1949. The dust was often thick at Penney-Royal. Moore recalls that he looked up to locate a big Maple tree so that he knew when to start turning for turn three.

Some of the racers who did well at Penney-Royal were Lloyd Moore, Mike Egan, Bud Fanelli, Jimmy Peoplecorn, Carl Pintegro and Glenn Davis from neighboring Pennsylvania. Racing at Penney-Royal ended late in the summer of 1950 when George Ott was killed during a race.

The same cars and drivers that ran at Penney-Royal raced on a fairgrounds track at Jamestown and possibly on other ovals in the area but no information is available. The Rochester cars and

Carl Pintagero accepts congratulations after winning a feature event at Penney-Royal. His #46 was powered by a Buick straight eight. (Lou Ensworth collection)

This Penney-Royal V8 seems to have all the normal speed goodies. (Lou Ensworth collection)

A typical roadster that ran at Penney-Royal Speedway in Leon, New York. (Lou Ensworth collection)

A pit scene at Penney-Royal in 1949. It is not known who drove #4.
(Lou Ensworth collection)

Lloyd Moore unloads his A-V8 from the "transporter." Moore won a lot of Penney-Royal races with this car.
(Lloyd Moore collection)

drivers occasionally raced at Penney-Royal. Lloyd Moore remembers that five cars from the Rochester Roadster Racing Association appeared at one race. Moore recalls that, "They were nice-looking cars, but we blew them off." (Odds are that there are Rochester drives who will dispute this statement.)

For some reason, roadster racing in New York apparently did not spread further east to cities like Syracuse. In the general area of New York City, a Metro Roadster Club was formed. This group supported races by the Eastern Racing Association in Delaware but, so far is known, never ran races of their own in New York State.

Another view of the Bud Fanale car. The original photo caption lists the car as having a Studebaker engine, but this engine appears to have overhead valves. (Lou Ensworth collection)

Liberal rules at Penney-Royal allowed almost everything to run. This car appears unfinished. (Lou Ensworth collection)

Lloyd Moore won the most money on this day at Penney-Royal. Note that dust conditions were severe. (Lloyd Moore collection)

rewsburg Jallopy Pilot Firsts At Penney-Royal

LEON, July 24 — Lloyd Moore, rewsburg daredevil jallopy pilot, ced away with the $75 first prize today's renewal of stock car cing on the Penney-Royal track ear here.

Other money-winners included rl Pintagreo, Billy Rexford and m Jackson.

The final race was abbreviated om 25 laps to 10 laps, due to tremely dusty conditions. The anagement has promised that the

track will be oiled and in firs class, dustless shape before nea Sunday's races.

Several of the cars, stripped down, souped-up vehicles of m thirties vintage, met minor m haps in the series of five rac during the day.

An even larger racing field is e pected at next week's field da The races are sponsored by th Leon Fire Department, on a di track said to be the fastes

FROM PENNEY-ROYAL TO NASCAR

Two of the drivers who raced roadsters at Penney-Royal, Bill Rexford and Lloyd Moore, moved on to NASCAR and did very well. With the backing of Julian Buesink, a Jamestown car dealer, Rexford and Moore ran most of the NASCAR Grand National (now Winston Cup) races in 1950. Stock car racing was exactly that in those days and Resford and Moore usually drove

cars right off Buesink's used car lot. The New York racers won a couple of times and ran consistantly. Rexford was the 1950 NASCAR champion and Moore finished fourth in points. Along with the racing rules, the NASCAR payoff has also changed a lot since 1950—Bill Rexford got $1,000, Moore $280.

Lloyd Moore in his neat A-V8 at Penney-Royal in 1949. This car was a winner and lots faster than Moore's first Penney-Royal car—a 1929 Marmon with a Model A body. (Lloyd Moore collection)

Bill Rexford was the 1950 NASCAR champion, but he didn't win too many races at Penney-Royal. This photo of his 1949 car indicates why he usually ran back in the pack. About all that can be said is, "Nice rollbar, Bill." (Adrain Ketchem collection)

NORTH DAKOTA

oadster racing in North Dakota and adjacent Minnesota began with the formation of the Valley Roadster Club in Fargo in early 1949. There was considerable interest in racing roadsters on the half-mile county fairground tracks in the area, and the purpose of the club was to establish car regulations and organize the races. The group drafted car specifications and rules that were better than those of most roadster organizations. Safety requirements seemed a bit lax, as seat belts and roll bars were left to "the option of the car builder-driver." Bruce Byers felt that Rule #5, which stated "Brakes are compulsory," was a bit loosely written, and he concluded that any means of slowing the car short of the driver dragging his feet would satisfy this rule. By the early summer of 1949, the Valley Roadster Club had about 20 cars ready to race or in various stages of construction. Most of the cars were A-V8s with some Model A and Model B Fords, a Fronty T and several other makes. There were some interesting sounding cars on the roster, such as Art Bayliss who had a

Harley Gunkle is pictured with his mechanic at a roadster race someplace in North Dakota. Gunkle later drove sprint cars and did well with a flathead V8.
(Dell Byers collection)

Hudson Eight "Pipe Organ" and Jerry Veslenden who had a huge Buick Eight in a early Chevy roadster.

The Valley Roadster Club was ready to race, and a small group called, Thrill Inc. was formed to promote the races. The first roadster race was at Ada, Minnesota, in July of 1949. The race was apparently a success, but the winner's name was not recorded. Other races in 1949 and 1950 were held under the promotion of Thrill Inc. at Detroit Lakes in Minnesota and at Fargo, North Dakota. The roadsters also competed under different promotion at Bismark, Forman and Andeda, North Dakota. The size of the purses are unknown, but it is a safe bet that most or all were under $500.

Despite the effort that had gone into organizing the roadster races, there were problems. The main one was dust—the drivers complained, the fans complained and so did people who lived anywhere near the race tracks. The "big money" that some racers may have anticipated did not materialize. Along with Thrills Inc. the roadster group built their own racetrack in Glyndon, Minnesota, a few miles east of Fargo. The track turned out to be

Action at Detroit Lakes. Red Stark is leading in #2, Jim Noel is on the outside, and Vern Selberg trails in his V8-powered hot rod.
(Dell Byers collection)

Harley Gunkle was the main event winner at Detroit Lakes, Minnesota, on July 2, 1950. Gunkle doesn't remember how much he won other than, "Not much."
(Harley Gunkle collection)

This may be Aneta or Foreman, North Dakota. Dave Bossjole is in the #17 '38 Ford convertible. On the pole in #97 is Orville Johnson— Johnson was killed in this car at Aneta in 1950.
(Dell Byers collection)

Bruce Byers drove this cutdown '40 Ford coupe in North Dakota roadster races. Byers later had a long career as a race promoter in the Fargo area. *(Dell Byers collection)*

poorly designed with long straightaways and sharp turns that the roadsters just could not negotiate. The roadsters never raced there.

Coupled with other problems of the roadsters was the death of Orville Johnson during a race in the fall of 1950 at Aneda, North Dakota. Johnson had the steering lock up on his Model A and was killed instantly when the car flipped.

Although no formal plans were made to end roadster racing after the 1950 season, racing just never started in 1951. Thrills Inc. began stock car races, and the brief era of the roadsters in North Dakota and adjacent Minnesota was over.

NOTE: *Most of the information on North Dakota and western Minnesota roadster racing comes from an unpublished history written by the late Bruce Byers in about 1953. Thanks to his widow, Dell*

Byers of Lakepark, Minnesota, for providing a copy of this material.

Harley Gunkle in #762 with Red Stark at dusty Bismark, North Dakota, in 1950. Stark is driving a Model T with a Roof head.
(Harley Gunkle collection)

This is probably Detroit Lakes, Minnesota, in 1950. The North Dakota roadster racers ran in both North Dakota and in western Minnesota.
(Dell Byers collection)

OHIO

● ●

The earliest evidence of roadster racing in Ohio is at Hamilton, near Cincinnati, in 1931. There is further evidence of racing at Hamilton in 1937, so it is logical that racing there continued throughout the 1930s. In the Columbus area, there was roadster racing at Newark at least in 1941. Since there was roadster racing for some 10 years in different parts of the state, it is quite possible that research has turned up only a fraction of the early racing in Ohio.

In general, even during the post-war years, there was never a really strong roadster organization in Ohio. One reason for this was the presence of the Mutual Racing Association in neighboring Indiana. Even though Mutual was busy racing at home, they were scheduling races at Dayton, Ohio, as early as 1946. Along with Dayton, Mutual was soon racing at the Cincinnati Race Bowl, and they had two of the best paying tracks in Ohio.

Apparently the Ohio Speedway Association was formed in the eastern part of the state in 1946. There is no documentation of this group's activities until 1948, but Spike Gilliland, who races with the OSA, was later referred to as the 1946 "Ohio State

Champion." In 1948, the Ohio Speedway Association somehow became aligned with NASCAR, and there was considerable publicity in *National Speed Sport News* and in *Hot Rod Magazine*. A few photos of the Ohio Speedway Association cars appeared, and these were obviously "seasoned" track roadsters that had been racing for a couple of years. In early 1948, roadster races were held on half-mile fairground ovals at Newark, Norwalk, Dover and at Berea near Cleveland. Most of the races were advertised as being sanctioned by both NASCAR and the OSA. NASCAR's interest in roadster racing was obvious, and, who knows, this may have been the beginnings of further involvement in hot rod racing in other parts of the country. The Ohio Speedway Association-NASCAR racers were victims of dreadful racing luck during the summer of 1948. Three drivers died during a short period of time, and a fourth died a few months later. Eddie Dean was killed at Norwalk on May 31, 1948. In early July

Marion—circa 1949. The driver of the "Flying Dragon" is not identified. (Lowell Sherer collection)

Warmups at Shady Bowl in about 1950. That is probably Harold Mowell in the lead car.
(Izor collection)

Paul Hooper in Doggie Sheldon's Miller-Schofield Model A Ford at Newark on July 8, 1941. Hooper became a fine driver in the roadsters, midgets and big cars. (Ron Williams collection)

This car is obviously a converted street rod, and it still uses a generator. Marion—circa 1949.
(Lowell Sherer collection)

Lee Izor owned some nice-looking Chevy roadsters, and this was one of them. Harold Mowell usually drove it. (Lowell Sherer collection)

Harold Hartley died at Dover and the popular Steve Lesick at Berea. A few months later, another driver, possibly Tiny Quillen, lost his life. NASCAR appears to have lost interest in the roadsters sometime during the summer of 1948. The Ohio Speedway Association had also been sanctioning stock car races, and they may have concentrated on these cars after the series of accidents. No further information on OSA roadster activities was found until a few brief articles appeared in *National Speed Sport News* in 1952. Some very good drivers raced with the Ohio Speedway Association in 1948. Names like Bob James, Gib Orr, Dick Jordan and Spike Gilliland would appear as winners of races with other roadster organizations in Ohio, Indiana and Pennsylvania.

There were other roadster groups formed in Ohio, one of which was the Triangle Racing Association. Just when Triangle was formed is not clear. It was apparently based in Dayton, but it

This Ohio car ran in the NASCAR roadster race at Davie, Florida, in 1949. Willy Sternquist drove it there, but who drove in Ohio is not known.
(Lou Ensworth collection)

Curley Cotner's name is on the side of the roadster at Marion, so it is assumed that he drove it.
(Lowell Sherer collection)

Barberton—circa 1948. No information on car #13 or it's driver. (Lou Ensworth collection)

DeGraff in 1946. Paul Hooper is shown in action. (Ron Williams collection)

A car in action at Norwalk in about 1948. No identification, but this is probably an Ohio Speedway Association event. (Don Boucher collection)

never sanctioned a race in that city. Triangle did race at Shady Bowl near DeGraff and possibly at Greenville. Information on Triangle is sketchy, and it does not seem like it was a strong organization. Some good drivers like Paul Hooper, Pete Allen, Don Jones, Harold Mowell and Chuck Farquer ran with Triangle, but they also crossed over and competed with other groups. Occasionally, some drivers from the Mutual Racing Association would come from Indiana to race with Triangle at Shady Bowl. Apparently these visitors were not always welcome. Don Anderson, currently the president of the Antique Auto Racing Association, remembers going to Shady Bowl with his roadster and three other Mutual cars. The Mutual drivers finished first through fourth in the feature and figured they had a pretty good payoff coming.

Not so—there was no payoff to the Mutual members. Just what pretense was used has been forgotten, but there must have been one heck of an argument!

Another hot rod group in Ohio was the Buckeye Roadster Association. Buckeye was formed in western Ohio in 1949 and raced almost exclusively on a track in the tiny town of Landeck. The Landeck races were on Sunday afternoons, so they seldom conflicted with other schedules, and Triangle and Mutual drivers were occasional visitors. Mutual driver, Smokey Stover, was one of these in the Joe Walls Hudson, and so far as is known, he even got paid.

There was other roadster racing in Ohio in a number of cities—

A car in action on the Marion track in about 1949. (Lowell Sherer collection)

Below—One of the better looking cars at Marion. This was 1949, and the sanctioning body for the races is uncertain. (Lowell Sherer collection)

Bob James heads onto the track at Barberton. James won a lot of roadster races in #45. (Lou Ensworth collection)

usually these races were on county fairground horse tracks. Many of the races were unsanctioned "outlaw" races, but some were sanctioned by the Northern Ohio Roadster Association. There may have also been a Ohio Roadster Association that was active in central Ohio.

Most roadster racing in Ohio ended about 1951 as the stock cars took over the fans interest. Mutual ran a few races at Dayton as late as 1952.

Amos Place owned and drove this Hudson Six, but it just would not stay cool. (Place collection)

George Place wrecked this car at New Brenen in about 1950. The car is the ex-Joe Walls' Hudson from the Mutual Racing Association.
(Place-Fairfax collection)

Elzie Whetnall usually ran with the Triangle Racing Association at Shady Bowl. The car originally ran with the Ohio Speedway Association.
(Place collection)

BUD CLAYPOOL'S ROCKET

Sometime in 1949, Bud Claypool bought the Hudson-powered hot rod that George Place had been running at Landeck. Claypool raced the car with moderate success, but soon ran into financial problems—he couldn't make the payments on the car to Place. An agreement was reached whereby Place got his Hudson engine back and Claypool kept the car.

Like most racers, Bud Claypool looked for a way to continue racing. He did so by finding a huge 320-cubic-inch Buick Straight Eight and putting this in the car. The Buick probably weighed 300 pounds more than the Hudson it replaced.

Bud Claypool in his "rocket." Originally built by George Place, this was one of the early Landeck roadsters. (Hardesty Photo)

The car had plenty of speed, but simply would not turn. George Place remembers that the car, "would go like a rocket and steer like a rock!" Claypool fought with the handling problem and finally resorted to a bit of "weight jacking." He filled a large sack with crushed stone and tied it to the frame over the left rear wheel. This may have helped the push a bit, but the sack shifted during the race and soon there was a hole in it. The crushed stone ran out onto the track like a stream of water. This just may be the origin of the term, "The handling went away." Claypool became a fine driver in the roadsters, ran modifieds and had several sprint car starts in the Little 500.

Bud Claypool in the former Place Hudson. Place's memories of the car: "Went like a rocket, steered like a rock." (Place Fairfax collection)

A KENTUCKY MYSTERY

With all the roadster racing that went on in the adjacent states of Ohio and Indiana it is logical that some racing would spill over into Kentucky. It is also logical that a roadster group would have been formed in Kentucky.

Armed with the above logic I did my best to find out something about Kentucky roadsters but came up empty. Only nomadic Red Amick (he raced roadsters in at least 12 states) could provide anything about hot rods in the Bluegrass State. Red remembers racing in Kentucky but doesn't remember in what city. He recalls that there wasn't much money but, "The pickin's were easy!" Perhaps these words will turn up some irate Kentucky hot rodders.

This Lee Izor Chevy featured a semi-detachable body that swung up out of the way while someone worked on the car. (Izor collection)

A car takes the checkered flag at Norwalk in about 1948. This was probably an Ohio Speedway Association event. (Don Boucher collection)

Landeck— circa 1950. Not the neatest of the Buckeye cars. Tim Rhondes is the driver. (Hardesty Photo)

Smokey Stover in the Joe Walls Hudson visited Landeck in 1950. Note the Riley sidedraft carburetors. (Fairfax collection)

Don Jones drove this Gene Schaffler V8 at Landeck. Jones later moved into the Hardesty Chevy and went very fast. (Place-Fairfax collection)

Bill Morgan of Nevada, Ohio, drove this V8 with the Buckeye Roadster Association. (Place collection)

DeGraff in 1946. Paul Hooper is on the outside. This is probably Shady Bowl, a track that was later paved—wonder why? (Ron Williams collection)

This is the Buckeye logo. (Fairfax collection)

There was off-road "Pasture Field" racing in Ohio. This is Dick Houser after breaking a spindle on his cut-down sedan at a track near Ashland. (Dick Houser collection)

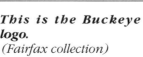

This is the Dick Andrews owned "Even Special" at Landeck in about 1949. (Fairfax collection)

Landeck Speedway in 1949. The driver of this early Buckeye Roadster Association car is unknown. (Hardesty Photo)

Gib Orr is pictured at an Ohio Speedway Association race at Barberton—circa 1948. (Lou Ensworth collection)

A field of Mutual Racing Association cars at Dayton on June 9, 1946. The roadsters are running on the quarter-mile track that was on the inside of the famed high bank speedway. (George Tichinor collection)

THE LANDECK RACERS

The story of racing in Landeck began in the spring of 1948 when two farmers in this tiny town in western Ohio decided to build a racetrack. These men were Leo Bonafas and Mike Kill. Both were confirmed race fans who often journeyed to Indiana to see roadster and big car races. Bonofas simply wanted to provide a track for local racers—even though there were none. Kill was more practical minded—he saw a chance to make a few bucks promoting the races.

In due time, a cornfield was demolished and construction of a half-mile dirt track was underway. The next step was to find some race cars. While "Build it and they will come" worked in the movie, *Field of Dreams*, it wasn't going to bring any race cars to Landeck. The existing roadster and big car groups were a considerable distance away, busy with more important matters, and not interested in a new and unproven track.

As the track neared completion Mike Kill went to the nearest "big" town of Delphos, population 6,000, to drum up something that could be called "race cars." One of Kill's first stops was at George Place's auto repair shop. Place was definitely interested in racing and soon set about building three cars for the races. Two of the cars were "built" in a hurry. The "building" consisted of butchering a couple of coupes—a '32 Ford and a '32 Plymouth. After a few hours work with a cutting torch, these cars became "roadsters." George Place put a lot more time, effort and money into constructing the car that he intended to drive at Landeck. The result was a rather odd combination of Hudson, Plymouth and Ford parts that had a very sleek "street rod" appearance, but it certainly wasn't a track roadster. Place later admitted, "I'd

never really seen a race car up close. I would have done a better job if I'd gone someplace and looked at one."

Mike Kill found a few more potential racers in nearby Spencerville. His efforts resulted in there being a field of nine, mostly strange-looking hot rods at the first Landeck race in the summer of 1948. The racing fever caught on in the area and soon the races were attracting full fields of cars and good crowds.

During the winter of 1948-49, the need for an organization was recognized and the Buckeye Roadster Association was formed. In some areas, the roadsters evolved slowly, but this was not to be true with Buckeye. The track roadsters of the Mutual Racing Association weren't too far away and there were some fast cars that could be copied. With this help available the Buckeye racers crowded years of racing technology into a few short months. Spencerville Chevrolet dealer, Jack Hardesty, fielded a very fast Chevy roadster for Don Jones to drive. Frank Crane did it the easy way and bought the McCormack Merc, a rapid Mutual Racing Association car. A couple of Tom Cherry-built Mercury engines found their way to Landeck Speedway. One of them, in Dick Andrews' car driven by George Place, won the 1949 Buckeye championship. George Place and his brother, Amos, later fielded lightweight T-bodies with Joe Walls inspired Hudson Sixes.

The Landeck racers learned to go fast in a hurry.

Note: *This story is essentially the same as that of racers all over the country. A small town, a racetrack and some hot rodders. Dale Fairfax of Indianapolis has provided excellent documentation for this tale.*

Tex Shackleford was the driver of the Joe Maddes' V8. Landeck—circa 1949. *(Place collection)*

Jimmy Brese in the Ray Spears car at Landeck. Brese has a rather uncomplimentary nickname. *(Hardesty Photo)*

Speed Rucker stands by the Walter Moorman V8 that he drove in Buckeye Roadster Association events. *(Place-Fairfax collection)*

Jim Cooley drove this car at Landeck. It had a Nash Ambassador six-cylinder engine—unusual, but it ran well. *(Place collection)*

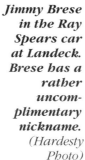

Action at Landeck in 1949. George Place is leading. *(Place collection)*

George Place owned a number of Hudson-powered cars, which he raced at Landeck. No identification on the driver of this one. *(Hardesty Photo)*

The start of a race at Landeck. George Place is on the pole, Dick Jones in #66. The second row is Bobby Lynn on the inside and Tim Rhode. In the third row is Junior McDonald in #53 and Bud Wilson on the outside. *(Place collection)*

The Don Jones-driven Hardesty Chevy outside of Jack Hardesty's Chevrolet dealership in Spencerville. *(Hardesty Photo)*

This is Don Jones in the Hardesty Chevy. It is a night race someplace—perhaps Dayton? *(Hardesty Photo)*

Jimmy Garmotta grins for the photographer after a race at Landeck. *(Hardesty Photo)*

Mutual Racing Association cars on the Dayton half-mile on July 4, 1950. Roy Prosser is leading followed by Everett Burton, Larry Crockett in #98Jr, Pat O'Conner, Bud Randall and Sam Skinner.

Dayton—circa 1952. This is the Leo Stabler Merc after a high-speed crash.
(Remington-Hurst collection)

Bud Claypool drove this Buick-powered car that was owned by Curley Ebbercote and the Kessel Brothers. Claypool later destroyed the car in a crash.
(Place-Fairfax collection)

Lee Izor built his own quick-change rear end in 1950. He used two stock Ford center sections to build the unit.
(Izor collection)

A Lee Izor Chevy Six as installed in one of his roadsters.
(Izor collection)

A typical county fair horse track at Norwalk—circa 1948. No identification on car #5.
(Don Boucher collection)

Jimmy Garmotta in the Frank Crane Merc. This car formerly ran with the Mutual Racing Association in Indiana. (Place collection)

A good view of Shady Bowl with cars from the Triangle Racing Association in action.
(Place collection)

Dayton—circa 1948. Junior Fort in the Van Dyke car. Fort died in an airplane crash in 1949.
(Zane Howell collection)

OKLAHOMA

roadster racing in Oklahoma began in 1946 when races were held at Woodward and Hobart. Very likely there was similar racing in other parts of Oklahoma, but research in nearly a dozen likely cities was not productive.

The races at Woodward were a typical small town effort with local cars, local drivers and cooperation from the city in providing a race track. The races were held at the city-owned Crystal Beach Track. This was a half-mile horse track built in the 1920s—in fact the roadsters and horses often raced on alternating weekends. Most of the Woodward cars were cut down from coupes of various makes: Were roadsters rare in Woodward? The race cars could be, and were, called "jalopies" in some locations, but in Woodward they were billed as hot rods. There were Dodges, Plymouths, a couple of Buick Eight-powered cars and a number of Model A-V8 combinations. Engine modifications were permitted and a four-cylinder Chevy with the Olds three-port head ran fast, although something usually broke. Of interest is a car that was built and sponsored by the local Chevrolet dealer. The car was constructed from, of all things, a 1937 Chevrolet Master four-door Sedan. The Chevrolet mechanics stripped the car to near nothing, installed primitive roll bars and a freshly rebuilt Chevy Six with a few hop-up tricks. On the track, they found they had a big problem. This Chevy had "Knee Action"—GM's early attempt at independent front-wheel suspension. This was bad enough on

The wreckage of Jack Miller's car after his fatal crash at Crystal Beach Track. The path of a piece of the four-by-four fence as it ran through the grill and firewall of the car is evident. (Don Baxter photo)

the highway and terrible on the race track. The "Knee Action" was quickly replaced by a straight axle.

After a season of racing at Crystal Beach and the inevitable hassles with the horsemen, another track was built near Woodward. This was the Covalt Dirt Track—a half miler that was anything but flat, and close to an off-road course. The races here apparently did not draw the fans so, it was back to the Crystal Beach Track where hot rod racing continued until about 1950. One of the top Woodward drivers was Ben Stedman. Stedman drove for John and Joe Loch, who built some very fast Dodges and Plymouths. When these engines wouldn't go fast enough, the Loch brothers talked the local Hudson dealer out of a brand new and potent Hudson Hornet motor. Other drivers who did well were Glen Hessy, Curt Sidders and Dutch Bodenhimer.

There was other roadster racing at Hobart and probably Lawton. For a brief period in the late 1940s, there was sort of a circuit for racing Model T roadsters—these may have been stock Ts. Races were run at Hobart, Elwood, Clinton and Shaddock. Ralph Hobbs remembers that his T won the race an Shaddock and that the payoff was all of $5.

As recorded by Don Baxter, cars from other parts of Oklahoma (as well as Kansas) competed at Woodward. Whether or not these cars were visitors from other places where there was racing, or just hot rodders looking for a race is not known. Bill Flintchem did a lot of racing in Missouri and Kansas

This is the Covalt Track near Woodward in about 1947. Two hot rods come out of the gully at one end of the track.
(Don Baxter photo)

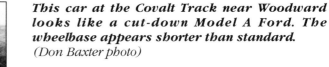

This car at the Covalt Track near Woodward looks like a cut-down Model A Ford. The wheelbase appears shorter than standard.
(Don Baxter photo)

and was usually billed as the "Oklahoma State Roadster Champion." Was this a real title, which means there is a lot of Oklahoma hot rod history missing, or was Flintchem simply from Oklahoma and the title was dreamed up by a publicist?

The Woodward racers were a determined bunch. A tornado that devastated the town on April 9, 1947. stopped racing for only a short time. They also suffered two fatalities. Jack Miller was killed when his car struck the infield fence at the Crystal Beach track. A four-by-four board came completely through the car and struck Miller with fatal results. The other victim was Bud Yearick, who died when his car slammed into a dust-obscured tangle at Crystal Beach.

None of the Woodward racers made it into big-time racing, but the town and the hot rodders shared the excitement of Troy Ruttman's 1952 Indy win. Ruttman's dad, Ralph, was born a few miles from Woodward, and Troy's grand-mother still lived in the area in 1952.

Note: *Most of the information on Oklahoma roadster racing came from an unpublished manuscript "Hot Rod Racing History in Woodward, Oklahoma" by Don Baxter of Wood-ward.*

Most of the Woodward cars were cut down from coupes and even sedans. It is hard to say just what the origin of #55 is. (Don Baxter photo)

This is the main straightaway at Covalt. There was no grandstand and no guard rails.
(Don Baxter photo)

OREGON

● ●

The Oregon Roadster Racing Association was formed in 1946 before there was any roadster racing in the state. There had been roadster races in Centralia and Yakima, Washington, early in 1946 in which Oregon drivers had participated. The Washington roadster racers had begun to organize after these races, and the Oregon owners and drivers did the same, so that they'd be in a better position to bargain with promoters. The first Oregon Roadster Racing Association event was actually a series of timed laps at Portland Speedway during a big car race. Dick Martin was one of the drivers who timed their street roadsters. Martin was among the fastest and he remembers that his time would have been good enough for the fast heat in the big car races. Within a few weeks a roadster race was held at Portland Speedway, and a reported 10,000 fans turned out for the event. Subsequent races also drew large crowds, purses were probably near $2,000 and soon street roadsters were flocking to join the Oregon Roadster Racing Association and pick up some of this "easy money."

One of the drivers who showed up for some of this money was Len Sutton. Sutton would become one of the Pacific Northwest's best drivers and go on to have a successful career at Indianapolis. Sutton didn't do too badly in his first roadster race—he managed a second in the semi-main and picked up $46. Most of the 1946 races were at the five-eighths mile Portland Speedway and most were won by Frankie McGowen in George "Pop" Kock's Lincoln Zephyr V-12 T-bodied car. The heavy V-12 was far from an ideal racing engine, but

Koch's car was lightweight, McGowen, with midget experience, drove it well, and it was one of the few cars running without a flywheel and clutch.

During the winter of 1946-47, new roadsters were built and the old ones lightened and improved to be more like track roadsters. In May of 1947, the Oregon racers found out that further improvements were needed. Southern California hot-shots Jack McGrath and Manual Ayulo showed up for a race at Portland Speedway and promptly knocked two seconds off the roadster track record. McGrath and Ayulo ran one-two in the feature race, and then did the same thing at a dirt track race in Salem the next day. The McGrath and Ayulo cars were "state of the art" track roadsters with bored and stroked Mercury engines, gearboxes, center steering, lightweight T-bodies and used alcohol fuel. The Oregon racers had a lot of copying to do, most of them took note, and Oregon roadsters were soon a lot faster.

During the 1947 season, races were held not only at Portland Speedway but at several other Oregon tracks, including a 300-mile tow to race at Klamath Falls in southern Oregon. All during that season there was cooperation with the Washington roadster organization and the two groups exchanged cars freely. The Washington roadsters were drawing big crowds at Seattle's Aurora Stadium. These races were held every Friday night and half a dozen or more Oregon cars would make the 180-mile trip north for the races. At the last race of the season, Len Sutton stepped into the Pop Koch-built Rolla Vollstead Merc. This combination dominated Oregon and Washington roadster racing for

Portland—1946. Jimmy Martin and mechanic Tom Story get ready to head for one of the first roadster races held in Portland.
(Dick Martin collection)

No need to worry about a trailer in the early days of Oregon roadster racing. Just drive the hot rod to the track. Jimmy Martin is the driver and Tom Story owns #33. (Dick Martin collection)

Three abreast action at Jansen Beach. Washington driver, Ray Davidson, is on the outside.
(Gordy Sutherland collection)

Lined up for the start at Portland Speedway— probably September 1946. Look at that crowd!
(Dick Martin collection)

the next several years.

At sometime during the 1947 season, the name of the Oregon roadster group was changed from the Oregon Roadster Racing Association to the the Roadster Racing Association of Oregon. Nobody seemed to know just why at the time, and surely nobody knows now.

In 1948, roadster racing in Oregon was flooded out for most of the season. The Columbia River flooded and Portland Speedway was under 10 feet of water for most of the summer. Most of the action for the Oregon racers was at Aurora Stadium in Seattle. Len Sutton was one of the drivers who made a weekly trip north and he, along with Ernie Koch and Mickey Shelton, took home a lot of Washington dollars.

In 1949, roadster racing was still going strong in Oregon. It was a prosperous season, but trouble was brewing. In general neither the Oregon or Washington roadster groups had enough cars to provide full fields. Cooperation between the groups was essential. The groups had similar rules so the cars could cross over. The Washington rules required that cars be fully upholstered—Oregon had no such requirement. The fine was only $5 or $10 so it was cheaper for the Oregon owners to pay rather than upholster their cars. There were complaints by both Oregon and Washington drivers of favoritism by officials—the hometowner always seemed to get the break. These were trivial things, but the main problem was probably that the Oregon drivers won too many races. In 22 races held at Aurora in the 1949 season, Oregon drivers won 14 times. On the other hand, Washington drivers seldom won in Oregon. Late in 1949, the two groups were at war and refused to support each other's races.

In 1950, the Oregon roadsters were not as active as in previous years, but there were races at the Hollywood Bowl in Salem and on nasty dirty tracks at Tillamook and Lebanon. A new track had been built in the infield of the Portland Meadows horse racing facility and races were held on this half miler. There were no races at Portland Speedway—perhaps because of politics between the two Portland tracks, which were actually adjacent to each other. Typical of the non-cooperation with the Washington roadsters was the fact that this group held a roadster race at the

Jansen Beach midget track in Portland.

In 1951, peace was restored among the Pacific Northwest roadster racers and the Oregon cars could once again race at Aurora Stadium. Len Sutton won four of the seven races there and Ernie Koch another. At home there were seven races at Portland Speedway and four at Salem—Sutton won seven of these 11. The Merc in the Vollstead hot rod that Sutton drove had been replaced with a GMC with a 12-port Horning head.

By 1952, roadster racing was about finished in Oregon and only seven races were run. Sutton won five of these, but a Washington visitor, Shorty Templeman, normally a midget driver, hit the winners circle at Portland Speedway. There were only a few races in 1953.

The story of roadster racing in Oregon reads like it was a Len Sutton benefit; he won a lot of races. Len Sutton was a fine driver, and in the Pop Koch-built Rolla Vollstead roadsters he usually had the best car. Sutton thinks he won about 100 roadster main events—probably about 75 of these were in Oregon. There were some other very fine drivers racing hot rods in Oregon. Ernie Koch was one of the best and later drove the Vallstead Offy in Championship Car races. Other drivers who were winners were Bill Hyde, Palmer Crowell, Bob Gregg, Gordy Livingston, Max Humm, Darmon Moore and Mickey Shelton.

Another Oregon roadster name very much worthy of mention is that of Pat Vadan, who was the starter for the Roadster Racing Association of Oregon. Vadan's talents were obvious from the beginning, and he moved on to become the chief starter at Indianapolis for some 15 years.

The Oregon roadsters suffered only one fatality during the years of racing. This was in 1947 at Portland Speedway. This track was also a drive-in movie theater and had the screen at one end. Dan Weeks, driving under the name of Danny Freeman, ran off of the track and crashed into the bracing for the screen. He was killed instantly.

The Oregon roadster champions were:

1946 Frankie McGowen	1950 Frank Koch
1947 Frankie McGowen	1951 Len Sutton
1948 Len Sutton	1952 Len Sutton
1949 Mickey Shelton	1953 Ernie Koch

One of the cars that competed in the first roadster race at Portland Speedway. That's an early model (pre-1937) V8 engine, and it is not going to be competitive for very long. *(Jay Koch collection)*

License plate and all, this is one of the street rods that competed in early races at Portland Speedway. Driver is Bill Weimar who had some midget experience. *(Dick Martin collection)*

Bill Marcos drove the Hudson roadster at Portland in 1946-47. It looks heavy; it was probably not competitive. *(Jay Koch collection)*

Portland Speedway April 13, 1947. Driver Kuzie Kuzmanich (left) crashed that day when the right front hub broke. Kuzmanich suffered a broken arm. *(Dick Martin collection)*

Portland Speedway in 1947— this is probably a practice session. *(Gordy Sutherland collection)*

Left—The pits at Portland Speedway. Mechanics are working on car #5—apparently trying to repair crash damage. *(Dick Martin collection)*

Dick Stanley's T-V8 at Portland Speedway. Several of the Oregon cars used pickup beds rather than the roadster tail. *(Dick Martin collection)*

This is the George "Pop" Koch Lincoln Zephyr V-12 Model A in 1946. With Frankie McGowen driving, this car won the 1946 Oregon Roadster Racing Association championship. The car had no firewall! *(Dick Martin collection)*

Left—Frankie McGowen in the 1947 Koch car. The Lincoln V-12 is still in place, but it has a lighter '27 T body. The car had no clutch or flywheel so Koch was a bit ahead of his competitors. *(Jay Koch collection)*

Darmond Moore drove this T-V8 in Oregon races. Moore was a front runner. *(Jay Koch collection)*

Frankie McGowen owned this roadster, but he was usually busy driving for Pop Koch. It is not known who drove this car. *(Jay Koch collection)*

Portland Speedway—1947. Russ Gilbertson probably drove this car. *(Jay Koch collection)*

There is no data available on this low-slung four banger. Portland—1947. *(Jay Koch collection)*

Armand Mullens drove this T-pickup. It has four-spring suspension—maybe a Chevy? *(Jay Koch collection)*

Portland Speedway in 1947 and the California invaders have arrived. Jack McGrath's #1 is on the pole and Manual Ayulo's #44 just behind. The California racers ran one-two although Dick Martin's #14 was leading when a head gasket blew. *(Dick Martin collection)*

The next day the roadsters ran at the Oregon State Fairgrounds in Salem. Ayulo is on the pole with McGrath outside—the pair finished first and second. *(Dick Martin collection)*

Klamath Falls, July 15, 1947. Jimmy Martin flipped and wound up with his head between the car body and the ground. The Cromwell helmet did its job and Martin was OK. *(Dick Martin collection)*

Hollywood Bowl in Salem. The driver of #36 has abandoned his machine, and the race goes on. Max Humm is in #73. *(Jay Koch collection)*

Action at the Portland Meadows half-mile track in 1950. The grandstands of next-door neighbor Portland Speedway are in the background.
(Don Gilchrest collection)

Ernie Koch was one the best Oregon roadster racers. This is Portland Meadows in 1950.
(Jay Koch collection)

Portland Meadows in 1950. Bob Gregg in #9 battle with Ernie Koch. (Jay Koch collection)

The start of a heat race at Portland Meadows. Ernie Koch is on the pole. and Damon Moor is in #81. Starter Pat Vidan is in the background.
(Jay Koch collection)

This is probably Jansen Beach Speedway—the third track that operated in Portland. All were within a few miles of each other.
(Jay Koch collection)

This is one of George "Pop" Koch's roadsters. His brother, Ernie, drove it. (Jay Koch collection)

This is one of the first roadster races at Portland Speedway. Jimmy Martin is in #33 and Don Moore in #57. (Dick Martin collection)

Portland Speedway. No certain identification, but it may be Ernie Koch in #25. (Jay Koch collection)

The lineup for a main event at Portland Speedway. Car #5 is Bob Donker's ride. Pete Lovely was on the outside and #26 was driven by Max Humm. (Don Gilchrest collection)

Car owner, Don Walters, and driver, Max Humm, are all smiles in this photo. (Don Gilchrest collection)

In the center with #17 on his jacket is Len Sutton, a three-time Roadster Racing Association of Oregon champion. (Gordy Sutherland collection)

Bill Hyde clowns with starter Pat Vidan at a race someplace in Oregon. (Jay Koch collection)

Ernie Koch has won a big trophy. Possibly this is for his 1950 Roadster Racing Association of Oregon championship. (Jay Koch collection)

Gordy Livingston was one of the Oregon midget drivers who also ran the hot rods. (Gordy Sutherland collection)

Bob Gregg was fast in the roadsters, midgets, sprint cars and later on in the super-modifieds. (Gordy Sutherland collection)

CROSS DRESSING

By the end of the roadster era most track roadsters evolved to the point where they were basically sprint cars underneath that Model T today. Despite the similarity of the the two types of cars, there were a few areas where the sprints and roadsters ran in the same races.

As the numbers of hot rod races declined, some roadster owners converted their cars to sprinters. The main problem in this conversion was that, in general, the roadster frame was too wide to make a good sprint car. A sprint car body could be fashioned to fit the roadster

Len Sutton is at the wheel of the Vollstead Horning-GMC for a 100-mile race at the Portland Meadows one-mile track. Car builder Pop Kock is at the left, and Rolla Vollstead is leaning over talking to Sutton. (Don Radbruch photo)

Ray Hiatt's #6X is an example of a roadster that has been converted to a sprint car. An expert body man, Hiatt was able to build a very good-looking sprint car body for the roadster chassis. Hiatt built the car in about 1960, so he used a Chevy V8 engine instead of the faithful flathead. (Russell Hiatt photo)

frame, but unless a lot of care and expert craftsmanship was used the result could be one god-awful ugly sprint car.

The other way for a roadster racer to go sprint car racing required a few more dollars and a lot more work. This was to build a sprint car frame and body and use the roadster engine, running gear and miscellaneous other parts. If a roadster race was available, it was not big job to convert the sprint car to a roadster. The only major change was a different fuel tank. With a few nuts and bolts, quite a few of hose clamps and perhaps a bit of bailing wire the roadster body could be attached to the sprint car chassis. Presto—a track roadster!

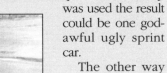

This is the same car with a roadster body on it. The back of the car looks a bit strange, but it is not a bad-looking track roadster. (Jay Koch collection)

Ed Elisian in the Hiatt sprint car during its roadster days. Johnny Obnesian built and owned the car, and it won a lot of roadster races from 1950 until 1953. Ed Elisian and Bob Veith were usually the drivers. (Ray Hiatt collection)

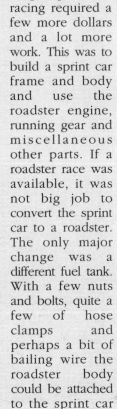

Ernie Koch in action at Jansen Beach—circa 1951.
(Jay Koch collection)

Trophy dash action before a good crowd at Jansen Beach. Ernie Koch is in #3, and Bob Gregg races in #12. *(Jay Koch collection)*

Ernie Koch journeyed north to a race at Silverlake Speedway near Everett, Washington, in 1951.

Roadster action at Portland Speedway in 1952 or 1953. Len Sutton leads in what is really a sprint car. Ernie Koch is in #1. *(Jay Koch collection)*

AN IDAHO MYSTERY

There may have been a few Idaho roadsters at a California Roadster Association race in Salt Lake City in about 1950. Former CRA president and driver, Walt James, thinks he remembers that a few Idaho drivers took part in the Salt Lake City race. Where these Idaho cars came from, and if they even raced in that state, is unknown.

The only documented information of roadster racing in Idaho comes from the unlikely location of Moscow, a college town in the northern part of the state. A report of roadster racing in the other Moscow would be only a little less believable. The races definitely did take place and were probably held in the late 1920s. As indicated in the photos the cars are quite well built and about as much a true race car as any roadster in that era.

These photos came from the Latah County Historical Society in Moscow. The information was quite positive that the races were at the Riverside Racetrack—only there is no river in Moscow. A possibility is that the track was near the Palouse River—a tiny stream some 10 miles from Moscow. Some very vague information did turn up indicating that there was once a race track in that area. From the photos the track does not look like the normal county fairgrounds horse track but, rather, more like a track constructed for auto racing.

The cars and drivers could be a bunch of touring "pros" who put on fake, or "hippodromed," races, but that would be a one-shot deal and held on any track available. Were a series of races held so that a special track was constructed? Were local cars and drivers competing there? Was this some of the earliest roadster racing in the country?

Nobody seems to know.

A driver stands by his car at the Riverside Racetrack in the late 1920s. Note that the roadster in the background has wooden wheels. The shape of this car's body looks a bit like a '26 Dodge. *(Latah County Historical Society collection)*

The field lines up for a standing start at Riverside Racetrack near Moscow, Idaho, in the late 1920s. Can anybody identify any of these cars? *(Latah County Historical Society collection)*

PENNSYLVANIA

There was roadster racing in Pennsylvania as early as 1940 when races were held at the Latimore Valley Fairgrounds south of Harrisburg. It is probable that these were the same "barrel hoop" cars similar to the ones that ran in neighboring Maryland—perhaps they were the same cars. These cars were stripped and primitive machines that used parts of farm equipment wheels as roll bars. Although it is known there were races, no information on the Latimore Valley events has been found.

After World War II, it is logical that there was roadster racing (of a sort) in a number of Pennsylvania towns. Thanks to John Way, there is information available on the races that were held at Zellers Grove near Myerstown. There were some of the pre-war "barrel hoop" cars competing, plus a mixture of many things—some of them actually roadsters. The promoter would allow just about anything to run—coupes, pickups, hot rods, sprint cars and, one day, even an old two-man racer showed up. This racing went on throughout 1946

and 1947 with moderate success and lots of arguments. In early 1948, the need for an organization to properly set up rules and car specifications was recognized. The roadsters were booming in other parts of the country, so that seemed the way to slant the organization. Car owners, Ray Madera and Dutch Heilman with the help of J. Earl Way, formed the Keystone Roadster Racing Association. The group was chartered on July 6, 1948, and it began sanctioning races at Zellers Grove a few weeks later.

The races were an immediate success and drew fine crowds to Zellers Grove. Keystone quickly expanded its operations to nearby Hilltop Speedway, to Sinking Springs Speedway some 30 miles to the the east, and later to Mahoney City. During the remainder of the 1948 season, Keystone kept busy with two to three races a week. Drivers like Bob Rolland, Vince Conrad, Charlie Felten-

(Unless otherwise noted all photos are from the Eastern Museum of Motor Racing and Ray Madera Collection.)

Williams Grove, 1948. Bob Flock is a visitor from Florida in #14. Flock's car sits high and was probably built from a NASCAR modified coupe. He finished fifth in the main that day.

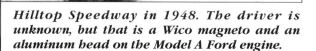

Zellers Grove in 1948. That's Toby Tobias on the pole. (Toby Tobias collection)

Hilltop Speedway in 1948. The driver is unknown, but that is a Wico magneto and an aluminum head on the Model A Ford engine.

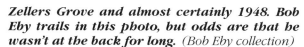

Zellers Grove and almost certainly 1948. Bob Eby trails in this photo, but odds are that he wasn't at the back for long. (Bob Eby collection)

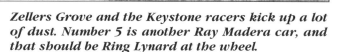

Ray Madera's #3. It is probably the same driver in all the photos of #3, and he's probably a top-ranked driver, but there is no identification available.

Zellers Grove and the Keystone racers kick up a lot of dust. Number 5 is another Ray Madera car, and that should be Ring Lynard at the wheel.

A fine action shot at Zellers Grove. Number 11 is probably Clarence Bear. Ring Lynard is on the outside in #5 and M. Reanachi pushes hard in #8.

Number 55 is a flathead Model A Ford. This is Zellers Grove in 1948, and there is no identification on the driver.

This is Hilltop Speedway. Vince Conrad kicks up some dust and Ring Lynard eats it in #5.

An unknown driver gets a trophy from Williams Grove promoter Roy Richwine.

A tangle at Williams Grove—circa 1949. Only Matt McKeon in #51 can be identified.

This looks like turn two at Zellers Grove. Vince Conrad is in #7.

burger, Ringy Lloyd and Red Dieter were race winners. Bob Eby won a lot of races, and he was the 1948 Keystone champion.

There had been roadster races at the famed Williams Grove oval during 1948. These races were under the sanction of the Eastern Roadster Association—primarily a Virginia group. (Eastern was formed in 1947 and may have raced in Pennsylvania in that year.) Roy Richwine was the promoter at Williams Grove and he scheduled a "National Roadster Championship" race for October 12, 1948. This race, for a $2,500 purse attracted an excellent field of 56 hot rods. Drivers came from as far as Minnesota, and the starting lineup included Dick Frazier, Willy Sternquist, Bob James, Paul Hooper and Ronnie Cash. Dick Frazier out qualified the field by nearly three seconds, won a head race and the semi-final. In the 50-lap main Frazier had problems, and Willy Sternquist was the winner over Dick Jorden and Steve Lesick.

In 1949, most of the roadster racing in Pennsylvania was under the Keystone banner although Eastern did hold spot races at Williams Grove. The two groups must have cooperated, as the Keystone drivers did race with Eastern at Williams Grove. Keystone, for the most part, confined its activities to Zellers Grove, Hilltop and Sinking Springs. The purses ran between $500 and $1,000—probably more near the latter figure. Bob Eby continued to win and racked up eight straight feature wins at Zellers Grove. He remembers the payoffs as being between $40 and $50 a race.

Since the first "National Roadster Championship" had been a success, Roy Richwine set another for Williams Grove on October 30, 1949. Once again the race attracted a stellar field of roadsters. Although Dick Frazier drove roadsters only a few times in 1949, he was back at Williams Grove with his famous #32. He was the class of the field, but had problems in the feature after leading for 29 laps. Indiana driver Smokey Stover in the Joe Walls Hudson won the 50 lapper. Ohio's Bob James was second and Eastern regular Carl Anderson third. Only nine of the 20 starters finished the race. The track was very loose and mud clogged radiators, causing cars to overheat.

In 1950, not too many roadster races were held in Pennsylvania as the stock cars were taking over. Keystone must have raced someplace but their regular track, Zellers Grove, was now under Eastern Roadster Association sanction. There was a roadster race at Williams Grove on June 5, and Charlie Feltenburger was the winner over Matt McKeon and Bob James. There was no "National Roadster

Zellers Grove in 1948. The Ray Madera-owned #3 looks like a street rod, but it ran fast on the track.

Bob Rolland is on the pole at Zellers Grove. That's a Ray Madera V8 on the outside, but its driver is unknown. (Bob Eby collection)

Early Keystone roadster action. That's Bob "Leadfoot" Eby in #710, and #3 is a Ray Madera car with an unknown driver at the wheel. Note that these cars have a stock wishbone setup.

The Keystone Roadster Racing Association cars line up for a heat race at Zellers Grove.

Carl Anderson gets his Williams Grove trophy from Eastern Roadster Association boss Doc Benson. (Lou Ensworth collection)

Crowded racing at Zellers Grove. Note that most of the cars use "barrel hoop" roll bars. These were made from the steel wheels of various types of farm equipment.

Bob Rolland and Williams Grove—circa 1949. The body looks like it has been cut down from a Model T coupe.

It's #711 again at Williams Grove. Another paint job, a few changes and a new (and unknown) driver.

Pat Patterson qualifies at Hilltop in 1949. (John Way collection)

Championship" race at Williams Grove that fall. Perhaps promoter Roy Richwine didn't like only nine finishers the previous year—perhaps it was the stock car invasion.

In 1951, there were only a few Pennsylvania roadster races. Wally Gore won a Zellers Grove race on March 25, but despite support from both Keystone and Eastern there were only 13 cars on hand. A *National Speed Sport News* columnist wrote that a roadster race was scheduled at Williams Grove for April 15, 1951, but the track's advertised schedule listed no such event. Another *NSSN* article mentioned an Eastern Roadster Association race to be held at Williams Grove on April 24, 1951. If any hot rod race was held at Williams Grove that April the results have been lost. Roadster racing was about finished in Pennsylvania.

A group of Keystone members pose for the cameraman in 1949. Top row—left to right. Mr. Leaman, owner of Hilltop Speedway, promoter Red Marshall, J. Earl Way and Loring Emory. In front, John Way is at right with Loring Emory Jr. John Way is now a racing historian and helped a lot with this chapter. (John Way collection)

The bulk of Pennsylvania roadster racing was sanctioned by Keystone and Eastern, but there were two other groups. Lynn Paxton of the Williams Grove Oldtimers remembers roadster organizations called "Southern Tier" and "National Auto Racing." Somebody out there must remember the "where, when and who" of these groups.

There were two known fatalities in Pennsylvania roadster racing. Red Deiter died at Williams Grove, and Mel Kieister lost his life at Hilltop Speedway.

Wally Gore at Williams Grove in about 1949. This car is still in existence.

This is Hilltop Speedway. Toby Tobias is in #27, #710 is Bob Eby and Art Ellison is in #91. A trio of top Keystone drivers. (*John Way collection*)

Pat Patterson warms up his #7 Model A Ford flathead at Zellers Grove. (*John Way collection*)

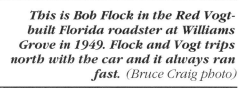

This is Bob Flock in the Red Vogt-built Florida roadster at Williams Grove in 1949. Flock and Vogt trips north with the car and it always ran fast. (*Bruce Craig photo*)

Mel Weidener smiles from his flathead Model A Ford. This could be one of the early "barrel hoop" cars—if so, it is one of the better-built ones. (*John Way collection*)

Bob Eby and Vince Conrad in #7 battle at Zellers Grove. Eby has left some of the spokes in his "barrel hoop" type roll bar. (*John Way collection*)

Pat Patterson has the pole as Toby Tobias tries to get around the outside. Note that the crowd is right against the Zellers Grove fence. (*Toby Tobias collection*)

Ray Maderas, the president of Keystone, fielded two nice-looking '32 Ford V8s. Here they battle against each other at Hilltop Speedway.

Sam Brubaker qualifies #22 at Hilltop Speedway in 1949. (*John Way collection*)

Zellers Grove in 1948. No identification on the drivers. The car at the rear is a "barrel hoop" car, and it may have raced as early as 1940. (*Bob Eby collection*)

Someplace in Pennsylvania—who, where and when? (Larry Jendras Jr. collection)

Action at Williams Grove in 1948. There is no identification on these Eastern Roadster Association drivers.

A car winds up in the weeds outside of Hilltop Speedway. The driver's fate is unknown.

A RARE ROADSTER

There are many now rare cars that were chopped up to build track roadsters. Toby Tobias' #127 was scarce when he built the car in 1948. It is a 1932 Ford Convertible—less than 500 of these gems were ever built. It differs from the common '32 Ford Roadster in that it had a more substantial top and windows that rolled up and down. There was certainly no advantage to using the convertible as a track hot rod. It was heavier than the roadster model, and the rather large area where the top folded down gave the car an ungainly look. Tobias remembers only that it was "available." He doesn't even want to think about how much the car would be worth today.

To anybody who has been around racing for 40 or so years, it would seem that there have been more Tobias' driving race cars than were 1932 Ford Convertibles. It also seems that many of the Tobias racers wind up nicknamed "Toby." The Tobias in #127 is the Original Toby Tobias.

In the dust at Zellers Grove, Bob Eby is in #710. The driver of the car on the outside sits way up high in what is probably an early 1940s "barrel hoop" car.

Keystone drivers Red Dieter (left) and Charlie Feltenburger are a bit dirty after a race at Zellers Grove. Dieter raced sprint cars and perhaps roadsters before World War II. He died in a roadster crash at Williams Grove. (John Way collection)

This is Carl Anderson at Hilltop Speedway. Anderson usually raced with the Eastern Roadster Association and must be just visiting at this Keystone race.

A big tangle Hilltop Speedway as the cars come out of turn four involves Vince Conrad in #7. (Toby Tobias collection)

Hilltop in 1948, and the cars line up for the feature race. Spectator protection is minimal. (John Way collection)

*Another tangle at Hilltop. That's Bick Bickleman in #36, Ring Lynard in #5, and Vince Conrad is about to pile into the mess in #7. **(Toby Tobias** collection)*

A bad crash at Hilltop Speedway as two cars head over the fence. Neither driver can be identified.

This is Hilltop Speedway in 1949 or 1950, and Charlie Feltenburger is driving #711. (John Way collection)

SOUTH DAKOTA

S outh Dakota roadster racing was the outgrowth of a street hot rod club formed in Huron in 1947. The club was first called the Century Club because the members had driven at 100mph on the highway—no mean feat on the narrow two-lane roads of that period. The club soon changed its name to "The Snails." (Perhaps better for the public image, but a strange name for a hot rod group.) There was no actual roadster racing group formed in South Dakota. All track racing was under the loose organization of The Snails with local service clubs sponsoring the races.

Racing began at Huron on the state fairground's half-mile track in 1948. A field of 10 roadsters competed, and it is believed that Bob Osmanson won the 15-lap main event over Merlin Twogood.

Roadster racing continued for the next several years at various South Dakota cities. Races were held at Huron, Glenwood, Mitchell, Gettysburg, Aberdeen, Sioux Falls, Winner and several other locations. It appears that the South Dakota racers pretty well kept to themselves and that the normal car counts

(Unless otherwise noted all photos are by Frank Hughes—Jim Johannson Collection.)

Forrest Hurd cranks out a fast lap at Winner in 1950. The 11.8:1 compression ratio was too much for the Merc, and it is about to let Hurd know this.

Forrest Hurd bails out of his Merc as it blows at Winner. Note how far back in the chassis the Merc is placed—a bit too far back by normal track roadster standards.

Forrest Hurd now has a flathead Ford Six in his car and performance was greatly improved over the Merc. Hurd still uses propane fuel. This is Huron, and Hurd won the 50-lap main event that day.

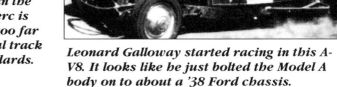

Leonard Galloway started racing in this A-V8. It looks like he just bolted the Model A body on to about a '38 Ford chassis.

Huron—circa 1950. Pappy Woods in a Fronty big car that he converted to a track roadster. The car was built in 1929 by Kenneth "Cementhead" Larson. It had a Star frame and a T rear end with Studebaker axles. Note the knock-off hubs.

Lyle Newland put the Glenn Johnson V8 into a haystack in this crash at Mitchell in 1950. Better the haystack than the barbed wire fence in the background.

were 10 to 12 roadsters. An exception was a race at Sioux Falls on Labor Day of 1949, when visiting Minnesota and Iowa cars swelled the car count to near 30.

The available records are far from complete but Forrest Hurd, Wally Warner and Bob Osmanson were consistent winners. By 1949, Hurd was running a car that would have been competitive anywhere. Along with his brother, Jack, and Jim Johannson, Hurd built the car from the ground up. He used a Merc with all the latest speed equipment and a Halibrand quick change rear end. Hurd was a farmer and it seemed to him that propane worked better in farm equipment than gasoline so he decided to try this in the race car. An engineer at the Huron propane company convinced Hurd that a compression ratio of 11.8:1 was the way to go. (Hurd learned a few years later that 10.5:1 would have worked much better.) The Merc tolerated the high compression ratio for awhile and ran fast, but it exploded in a cloud of steam during a race at Winner. Forrest Hurd replaced the Merc with a Ford Six flathead and with this motor won most of his races.

A car and driver combination that attracted a lot of fan support was Merritt "Pappy" Wood and his Fronty T. Wood had been a dirt track racer in the 1920s and he converted a Fronty race car to run with the youngsters. Wood was 65 at the time, but he held his own against the modern and bigger hot rod engines. The Fronty T had a throaty roar that sounded like an Offy—the fans loved it!

The purses for the South Dakota roadster races ranged from excellent to very bad. For the most part purses were based on a percentage of the gate receipts. Forrest Hurd remembers running at some South Dakota town for a total purse of $10. On the other hand, the roadster did run at Huron a couple times a year and the purses, with community backing, were excellent—tops was $1,600. On July 4, 1950, Wally Warner did OK at Huron with a second in the trophy dash, a heat race win and another victory in the main event. Driving the Woonsocket Super Service sponsored Merc, Warner took home $360. The payoff was heavy towards the front, drivers finishing worse than fourth in the main got nothing.

All the South Dakota roadster races were on half-mile county fairgrounds horse tracks. Given these racing conditions the safety record was not too bad, but the deaths of two Huron drivers in separate accidents hit that small community very hard. Roger Bolte died at Huron during time trials when the throttle apparently stuck open and he went through

While hardly a roadster, this Model T with Merrett "Pappy" Woods at the wheel won a 100-lap old car race at Huron on July 4, 1947. When roadster racing started the next year, Woods was one of the drivers.

Hot rodders prepare for a race at Glenwood Park in Mitchell. Car #1 in the foreground was driven to a number of South Dakota wins by Wally Warner.

This is the pits at Huron in 1950. The Pappy Woods Fronty T is at the left and #4 is the Leonard Galloway V8.

Wally Warner is shown on this 1950 poster for a South Dakota roadster race.
(Elaine Walker collection)

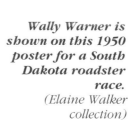

HOT-ROD RACES

10 EXCITING TIME EVENTS!

2 p. m. Sunday, Sept. 10
Mobridge Rodeo Grounds
MOBRIDGE, SOUTH DAKOTA
Adm.: Adults, $1.25; Children Under 12, 50c, Tax Incl.

the board fence sideways. At Sioux Falls Richard Barnes rolled off the track and suffered fatal injuries. The South Dakota racers also had some good luck. At Mobridge, a car flipped a half dozen times, sailed through a chain link fence and the driver emerged with only a broken tooth.

Roadster racing in South Dakota ended during the 1952 season.

This is Ronnie Bushoff's car after he and Leonard Galloway crashed at Winner. The roll bar design leaves something to be desired and this may have contributed to Bushoff's shoulder injuries.

Leonard Galloway in a T-V8 at the Tripp County Fairgrounds in Winner. It appears there are two radiators soldered together in an attempt to cool the V8.

Warmups at Huron. Bob Osmanson is on the pole, Forrest Hurd in #4, Ronnie Bushoff in #12 and Pappy Woods in #9.

The crew of #2 prepares for action at a South Dakota track in 1950. Jim Johannson stands in the car that he and Forrest Hurd built.

Gettysburg, South Dakota—circa 1949. Number 7 is Ed Stahl in a Model A flathead. Check that crashwall!

The location is unknown, but it is probably 1949. Forrest Hurd in his first track roadster. Hurd soon built another lighter and faster car.

Forrest Hurd in action—circa 1949. Richard Barnes was killed in this car at Sioux Falls in 1950.

Pappy Woods and his Fronty T in action at Gettysburg, South Dakota. While not a winner, the 65-year-old Woods was competitive and a crowd pleaser.

Leonard Galloway and Ronnie Bishoff crashed at Winner in 1950. Both suffered severe shoulder injuries. Note the bent roll bar on Galloway's #4.

THE STORY OF THE
BIJOU HILLS BOBTAIL

It was common for roadster racers to use parts, such as Model T bodies and Franklin steering gears, from cars built in the 1920s, but to build a hot rod from a 1920s bobtail race car was unusual.

From historian Jim Johannson in Huron, South Dakota comes this tale of how the "Bijou Hills Bobtail" became a track roadster.

The car was originally built in the early 1920s by A.J. Gephart of Bijou Hills, South Dakota—a tiny hamlet that no longer exists. The bobtail design was common in those days as builders saw no reason to bother to build a tail to enclose the fuel tank. For power Gephart used a four-cylinder Dodge engine with Morton and Brett speed equipment—a setup competitive with the Fords and

It is 1950 and a few modifications have been made to the Bijou Hills Bobtail. The frame rails are the same, the Model T rear end is still in place and that radiator shell looks like it came from 1925. (Hughes-Johannsen collection)

Pete Berens in action at Glenwood Park in Mitchell, South Dakota, in 1950. Lyle Hopper climbs over a wheel of Berens' Buick-powered roadster. (Hughes-Johannsen collection)

Chevys of the era. A.J. Gephart successfully campaigned the car on South Dakota dirt tracks for many years—the car became well known as the "Bijou Hills Bobtail." Just when the car's racing days ended (the first time) is not known, but odds are it was outclassed by about 1935.

The car sat outside in the harsh South Dakota climate until 1949 when three Huron men bought it from Gephart. The new owners made some modifications to convert the car to a track roadster, but many of the old "Bijou Hills Bobtail" parts were used. These included the Ruckstell (two speed) Model T Ford rear end. They even got the Morton and Brett-Dodge running and raced with this engine until it swallowed a valve and destroyed itself. Pete Berens had been driving the car and, as is obvious from the photos, Pete was a big man. Perhaps this influenced the owners thinking when they replaced the little Dodge with a big engine—a 320-cubic-inch 1941 Buick Straight Eight!

It seems impossible that the ancient frame and that Model T Ford rear end could handle the weight and power of the big Buick, but it did. It also handled Pete Berens' 275 pounds. Although it was not a winner, the updated "Bijou Hills Bobtail" ran well on the South Dakota roadster circuit.

A.J. Gephart is the driver of the Bijou Hills Bobtail at the Ruskin Park track—circa 1925. This South Dakota car used a four-cylinder Dodge with a Morton and Brett overhead valve conversion. (Hughes-Johannsen collection)

This is Frank Osmanson in his Cragar-powered hot rod. The body is obviously home-made.

Merlin Twogood at the Tripp County Fairgrounds in Winner. The Clayton Carter owned V8 has a strange-looking intake manifold.

Bill Aker came up from Rock Rapids, Iowa, to race at the Tripp County Fairgrounds. Aker used two radiators but it's a safe bet the V8 still overheated.

Someplace in South Dakota— circa 1950. Merlin Twogood in #5 and either Clayton Carter or Lyle Hooper in #11.

Glenwood Park in Mitchell. This is Lyle Hooper in his Merc.

Frank Osmanson at Winner in about 1951. The engine is a Cragar Model B Ford.

Merlin Twogood at Glenwood Park. The pipe on the ground in the background is part of the track sprinkler system—it didn't work very well.

TEXAS

• •

Roadster racing in Texas began in the late 1920s, and by the early '30s races were held on an intermittent basis in a number of Texas cities. Races were held in San Antonio, Houston, Dallas, Corpus Christi, Austin, El Paso and several other Texas towns. There was no actual roadster organization formed, but a dozen or so cars and drivers traveled this very long circuit.

Races were held on the familiar half-mile county fairgrounds track and on a track in Houston that measured one and a half miles. The races were usually billed as "Modified Stock Car Races," but were open to only roadsters. There were no engine restrictions. Racer Lee Wick remembers that, "They never lifted the hood. We could do anything we wanted." Wick had a '31 Model A roadster and used a Riley Rockerarm head but had a lot of head gasket problems and finally settled on a Cragar Overhead Valve engine. This engine would have been very competitive in most big car races. Wick won regularly on the roadster circuit.

San Antonio in 1932. The $50 Lee Wick won in the "Sweepstakes" was more than a month's salary for the average working man. (Lee Wick collection)

Beesville in 1931. Jim Davis is on the pole, Matt Ward in the center and Cotten Grable on the outside. (Lee Wick collection)

While Lee Wick had success with the modified Ford engine, other Texas racers used a variety of engine makes. Following is the entry list for a July 1, 1933, race at Exposition Speedway in San Antonio:

Driver	Residence	Car	#
Lee Wick	Victoria, TX	Ford A	#77
Grady Sexton	San Antonio, TX	Chevy Six	#44
Henry Seiler	Kenedy, TX	Willys Six	#11
Benny Sagle	Karnes City, TX	Chevy Six	#31
Luther Day	San Antonio, TX	Chevy Four	#10
Jimmie Davis	San Antonio, TX	Ford A	#7
Fred Ruth	San Antonio, TX	Chevy Six	#27
Earl Allen	San Antonio, TX	Chevy Six	#22
Eddie Boyle	Seguin, TX	Chevy Six	—
Eddie Byers	Austin, TX	Ford A	—
Truman Brooks	Austin, TX	Ford A	—
Henry Meider	Pittsburgh, PA	Terraplane	#0

RACES
Exposition Speedway

Cash **$250.00** Purse

FIRST EVENT
Time Trials — 2:30 P. M. — All Cars — 1 Lap
SECOND EVENT
Class "A". Six Fastest Cars. 15 Laps
First Place $31.25
Second Place 18.75
Third Place 12.50
THIRD EVENT
Class "B". Next Six Fastest Cars. 15 Laps
First Place $18.75
Second Place 11.25
Third Place 7.50
FOURTH EVENT
Consolation Race. Non-Winners, A and B. 10 Laps
First Place $12.50
Second Place 7.50
Third Place 5.00
FIFTH EVENT
Sweepstakes. 30 Laps
First Place $50.00
Second Place 37.50

B.C. Ryan gets a thrill at Pan American Speedway in San Antonio. Henry Majors is in Don Braggs #11 V8. Ryan's car is Ardun-powered— unusual for a track roadster. (Wade Bedell collection)

Lee Flowers and passenger go sailing over a hill at Devil's Bowl in 1946. Flowers drove track roadsters and later was a midget champion in the Kansas City area. (Don Fowler collection)

The purse that day was a guaranteed $250—perhaps the first guaranteed purse for the roadsters anyplace. Lee Wick, with the Cragar Model A Ford, had fast time, took second in a heat race and won the feature event. Wick won $88.75 that day—big money in 1933. Probably less than 10 percent of the later roadster racers ever won this much money in one race.

There is a gap in Texas roadster racing as Lee Wick, who supplied most of the information on early racing, quit competing in 1933. There is little doubt that roadster racing continued until it was interrupted by World War II in 1941.

The first post-war roadster racing in Texas was at Devil's Bowl in San Antonio where off-road races were held in 1946. The Texans called this "Gravel Pit" racing, and that's exactly what Devil's Bowl looked like. Around the same time, another San Antonio track called Spillway was operating, and it is here that post-war Texas track roadster racing probably began. Spillway was kind of a primitive

B.C. Ryan—circa 1950. A nice-looking roadster. (Wade Bedell collection)

Grady Sexton drove the #44 Chevy in Texas roadster races. It had the late model six-cylinder engine. (Lee Wick collection)

This is a match race between Grady Sexton in #44 and Luther Day in #10. Location is unknown. (Lee Wick collection)

Devil's Bowl—circa 1946. Some very primitive cars raced here. (Don Fowler collection)

Action at Devil's Bowl in about 1946. (Don Fowler collection)

Lee Wick in about 1932. The roadster was obviously driven to the race track and sports a license plate, lights and even a horn! (Lee Wick collection)

place, and apparently, so were the roadsters—they were more like jalopies, and some had 300 pounds of angle iron and pipe as bumpers. Wade Bedell remembers one night West Coast racer, Ken Stansberry, showed up with a lightweight Southern California car and blew everybody off. Out came the cutting torches, off came a lot of iron and real roadster racing began in Texas. The transformation was probably in 1947.

It is documented in *Hot Rod Magazine* by Pauline Bayer that the Texas Roadster Racing Association was formed in early 1948. Several other roadster groups would spring up, but the TRRA was the dominant organization. At about this same time, Pan American Speedway was built in San Antonio, and this became the home track for the Texas hot rod racers. For the next couple of years, roadster races were held on a fairly regular basis in San Antonio, Austin, Loredo, Corpus Christi, San Angelo, Houston and rarely in Dallas. For a short period, there was a roadster circuit that required towing some 1,140 miles per week. The purses at Pan American Speedway were the highest with about $2,500 being tops, but most purses were much lower. Wade Bedell won a lot of races and thinks about $50 to win the main was average. B.C. Ryan was also a winner and recalls winning more than the $50 and also a lot less.

In Texas, the roadsters lasted until about 1951. The Texas Roadster Racing Association crowned champions in at least three seasons. B.C. Ryan won two championships, and Henry Majors in the Don Bragg V8 won in 1950. Some of the other top drivers were Harry Elbel, Wade Bedell, George Carrvel and A.M. Farris. Future Indy drivers, Jud Larson and Jimmy Reece both started racing in the Texas roadsters but rather quickly switched to the midgets.

Details on possible fatalities in Texas roadster racing are rather sketchy. Lee Wick is certain that there were no fatal wrecks in the early 1930s. During the period from 1946 to about 1951, there were probably two fatalities. A driver died of a broken neck at Alamo Downs and another at Austin, where a stuck throttle resulted in an end-over-end crash. It is sad that the names of these men who gave their lives to Texas roadster racing have been forgotten.

A LOUISIANA MYSTERY

The only available information on Louisiana roadster racing comes from a short article that appeared in *National Speed Sport News* late in 1951. This reports the death of Bob Hammuller during a hot rod race at the Louisiana State Fairgrounds in Shreveport on October 30, 1951.

October 30 is around the normal date of the state fair in Louisiana, and for years, these fair dates were the private property of the IMCA sprint cars. It is unlikely that the then mighty IMCA would take kindly to hot rods racing during the fair. Where did the roadsters come from? There were no organized track roadster groups within 500 miles of Shreveport. Perhaps the cars and drivers came from San Antonio, but none of the Texas racers remember a Louisiana race. Attempts to find out more about this race from the Louisiana State Fair, the *Shreveport Times* and individuals turned up nothing.

Seemingly there were no roadsters available, and the IMCA wouldn't have let them race if there were. Yet the race took place, and Bob Hammuller died. Was it perhaps some sort of exhibition race for street roadsters? Or maybe the term "hot rod" was misused and it was really some sort of modified stock car race?

Note: *Another issue of* National Speed Sport News *reports the driver's name as Bob Hamilton.*

The date and place this car raced is uncertain Wade Bedell (center) became a top-ranked roadster and midget driver. (Don Fowler collection)

Chief Swinford drove this neat-looking '32 V8 in Texas roadster races. (Wade Bedell collection)

Right—The Texas roadster racers got good publicity in the sports section of a San Antonio newspaper. (Lee Wick collection)

Above—The date and location of this Texas roadster race is uncertain. The best guess is Alamo Downs in the late 1930s. (Don Fowler collection)

Dusty! Are there more than two cars in this race? (Don Fowler collection)

No identification available on these drivers. Since it is probably a hot day in Texas, the driver of the lead car has a practical sponsor. (Don Fowler collection)

Devil's Bowl near San Antonio in 1946. This was off-road or "gravel pit" racing. (Don Fowler collection)

Fred Elbel in #8 crowds Charles Ferrell at Pan American Speedway in this 1948 action. B.C. Ryan stays up high and out of trouble. (Charles McQueen collection)

Lee Wick's note on this pit pass indicates that he did not have a good day at Houston. Despite the lack of a seat belt and a helmet Wick had only minor injuries.

(Lee Wick collection)

Mid-1960s at Austin. Bud Jenkins in the Don Bragg car that raced as a roadster around 1950. The flathead V8 has been replaced by a Chevy V8. (Charles McQueen collection)

The Graphite Oil Company sponsored the races at San Antonio's Exposition Speedway in 1933. They put out an eight-page newspaper for publicity. (Lee Wick collection)

Lee Wick in his rather innocent looking '31 Model A. The car housed a full race Cragar Overhead Valve engine. It would fly! *(Lee Wick collection)*

Left—Luther Day drove this car powered with a four-cylinder Chevy. We can assume it had a three-port Oldsmobile head commonly used to hop up the Chevies. *(Lee Wick collection)*

This could be Alamo Downs in about 1931. Looks like the race is in a ballpark, and the protection for spectators is minimal. *(Don Fowler collection)*

Kenedy, Texas, in 1931. There was a "Powder Puff," race and this determined-looking young lady is in a Willys roadster. *(Lee Wick collection)*

Action at Pan American Speedway in about 1950. Henry Majors is in #11. This car raced as a super-modified until the mid-1960s. *(Wade Bedell collection)*

A MEXICAN ROAD RACE

Almost lost to history is the story of a road race in Mexico in the early 1930s. This was an open race from Loredo, Texas, to Monterrey, Mexico. It was a distance of 140 miles, and one can only imagine what the road was like way back then. The first Loredo-Monterrey race was held in 1931, and Hal Tice was the winner in a Ford roadster. In 1932, Tice won again, and for his second victory was presented with the President of Mexico Gold Cup. Unfortunately, Tice was killed on his way home from Monterrey when his racer crashed into a truck.

In 1933, a purse of $3,000 was posted for the race. Although part of the purse was slated for a motorcycle division, a half-dozen Texas roadster racers planned to enter the event. Lee Wick was among these drivers, and, with his Cragar-powered roadster, Wick had to be one of the favorites. Unfortunately Wick's hopes for a big payoff were dashed a few days before the race when the Rio Grande flooded and all access to Mexico was blocked. Wick and his fellow racers were trapped in a Loredo hotel for a week waiting for the floodwaters to subside. The race was cancelled, some of the racers had to sneak out of the hotel without paying their bills, and a report Lee Wick would have made on the race is missing from *Roaring Roadsters*.

Eddie Callahan drove the Ray McCall V8 at Shadowland Speedway in San Antonio— circa 1948. *(Charles McQueen collection)*

Exposition Speedway, San Antonio in 1933. Looks like a dusty mile track . *(Lee Wick collection)*

Harry Elbel was one of the best Texas roadster drivers. Here he is at Devil's Bowl (or possibly Spillway) in one of his early cars. *(Charles McQueen collection)*

VIRGINIA &

○ ●

R oadster racing in this area probably started around 1939. The early cars were barely "roadsters" as most of them were stripped until only the cowl of the body remained. They were no doubt billed as "jalopies," but engine modifications appear to have been allowed. Some of the cars used the "barrel hoop" roll bars made from farm equipment wheels. As was common for that period, no actual organization was formed and the races were held on an intermittent basis with small fields. Racing is known to have taken place in Winchester, Virginia, and Cumberland, Maryland, and it is almost certain there was racing in other cities. Available information is sparse.

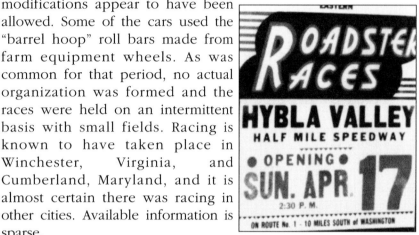

There is not much more information available on roadster racing in this area after World War II. The group of drivers that ran at Winchester resumed racing in 1946 with many of the same cars. It is probable that in 1947 there was an influx of new drivers, owners and later model engines and that races were held at tracks other than Winchester. Racing became more organized in 1948 when the Eastern Racing Association was

This poster advertises the opening of Hybla Valley Speedway. The race drew a reported 10,000 fans.

formed. The group, under the able leadership of Doc Benson, sanctioned most of the roadster races in Virginia, Maryland and Delaware for the next several years. The ERA raced at places like Winchester, Dover, Delaware, and Tappanhannok, Virginia. They also cooperated with the Pennsylvania-based Keystone group and raced at Williams Grove.

In 1949, Hybla Valley Speedway was built a few miles south of Washington, D.C. and the Eastern Racing Association roadsters were the opening show. This race, on April 17, 1949, drew a reported 10,000 fans and paid a purse of $1,700. Ronnie Cash won the main event and collected about $300. Eastern may have had other races in between, but they raced at Hybla Valley about once a month for the first part of the 1949 season. Bob James came down from Ohio to win one race, and on June 5, 1949, Shorty Bowers won the main event. It was in this race that the popular Ronnie Cash was killed when he tangled with Doug Bailey and flipped several times. A benefit race for Ronnie Cash was held at Hybla Valley on June 26, 1949. Dick Frazier, who came over from Indiana to help draw a crowd, knocked two seconds off the track record while

MARYLAND

qualifying and then won the main event. Eastern's schedule later that summer included acting as the sanctioning body at Williams Grove, Pennsylvania, for the "National Championship Roadster Races."

For the next couple of years, Eastern did not race very often, either that or pieces of history are missing. Most likely the latter, as Doc Benson was a very energetic business manager, had a good field of cars and drivers available, and almost certainly scheduled races someplace. It is known that races were held at Manassa, Virginia, and Pomonkey, Maryland, during this period. By 1952, roadster racing, so far as the Eastern Racing Association was concerned, was finished. The Mutual Racing Association came from Indiana to race at Manassa that year, and in 1953, it was mixed sprints and roadsters at Manassa.

The top Eastern Racing Association drivers, other than those previously mentioned were Carl Anderson, Joe Jerigen, Bob Whitbeck, Wally Gore and Chuck Feltenburger. Carl Anderson was the ERA champion in 1949, but who won in the other years is not known.

Ronnie Cash was the only known Eastern Racing Association fatality.

These ads for roadster races are probably from **National Speed Sport News.** *Note that in the 1950 ad from Mason-Dixon Speedway the stock cars are already pushing out the roadsters.* (Larry Jendras Jr. collection)

Hybla Valley Speedway hoped to attract large crowds from the Washington, D.C. area, but other than the first few races, failed to do so. (Larry Jendras Jr. collection)

Ken Cather leads the field at Winchester in 1946. The cars behind this trio are probably lost in the dust. (Frank Scheder collection)

Winchester in 1939, and this is Jack Boydon. Even though the car lacks a body it does have kick off bars. The roll bar leaves a bit to be desired. (John Jackson collection)

All of these photos were taken at Cumberland, Maryland, in 1939. Unfortunately, no driver identification is available. As is evident from the photos some of the cars have full roadster bodies while others are stripped to almost nothing. Apparently, the rules were rather open. It does look like some of the Model A Fords have non-stock down draft carburetors, so engine modifications must have been allowed. There are no Ford V8 engines. The cost of these late model engines may have been a factor, but the rules of groups like the Cumberland racers often barred engines made after 1931. Ford did not put out the V8 engine until 1932, so this rule kept out these potential engines.

(Larry Jendras Jr. collection)

ABOUT ROADSTER RACING IN THE 1940S

In the mid- to late 1940s, right after World War II when auto racing was bouncing back in several forms, Doc Benson, a skilled cabinetmaker and carpenter in Arlington, Virginia, and the Washington, D.C., area, was working hard to organize and create a racing circuit for roadster race cars ... "poor man's racing," it was nicknamed.

The Eastern Roaring Roadster Association ran some good races on some of the short tracks in Virginia and Maryland areas and even trekked into West Virginia. I did what I could to assist with some articles in *Speed Age* magazine, but Doc couldn't quite convince the major promoters such as Roy Richwine at Williams Grove, Pennsylvania, and Sam Nunis, who had races from New Jersey State Fairgrounds to Delaware and through the central East Coast and the South.

Like so many folks in the sport, Jimmy Quisenberry and I decided to have a fling at race promotion, just as a hobby, to try and prove we could do it, too.

We booked the AAA Contest Board Midgets into the Staunton, Virginia, fairgrounds, a short dirt track, on Fourth of July afternoon and into the Schrader Field dirt track at Lynchburg, Virginia, some 80 miles south of Staunton, but on the other side of the Blue Ridge Mountains, for that evening.

We arranged for a State Police, sheriff and local police escort for all the race cars and crews from Staunton to Lynchburg, and it was agreed that we would pay off the prize money for both races at Lynchburg.

There was a huge crowd at Staunton and some good midget racing. Jimmy and I collected our money from the fairgrounds' ticket takers and upwards of a hundred racers, mechanics, officials and fans hit the highways over the mountains to Lynchburg.

A county official and business man had built Schrader Field as a place for the locals to enjoy all kinds of sports. Entertain the folks and keep their votes for the next election.

Because we couldn't be in both Staunton and Lynchburg at the same time, we had arranged with the local Lion's Club to sell the tickets and collect the money, for a club fundraising commission.

The weather was great, there were 3,000 or more in the stands, the racing was good. Boy, we made money in Staunton and this looks great!

Midway through the race program Jimmy and I went to the office to collect our money, and the Lion's president handed us a couple hundred dollars and change.

"How come? There are about 3,000 folks in the stands."

"Oh, didn't you know? When Mr. Schrader built this place he gave almost everyone in the county lifetime passes."

Between the Staunton gate receipts and the *Speed Age* company check book every racing team received all their money for both races as AAA decreed, and all went home happy. Our fling at trace promotion had cost us (*Speed Age*) a bundle.

We couldn't give up losers: one more time. A Saturday afternoon AAA midget race at the Richmond, Virginia, fairgrounds, a beautiful half-mile dirt, called Strawberry Hill.

We were rained out! We had a rain date paid for, but the midgets were booked elsewhere.

What to do? Doc Benson suggested, "Let me bring the Roadsters next Saturday."

"Okay, wonderful. Thanks!"

Just to add to the show, we arranged for a midget to come up from Norfolk, Virginia, for a match race, for show. The fans knew it was not real. The only problem was, the midget engine actually conked out on the backstretch and the Roadster cruised around to the checker.

The crowd hooted and booed.

Max Ailor, sports writer for the Richmond newspaper, had really helped with some good stories during the week.

The racing for the first heat of the Roadster program was terrible. So was the second heat. People were demanding and getting their money refunded. Doc Benson felt bad. Normally, his boys put on good shows, but not today.

I was standing with Max Ailor. "Max, this is the worst racing I ever saw. I know you're going to have to write the story like it is. Don't worry about me. Do what you have to do. This is awful! I guess I had better stick with what I know, putting out a magazine."

In Sunday morning's paper, Max Ailor led with, "Last night, Don O'Reilly became an ex-promoter." He treated us pretty good, told a good honest story, but wrote it as, sort of, that's the way it is some times. By Don O'Rielly, Publisher/Editor Speed Age Magazine

A field of Eastern Racing Association roadsters taking the starter's flag at Winchester in about 1948.
(Eastern Museum of Motor Racing—Ray Madera collection)

A NEW ENGLAND MYSTERY—SOLVED!

Eastern racing historians pretty well agree that there was no roadster racing in the New England states. The above full-page ad that appeared in a 1949 issue of *Illustrated Speedway News* seems to dispute this contention.

Bob Silvia of Warwick, Rhode Island, is one of the better authorities on racing in that part of the country. This advertisement confused Silvia for awhile, but he did come up with an answer. The American Hot Rod Racing Club had ideas about racing roadsters, but their plans were well ahead of their actions. (As indicated on the ad they also planned speed trials on a "five mile straight-a-way course"—where in New England did they plan to find this?)

What happened was that in New England there was a lot more interest in racing modified coupes than in racing roadsters. By the time the American Hot Rod Racing Club got going, the roadsters had all but been forgotten.

(Ray Haitt collection)

Bob Silvia did find that a few roadsters probably ran as part of a AHRRC modified coupe event at Cherry Park, Connecticut, on October 2, 1949. That was the extent of roadster racing in New England.

Walter Nycomb came from Maryland for this 1939 race at Winchester. Looks like part of the "space frame" is two-by-12-inch lumber.
(Frank Scheder collection)

No identification on this Winchester driver—1946. Does he have a Farmall tractor engine in what is left of that Model A? *(Frank Scheder collection)*

The driver of #13 at Winchester is not identified. This car appears to have a down-draft carburetor and special headers.
(Frank Scheder collection)

Jimmy Shaw of Romney, West Virginia, at Winchester in 1946. Shaw's car has a full body that looks like the front half of some of today's sprint cars. *(Frank Scheder collection)*

The field lines up at Winchester, Virginia, in 1939. On the pole is Carl Anderson, who became a star roadster driver after World War II. Anderson won the Eastern Racing Association championship in 1949. (John Jackson collection)

A starting field at Winchester, Virginia in 1946. (Frank Scheder collection)

WASHINGTON

There was some roadster racing in Washington in the late 1930s. These were exhibition races for street roadsters during big car programs at Silverlake Speedway near Everett. There are vague reports that northwest drivers like Don Olds, Art Scovill and Allan Heath took part in these races but nothing definite could be found. Around 1940, there were a few track roadster races held in the Seattle area. Zeke Zeigler was one of the drivers and most likely he ran the Riley Four Port that he later used in his big car.

After World War II, Washington roadster racing got under way with at race a Tenino in the central part of the state. With the help of the Seattle-based Washington Hi-Winders roadster club both Oregon and Washington cars took part in this race. The cars were mostly right off the street, and the track was a rutted and narrow half-mile horse track. The main event was won by a Riley Four Port in a short wheel base Model A with a narrowed body. It may have been a pre-war Washington car or a Southern California "modified" from the late 1930s. A few weeks later another hot rod race was run at the mile and one-eighth fairground track in Yakima. Dick Hoag drove his '32 Ford V8 roadster to the race, won the main and drove it home again. A few more races were held during the 1946 season including a fiasco at Port Angles. *(See the sidebar in this chapter for the strange details of this mess.)*

During the winter of 1946-47 the need for a strong roadster organization was recognized, and the Racing Roadster Association of Washington was formed. During that winter, some of the street rods of the 1946 became a little more like race cars, but in general there were no major modifications. As in other parts of the country, midget racing was

Bob Ramstead in what looks like a street rod. This photo could have been taken at Port Angeles or Tenino in 1946. *(Gordy Sutherland collection)*

This is Aurora Speedway in 1947 and Whitey Lundsteadt is in #28. *(Gordy Sutherland collection)*

Gordy Sutherland at Aurora in 1947. The V8 engine has a McCullough supercharger on it. Howard Shelly died in this car at Yakima in 1948. *(Gordy Sutherland collection)*

A strange photo and a strange car. Number 26 with its low frame and high engine placement looks like something out of 1947, yet the car in the background with its center steering looks more like a 1949 or 1950 track roadster. The unidentified driver wears a football helmet—something the RRAW never allowed. *(Gordy Sutherland collection)*

booming in the Pacific Northwest, and RRAW Vice President Gordy Sutherland felt that the roadsters were ready to race on some of the midget tracks. He approached Earl Herous who owned Aurora Stadium Speedway with the idea of running the hot rods on his quarter miler. A roadster race was scheduled, heavily advertised and a record crowd showed up. The purse that day was $3,820; it was by far the biggest payday the Washington roadsters would ever enjoy.

Racing continued on a weekly basis at Aurora Speedway, and there were also some races on another midget speedway—Sea-Tac near Tacoma. There were also several races on the big dirt track at Yakima. The Racing Roadster Association of Washington cooperated with the roadster racing group in Oregon and many of the cars journeyed regularly to Portland to compete.

In 1948, the Washington roadsters really had cooperation from the Oregon group. The Columbia River flooded and put 10 feet of water over Portland Speedway and the Oregon racers lost their home track for most of the season. Len Sutton was one of the drivers who drove the 200 miles to Seattle to race at Aurora on Friday nights. Sutton made the trip with the Rolla Vollstead #27 weekly and won almost weekly. Bob Donker was one of the few Washington hot rodders to beat Sutton occasionally.

The roadsters continued to draw good crowds at Aurora for several more years. During 1949, they made several trips to Digney Speedway in Vancouver, British Columbia, to race, and they also competed in what looked like a cow pasture at Sultan, Washington. In 1950, there was trouble between the Oregon and Washington roadster groups. The drivers claimed that officials would not treat visiting racers fairly—sounds like both groups got mad at the other's officials. Without the Oregon support, car counts were down. Nonetheless, 20 races were held at Aurora Speedway, and there were some spot races at Bremerton and other Washington cities.

By 1951, the stock cars were taking over and only seven roadster races were held at Aurora. Indicative that things were bad for the midgets, too, was the fact that the great midget driver, Shorty Templeman, was racing hot rods. He did bull his way to a main event win at Aurora. A few races were held at other Washington tracks, including a best-forgotten race at Spokane. Only seven cars made the 200-mile tow to Spokane, and Bob Donker won the main. It is doubtful if Donker ever got paid; by the time he took the checkered flag

This was the first hot rod race at Seattle's Aurora Speedway in 1947. Del Fanning poses before winning the biggest payoff of his roadster career: $647 in the main event that day. (Gordy Sutherland collection)

Practice for the first roadster race at Aurora Speedway Stadium. Number 1 is Johnny Gorman, #96 is Armand Millins and #48 has a passenger along for the ride. (Gordy Sutherland collection)

This is Sultan, Washington. The roadsters are running on what looks like a cow pasture. The race was probably part of a local celebration. (Gordy Sutherland collection)

This is apparently a practice session for the first roadster race at Aurora in 1947. Johnny Gorman is in #1, Oregon visitor Armand Millins in #96, and Bob Donker is in his own #2. (Gordy Sutherland collection)

The owner of the Del Fanning-driven #42 shows off a fistful of money after leaving the Aurora Speedway payoff window. (Gordy Sutherland collection)

Phil Folbert in an early Washington track roadster. Note the strange-looking heads on that V8. (Gordy Sutherland collection)

Fred Dickie at Aurora in 1947. That's a Nash Ambassador Six engine, and it ran well. Dickie was 1946 Washington roadster champion—perhaps it was in this car. (Gordy Sutherland collection)

Kenny Baxter in 1947. Looks like the car could use a front bumper (nerfting iron). (Gordy Sutherland collection)

the promoter had skipped with the gate receipts.

By 1952, the roadsters were about finished in Washington—they managed only two races at Aurora Speedway. Only a few races were held in 1953—nobody seems to remember where.

While most the Washington roadster racing centered around the Roadster Racing Association of Washington, there were a couple of other small groups formed. In Yakima, hot rodders formed an association the name of which, unfortunately, has been forgotten. In Spokane, an attempt was made in about 1950 to form a track roadster racing association. It got off the ground far enough to have a name—the Spokane Roadster Racing Association. Some car plaques were made and a few of these even exist today, but nobody remembers anything about the Spokane Roadster Racing Association.

The safety record of the Washington roadsters was fairly good. The only fatal crash came at Yakima—probably one of the most dangerous places the roadsters ever ran. The mile-and-one-eighth track was very fast, usually dusty and had the normal horse-type wooden fences. Several serious accidents occurred there, including Howard Shelly, who died at Yakima in 1948. Shelly was primarily a midget driver, but he was at the wheel of a McCullough supercharged A-V8 on that day. He was leading the main event when he tangled with a lapped car and rolled endlessly down the main straightaway.

In another near-fatal crash at Aurora in 1950, Del Fanning slammed head on into the crashwall, and it was only a miracle that he survived. With Fanning facing a long hospital stay the Racing Roadster Association of Washington turned to their crash fund to pay the bills. Instead, they discovered that the group's treasurer had embezzled $4,700—there was no money available. Benefit races were held for Fanning, and the RRAW treasurer wound up in prison for five years.

Washington Roadster Champions:
    1946 Fred Dickie?
    1947 Johnny Gorman
    1948 Bob Donker
    1949 Johnny Gorman
    1950 Mickey Shelton?
    1951 Bob Donker
    1952 Shorty Templeman
    1953 Dick Brower

Bob Ramstead at Aurora. Note the low (stepped) frame. This was a better setup for the street rather than the track. (Gordy Sutherland collection)

State of the art firefighting equipment at an early Aurora Speedway race. The car did not flip; it was turned over by track workers in an effort to quell the fire. (Dick Martin collection)

*Bremerton in 1950. Bob Donker in W9 and Don Radbruch battle for the lead.
(Gordy Sutherland collection)*

Workers try to pull Kenny Baxter out of his over-turned hot rod. Baxter was OK. (Carl Payne photo—Ray Hiatt collection)

Ray Davidson smiles from #26—circa 1950. This car looks like it has Model T frame rails. (Carl Payne photo—Ray Hiatt collection)

*An Aurora Stadium Speedway program —1950.
(Ray Hiatt collection)*

*Kenny Baxter was the trophy dash winner at Sultan in 1947.
(Gordy Sutherland collection)*

*Phil Foubert slides upside-down in this Aurora action. Johnny Gorman in #9, Ray Davidson in #26 and Mickey Sheldon try to avoid contact.
(Gordy Sutherland collection)*

*Ray Davidson climbs the wall at Aurora in 1948. The pitmen scattered, but Davidson came down on the track and was OK.
(Carl Payne photo—Ray Hiatt collection)*

Bob Lange ran this neat-looking Plymouth Six at Aurora in 1948.
(Carl Payne photo—Ray Hiatt collection)

circa 1949. Fred Dickie sat high in his #88. That's a strange-looking intake manifold on the V8.
(Gordy Sutherland collection)

Chuck Cedar is pictured in Mickey Sheldon's V8. Those are Bendix brakes from a World War II aircraft. Roll bar is from the local plumbing shop.
(Don Gilchrest collection)

Whitey Lundsteadt tries to crawl out after flipping at Aurora. Lundsteadt was OK.
(Gordy Sutherland collection)

This looks like Bob Donker in his own car—circa 1947. Donker was a two-time Washington roadster champion. *(Gordy Sutherland collection)*

Number 81 has hit something solid at Aurora in 1949. Note the strange front spring perch on this car. *(Gordy Sutherland collection)*

Johnny Gorman at Aurora. There must be some sort of supercharger on that V8.
(Gordy Sutherland collection)

Lee Kirk came from Yakima to race at Aurora Speedway in Seattle. Races were every Friday night and Kirk was a regular. *(Lee Kirk collection)*

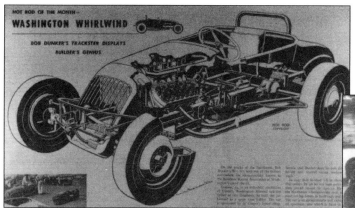

Hot Rod Magazine featured a centerfold with a Rex Burnett cutaway drawing of the Donker roadster in the July issue of the magazine. HRM did misspell Donker's name.
(Used with permission of Hot Rod Magazine.)

There's a good crowd on hand for this Aurora race in 1950. The only driver that can be identified is Pete Lovely in #7. *(Gordy Sutherland collection)*

Aurora action, probably in 1951. Number 1 is an Oregon car and the driver is Ernie Koch.
(Jay Koch collection)

Bob Donker built and drove this very nice looking roadster. The car was featured in Hot Rod Magazine in 1951. *(Gordy Sutherland collection)*

Oregon's Frankie McGowen visited Aurora quite regularly. McGowen was a top-ranked midget pilot.
(Gordy Sutherland collection)

HOT RODS TO FORMULA I

One of #55's drivers was Pete Lovely—a future Formul I driver. Lovely drove roadsters in Oregon and Washington and was the only hot rodder to make it to Formula I. His first track roaster in 1947 was a straight-off-the-street '32 Ford roadster. In 1948, he drove a '29 Model A with the V8 engine pushed way back in the chassis—Pete describes it as a "horrible car." During the next couple of years, Lovely, driving #55 and some other good cars, was one of the Pacific Northwest's top roadster drivers. When roadster racing died out, Lovely turned to the sports cars. In 1957, he won the first race ever held at Monterey's Laguna Seca, where he drove a two-liter Ferrari to victory and a payoff of—nothing! Sports car drivers in that era were so "pure" that money was a dirty word.

Lovely wound up owning a Volkswagen dealership and successfully raced sports car throughout the '50s and

'60s. In 1968, he bought a 1-year-old Lotus 49 Formula I car for $36,000 and the next year he drove it in the United States, Canadian and Mexican Gran Prix. As a private entry, Lovely had no chance of beating the factory teams, but he did manage a seventh place finish in Mexico and a ninth in Canada. In 1970, he updated the Lotus and took it to Europe. In the French Gran Prix, a broken suspension part sent him into the guard rail, but he had better luck in England and posted a tenth place finsih in the British Gran Prix. Had Lovely been able to afford to run the full Gran Prix circuit, it is almost certain that a better ride would have become available—his performance in an outclassed car was amazing.

Pet Lovely is still racing. Now it is vintage sports care that are, in Pete's words, "restored to an indecent level of perfection."

This is a local car at Yakima in 1946. The engine is described as a "Viking V-12." To "balance" the car there was a large chunk of concrete in the trunk. The car did not do well. (Dick Martin collection)

The serious Del Fanning crash at Aurora in June of 1950. Fanning tangled with another car and then hit the crashwall head on. He was very seriously injured. (Carl Payne photo—Ray Hiatt collection)

BIG LEAGUE RACING

BY DON GILCHREST

Traveling throughout the country is commonplace in racing this day and age, but in 1951 it was a little different, I like to call the "Hot Rod Era" the granddaddy of sprint car racing and present-day travel.

Think travel was easy in those days? C'mon along with my pal, a college student from Everett and owner and driver of Washington's #8 roadster, Roger Covert, and myself, his gopher, just out of high school, as we took on the "Big Leagues" of racing travel.

Our trip first took us from Everett to Salem, Oregon—about 200 miles—for a Saturday night visit to the Hollywood Bowl, a quarter-mile paved oval. Sounds easy? Try no freeways, but a windy highway that took you through each and every city along the way. Now pull the race car on the ground with a tow bar. How about a trailer? A few of the elite racers had trailers. These trailers were a far cry from present trailers, being whippy and a chore to tow. We had a trusty tow bar. The trip to Salem was without incident if you don't count using the license off my 1949 Ford on the race car. Of course, we were stopped 10 miles from the Oregon border. Given a ticket, made to leave the race car and drive Roger's 1947 Chevy to Vancouver, Washington, to obtain a temporary license, good for just the 10 miles to the border.

After this delay, we got into Oregon, went directly to the State Patrol and made ourselves legal. Oh yes, they confiscated my license plate in Washington.

My notes on the Salem race had Len Sutton winning in Rolla Vollstead's #27. (They had a trailer.).... Twenty six cars on hand for a purse of $942.65.... Covert had ninth fastest time and ended up in a shunt with Phil Foubert in the feature event, thus a DNF.

We left Salem about midnight and headed further south, roughly another 100 miles for a dirt race on the half-mile horse track at the Roseburg Fairgrounds. Yep, the big change from pavement to dirt involved different tires and a rear end change for the bigger track. We, like practically all the racers, did not have a quick change

rear end. So the long time it took for a change was spent under a neon sign at a gas station at about two in the morning.

Stopping on a dark stretch of Highway 99 for a little sleep in the car we woke up with the roadster sitting dead on the tracks of the Northern Pacific. Luckily, they had the day off.

To continue our trip into Roseburg, Sunday morning, we found we were running a little late, (what else is new) so we unhooked the roadster and Roger warmed it up, zig zagging through the churchgoers and travelers on 99.

At the track, we found about 100-degree weather, we kept cool laying in the shade under the race car. The track was not used to having machines, but horses, on it and so to say it was rough and extremely bumpy would be putting it mildly. In fact, Roger told me, "You drive the head race, it's too hot for me."

Here is what my fading notes said about the event: "Ernie Koch in his brother's Pop Koch #0-25 won the feature with Howard Osbourne second... Seattle's Johnny Gorman won the fast heat with Osbourne fast time.... Track conditions took a race-long toll that included a broken radiator, three lost gears and three lost batteries.... 16 cars were on hand for the first-ever roadster appearance. ... Purse $1,100." And last but not least, "It's hot, the track is not dusty, but it's *rough*."

How did we do? We used one hand to hold the battery in the car all day long, but it finally bounced out in the feature and Roger was out early. In the heat race, the battery shorted out. Roger's time came in at 32.09.

We left Roseburg in the early evening with giant mugs of beer, in milkshake containers, for refreshments and took turns falling asleep as we went straight through to Tacoma, where my car was and where Covert made classes and then for me, without license plate on either car or roadster sweating out the final 60 miles to Everett and work.

That's "Big League Racing" for a couple of neophytes.

Another view of the wrecked Del Fanning car. The engine is lying on the ground and Fanning's body has mangled the steering wheel. Del Fanning was out of racing for a year but came back to go as fast as ever. *(Carl Payne Photo—Ray Hiatt collection)*

Local driver Lee Kirk at Yakima in 1946. Kirk's street rod is powered by a supercharged Graham engine. Kirk remembers the car was "a bomb on the street and a bust on the track." *(Lee Kirk collection)*

Yakima in 1946. The Bill Brannin car is from Oregon and went very fast with what appears to be a stock engine. The engine is set well back in the chassis—unusual for 1946. *(Dick Martin collection)*

A couple of Washington roadsters tangle during a race at Wenatchee, Washington.
(Gordy Sutherland collection)

Yakima in 1946. Bill Hyde stands by what is obviously a street roadster. Hyde was a fine roadster and sprint car driver. *(Jay Koch collection)*

One of the early (1946) races at Yakima. Both Oregon and Washington cars were at this race, and most were driven to the track.
(Dick Martin collection)

The roadster on a tow bar someplace in southern Washington. This was just before the Highway Patrol arrived and trouble began. (Don Gilchrest collection)

Inset—Roger Covert at the wheel of the roadster that he and Don Gilchrest towed from Seattle to races in Oregon in 1951. Frank Billings is at left and current National Speed Sport News columnist Don Gilchrest at right. (Don Gilchrest collection)

Author Don Radruch visited the Pacific Northwest in 1950. He's shown here at Aurora Speedway in Seattle. The aluminum channel frame rails were common on West Coast cars.
(Don Radbruch collection)

Ernie Koch leads a pack of Aurora racers. It looks like Bob Donker close behind Koch.
(Gordy Sutherland collection)

A FIASCO AT PORT ANGELES

By late summer of 1946, the Oregon and Washington hot rodders had already competed in a race at Tenino in central Washington, and they were eager for more racing. Nobody remembers just why, but the next race was scheduled at Port Angeles, a remote town some 100 miles north of Seattle. Port Angeles did have a half-mile county fairgrounds horse track, but so did lots of more accessible towns. At any rate, a promoter appeared from somewhere and the Oregon and Washington roadster racers headed north to Port Angeles to race.

This was probably the first auto race of any kind in Port Angeles and the event attracted a large crowd. Despite the fact that the officials and drivers lacked experience and the cars were mostly street rods, it can be assumed that things went reasonably well until the main event.

By that time, the track was dusty and visiblity was nil. During the race a couple of roadsters got tangled up on the main straightaway and ground to a halt near the start-finish line. Another car piled into the wreckage, and its driver was thrown to the track. Two more cars appeared out of the dust, barely missed the stunned driver, and joined the growing pile of wreckage. At this point, the ambulance driver, who may or may not have been summoned by the officials, pulled his vehicle out onto the track. Other cars were still groping their way around in the dust and one of them slammed into the rear of the ambulance. The impact split the fuel tank of the ambulance and gasoline sprayed in all directions. It took but an instant for flames to burst out. Roadster drivers and the ambulance driver scrambled from the wreckage and spectators headed for safety as the fire threatened the grandstand. There was minimal, if any, firefighting equipment available, and the blaze had its way until the local volunteer fire department arrived long minutes later.

Amazingly enough there were no serious injuries, but a few hot rods and an expensive ambulance went up in flames. The promoter figured he'd better get out while the getting was good and did so—complete with gate receipts.

Racer Gordy Sutherland remembers that there wasn't much left of his battered and scorched roadster, so he simply left most of it at the track. He loaded the engine into the trunk of his '40 Hudson. The hot rod's rear end seemed OK so he hooked onto that and towed it back to Seattle.

This was the only roadster race ever held at Port Angeles.

THE STORY OF #55

Washington track roadster #55 has had a very interesting existence. It survived four years of action on Oregon and Washington race tracks. It made the pages of *Hot Rod Magazine*, was the subject of a *Saturday Evening Post* article, appeared in shows, trained a Formula I driver and, today, is in the process of making a comeback!

Pete Lovely in #55 at Aurora Speedway in Seattle in 1949. This is the "as built" version of the car with the Model A frame rails. *(Don Gilchrest collection)*

The car was built in 1948 by Minor Pelley and Pete Lovely. With a Merc engine, Model A frame rails and a '25 T body it looked like a dozen other Pacific Northwest track roadsters. It did have one very unusual feature. The '25 T body that Pelley and Lovely used was in exceptional shape and the passenger side door worked just fine. (1923 to 1925 Model T roadsters had only a passenger side door.) Rather than strip out the wood framing and weld the door shut, the builders left it in place as an operating door. The car was finished off with

Pete Lovely sits in #55 at a Seattle Sports Show in 1949. The car was chosen to represent the Roadster Racing Association of Washington in the show • *(Gordy Sutherland collection)*

a nice upholstery job and the result was #55—a nice-looking track roadster.

Pete Lovely, Ike Hanks and Chuck Cookson did most of the driving, and the car was campaigned with moderate success on the Oregon and Washington roadster circuit.

In 1950, the car ran as Number 7. Ike Hanks is at the wheel. The aluminum frame rails were installed after the original frame was bent in a crash at Portland, Oregon. *(Gordy Sutherland collection)*

Car #55 appeared in the 1949 Seattle Sportsman Show as a part of the Racing Roadster Association of Washington exhibit. A few months later it was in the pages of *Hot Rod Magazine* as the "Seattle Track Roadster."

In 1950, the car was sold to Fred Pierce and now carried the number 7. It had acquired an aluminum channel frame, but the trademark door was still in place. Fred's dad, Frank Pierce, was a freelance writer and wrote a story about the car for the *Saturday Evening*

Post, then one of the most prestigious magazines in the country.

The article, entitled "I've Got A Thunderbolt in My Backyard," told the story of how Fred Pierce had acquired the car, and how he and his friends were working on the car and racing it. From a technical and racing standpoint the article was terrible, but it was a good human interest story and created some favorable publicity for roadster racing and for #55.

Fred Pierce sold #55 to John Ryerson who, after the demise of roadster racing, stored the car for many years. It was then sold to former roadster racer Bob Ramstead, who made a few changes and converted the car into a street hot rod. If Ramstead drove it on the street it was illegally, as the car was never registered in the state of Washington.

In 1990, Ray Hiatt of Hayward, California, heard about #55 and bought the car. Hiatt, a self-admitted roadster nut, had seen the car race at Aurora Speedway in Seattle from 1949 until 1951. He has managed to obtain legal California registration for #55, and has driven it on the highway. At present, Hiatt is converting the car back to what it was some 40 years ago. He plans to run it in Western Racing Association vintage race car events. It won't be long before #55 is back on the track where it belongs!

Roadster racing got some national publicity in this Saturday Evening Post article by Frank Pierce. The article implies that Pierce's son, Fred, converted a beat-up jalopy into the track roadster. *(Ray Hiatt collection)*

Car #55 was featured in Hot Rod Magazine in 1949. Note the operating door in the lower HRM photo. *(Used with permission of* Hot Rod Magazine.*)*

This is #55 in 1992 with owner, Ray Hiatt, at the wheel. It is changed only slightly from its track roadster days. Hiatt is now converting the car back to a track roadster. *(Ray Hiatt collection)*

WISCONSIN

• •

Roadster racing in Wisconsin can be divided into two parts: the activity at the State Fairgrounds at Milwaukee and the racing in the remainder of the state.

Roadster racing at Milwaukee was apparently limited to 1948, and it was sanctioned by Andy Granatelli's Hurricane Racing Association. At least four events were held on the quarter-mile dirt track at the fairground's facility, attracting top drivers from both the Chicago-based Hurricane group and the Mutual Racing Association from Indiana. Drivers such as Jim Rathmann, Ray Erickson, Al Swenson, Smokey Stover and Dick Frazier were all in the starting fields. As was his habit with his #32 during the 1948 season, Dick Frazier ran off with most of the money. He swept the program on June 15 ($434), June 29 ($336), July 13 (winnings unknown), and July 27 ($418).

Andy Granatelli and Hurricane planned a "big race" on the then dirt Milwaukee mile for August 9, 1948. Perhaps "big race" meant a hundred miler, but

A program cover for one of the Wisconsin Roadster Racing Association races. Bill Fitzgerald is at the left, but the other drivers are not identified.
(Bill Fitzgerald collection)

Bill Fitzgerald has managed to hang on to his Wisconsin Roadster Racing Association card for all these years.
(Bill Fitzgerald collection)

for some reason the event was scaled down to a series of sprint races with an advertised 50-lap main that turned out to be 30 laps. The purse was apparently a flat $2,000, and once again it turned out to be a Dick Frazier benefit. Frazier qualified #32 in 42.78 seconds, which was no doubt faster than some of the AAA Indy cars of that era. Frazier won the main, but no other results are available.

It seems unlikely that Hurricane or Mutual did not sanction hot rod races at Milwaukee after 1948, but no evidence of any further racing has surfaced.

In the remainder of Wisconsin, track roadster racing was sanctioned by the Wisconsin Roadster Racing Association. This group had about 20 cars scattered throughout the state and held races at places like Manitowok, Lodi, Edgerton, Hales Corners and several other towns. The Wisconsin Roadster Racing Association raced for several years, but for some reason many of the cars did not develop into true track roadsters. They were basically modified street rods, and some of them were driven to the tracks to race. One of the first races was at Manitowok in about 1948 or 1949. Manitowok had a nasty and narrow fairground's half-miler with sharp turns. With mostly street rods, which at best could be classified as ill-handling, and inexperienced drivers, a lot of fence was knocked down that day, but there were no serious injuries.

"Wild" Bill Fitzgerald was one of the better

Roaring Roadsters

"Wild" Bill Fitzgerald at Lodi, Wisconsin in 1949. This is a typical county fair horse track— hazardous for both racer and spectator.
(Bill Fitzgerald collection)

WRRA drivers, and although he admits his car was "kind of roughshod," it was a true track roadster. Fitzgerald won a few main events but doesn't really remember what the payoffs were, "It couldn't have been much or I'd remember it—maybe $20 to $50." Drivers who ran with the Wisconsin Roadster Racing Association besides Fitzgerald include Jim and Bob Graff and Norm Hanson, who was probably a WRRA champion.

The Wisconsin Roadster Racing Association racers managed to survive the dangerous horse tracks without serious harm, but there were some bad wrecks. At Manitowok, a car went through a fence and into a barn. This car had a five-gallon "G.I. Can" as a fuel tank, which sat on the seat alongside the driver. The can got knocked over, caught fire and burned the driver, as well as nearly burning down the barn.

ROADSTER RACERS AND THE LAW

There is little doubt that most of us who raced roadsters did things on the highway that we should not have done—if we got in trouble we had asked for it. Many of us, however, got in trouble without asking for it while towing roadsters to the races. Few of us could afford trailers for the race cars so they were towed with a tow bar. This meant that the race car had to be a legally registered motor vehicle.

To legally register a track roadster was not easy. The car was built from bits and pieces of many cars so how did one get a legal registration? One way to handle this problem was to borrow a license plate from another car and hang it on the towed track roadster. Usually all was OK, but once in a while a highway patrol officer would want to check the roadster's registration. This could be trouble, and I'm sure every roadster racer tried a different excuse. Mine? I somehow acquired a registration and license plate from a 1935 Ford Sedan that I used for the roadster. When an officer would ask questions the standard reply was, "Oh, we changed bodies, Officer." It always worked.

MORE MYSTERIES

A mong the track roadster history that has been lost over the years are the identifications of some of the men who drove the cars. These are a few of the perhaps one hundred unidentified photos that were collected during book research.

Perhaps somebody out there can identify the drivers, cars or race tracks.

(Gordy Sutherland collection)

Possibly Agoura in Southern California.
(Greg Sharp— Vintage Racing Photos)

Penney-Royal Speedway, Leon, New York. "The Wild Irishman."
(Lou Ensworth collection)

Aurora Stadium, Seattle, Washington.
(Gordy Sutherland collection)

Aurora Stadium, Seattle, Washington.
(Gordy Sutherland collection)

Southern California?
(Johnny Klann collection)

Porterville, California.
(Steve Larson collection)

Check those headers!
(Izor collection)

Indiana—probably Mutual Racing Associations.
(Zane Howell collection)

This photo was originally captioned, "Pat Flaherty" (1956 Indy winner), but this is probably not correct.
(Bill Hill collection)

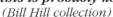

Probably Southern California.
(Greg Sharp—Vintage Racing Photos)

Brighton, Colorado.
(Leroy Byers collection)

Northern California.
(Bob Veith collection)

Where, who and when?

Aztec, New Mexico.
(Bob Noe collection)

Brighton, Colorado.
(Leroy Byers collection)

Englewood Speedway, Denver, Colorado.
(Leroy Byers collection)

Northern California.
(Bob Veith collection)

"Spillway", San Antonio, Texas.
(Don Fowler collection)

Arapahoe Fairgrounds, Littleton, Colorado. *(Leroy Byers collection)*

MORE HOT ROD HISTORY!

Complete your library. No serious hot rod or race car enthusiast should be without Tex Smith's HOT ROD HISTORY, Book 1 and Book 2.

Recognized around the world as the greatest hot rod history books ever printed, written by one of the world's most famous rodders, Tom Medley.

From legendary Ed Winfield well into modern rod times, these are companion books that are crammed with hundreds and hundreds of rare photographs, accompanied by stories from the people who lived those golden days. From the board tracks and dirt ovals of the earliest days to the famed dry lakes of southern California to land speed record setting efforts of current times.

Each book $19.95, plus $3 shipping

Mastercard/Visa 1-800-513-8133

•

Tex Smith Publishing
P.O. Box 726
Driggs, ID 83422

CarTech
11481 Kost Dam Rd.
North Branch, MN 55056